GERMAN
PHRASEBOOK

Franziska Buck
Anke Munderloh

German phrasebook
1st edition – November 1997

Published by
Lonely Planet Publications Pty Ltd ABN 36 005 607 983
90 Maribyrnong St, Footscray, Victoria 3011, Australia

Lonely Planet Offices
Australia Locked Bag 1, Footscray, Victoria 3011
USA 150 Linden St, Oakland CA 94607
UK 10a Spring Place, London NW5 3BH
France 1 rue du Dahomey, 75011 Paris

Cover illustration
Barred for Life by Penelope Richardson

ISBN 0 86442 451 5

text © Lonely Planet Publications Pty Ltd 1997
cover illustration © Lonely Planet Publications Pty Ltd 1997

Colorcraft Ltd, Hong Kong

All rights reserved. No part of this publication may be reproduced, stored in a retrieval system or transmitted in any form by any means, electronic, mechanical, photocopying, recording or otherwise, except brief extracts for the purpose of review, without the written permission of the publisher.

Lonely Planet, the Lonely Planet logo, Lonely Planet Images, CitySync and eKno are trade marks of Lonely Planet Publications Pty. Ltd. Other trade marks are the property of their respective owners.

CONTENTS

About the Authors

Franziska Buck is a linguist and a teacher of German as a foreign language. She has worked as a lecturer at Augsburg University and Lancaster University and is currently working on her PhD.

Anke Munderloh is also a linguist who has contributed to the Lonely Planet *Latin American Spanish* phrasebook. She currently works as an editor for the German magazine, *Outdoor*.

From the Authors

Thanks to Silke Holzäpfel for her work on the dialects, accents and specialities. Thanks also to Bernd and Tina Wiedemann, Anna Komutan and Peter Schindler for their support.

From the Publisher

This book was produced through an incredible combination of effort, determination and **chutzpah**, by a team led by Sally Steward, who, not one to be frightened off by the sight of **Pfälzer Saumagen**, supervised; Diana Saad, whose first edit made it easy for those who came after; Peter D'Onghia, who proofread and came up with 20 different ways of saying beer in German; Lou Callan, who proofread and found that too much **Schnaps** is never enough; Penelope Richardson, whose wonderful text design, cover design and illustrations don't make up for the fact that she just doesn't look right in canary yellow **Lederhosen**; Emma Powell, who laid out the book and discovered that grammar just ain't what it used to be, and Robyn Woodward-Kron, who proofread and actually enjoyed it. Thanks also to Richard Plunkett for his excellent crosswords and pleasant demeanour, Adam McCrow, who put the final touches on the cover, Magdalena Schmid, for additional proofreading, and Patrick Marris for refining the layout.

INTRODUCTION

It might be a surprise to know that German is, in fact, a close relative of English. English, German and Dutch are all known as West Germanic languages. This means that you know quite a few German words already – **Arm**, **Finger**, **Gold** – and you'll be able to figure out many others – **Mutter** (mother), **trinken** (to drink), **gut** (good). A primary reason why English and German have grown apart is that the Normans, on invading England in 1066, brought with them a large number of non-Germanic words. This caused English to have lots of synonyms, with the more basic word being Germanic, and the more literary or specialised one coming from French; for instance, the Germanic 'start' and 'green' as opposed to the French 'commence' and 'verdant'.

German grammar is often described as difficult – it is cited that there are many different ways to say 'the', and that words have 'lots of endings'. However, most of these concepts that seem so alien actually have remnants in English. German also has the advantage of being comparatively easy to pronounce. It is beyond the scope of this book to outline how to put your own sentences together from scratch, but there are many examples of model sentences where you can choose the key word you want: for instance 'It is too ... (big/small/short/long)'.

German is spoken throughout Germany and Austria, and in most of Switzerland. It is also extremely useful in Eastern Europe, especially with older people. Although you may hear different dialects, there is a strong tradition of a prescribed official language – Hochdeutsch (High German). High German is used in this book and will always be understood. In some tourist centres English is so widely spoken that you may not have a chance to use German, even if you want to! However, as soon as you try to meet ordinary people or move out of the big cities, especially in what was East Germany, the situation is totally different. Your efforts to speak the local language will be very much appreciated and will make your trip much more enjoyable and fulfilling.

Gute Reise!

INTRODUCTION

ARTHUR OR MARTHA?

German has three noun forms, known as masculine, feminine and neuter. Throughout this book we have used the abbreviations (m), (f) and (neut) to indicate the gender of a word. Where a word can be either masculine or feminine, the feminine ending is separated by a slash. For example **Sekretär/in** (secretary) indicates that the masculine form is **Sekretär** and the feminine form is **Sekretärin** (see Grammar, page 21, for how to make nouns feminine). In cases where the feminine is more complicated than adding – **in** to the masculine form, both forms of the word appear in full, masculine first, eg **Krankenpfleger/ Krankenschwester** (nurse).

ABBREVIATIONS USED IN THIS BOOK

Below is a list of abbreviations you will see used in this book.

acc	accusative
dat	dative
f	feminine
gen	genitive
inf	informal
lit	literally
m	masculine
neut	neuter
nom	nominative
pl	plural
pol	polite
S	southern Germany
sg	singular

(See Grammar, page 25, for an explanation of cases.)

HOW TO USE THIS PHRASEBOOK
You Can Speak Another Language

It's true – anyone can speak another language. Don't worry if you haven't studied languages before, or that you studied a language at school for years and can't remember any of it. It doesn't even matter if you failed English grammar. After all, that's never affected your ability to speak English! And this is the key to picking up a language in another country. You don't need to sit down and memorise endless grammatical details and you don't need to memorise long lists of vocabulary. You just need to start speaking. Once you start, you'll be amazed how many prompts you'll get to help you build on those first words. You'll hear people speaking, pick up sounds from TV, catch a word or two that you think you know from the local radio, see something on a billboard – all these things help to build your understanding.

Plunge In

There's just one thing you need to start speaking another language – courage. Your biggest hurdle is overcoming the fear of saying aloud what may seem to you to be just a bunch of sounds. There are a number of ways to do this.

Firstly, think of some German words or phrases that you are familiar with, such as **Auf Wiedersehen** and **Gesundheit!** You are probably already able to say these phrases fluently – and you'll even get a response. From these basic beginnings, provided you can get past the 'courage to speak' barrier, you can start making sentences.

The best way to start overcoming your fear is to memorise a few key words. These are the words you know you'll be saying again and again, like 'hello', 'thank you' and 'how much?'. Here's an important hint though: right from the beginning, learn at least one phrase that will be useful but not essential. Such as 'good morning' or 'good afternoon', 'see you later' or even a conversational piece like 'lovely day, isn't it?' or 'it's cold today' (people everywhere love to talk about the weather). Having this extra phrase

INTRODUCTION

(just start with one, if you like, and learn to say it really well) will enable you to move away from the basics, and when you get a reply and a smile, it'll also boost your confidence. You'll find that people you speak to will like it too, as they'll understand that at least you've tried to learn more of the language than just the usual essential words.

Ways to Remember

There are several ways to learn a language. Most people find they learn from a variety of these, although people usually have a preferred way to remember. Some like to see the written word and remember the sound from what they see. Some like to just hear it spoken in context (if this is you, try talking to yourself in German, but do it in the car or somewhere private, to give yourself confidence, and so others don't wonder about your sanity!). Others, especially the more mathematically inclined, like to analyse the grammar of a language, and piece together words according to the rules of grammar. The very visually inclined like to associate the written word and even sounds with some visual stimulus, such as from illustrations, TV and general things they see in the street. As you learn, you'll discover what works best for you – be aware of what made you really remember a particular word, and if it sticks in your mind, keep using that method.

Kicking Off

Chances are you'll want to learn some of the language before you go. The first thing to do is to memorise those essential phrases and words. Check out the basics (page 53) ... and don't forget that extra phrase (see Plunge In!). Try the sections on making conversation or greeting people for a phrase you'd like to use. Write some of these words down on a separate piece of paper and stick them up around the place. On the fridge, by the bed, on your computer, as a bookmark – somewhere where you'll see them often. Try putting some words in context – the 'How much is it?' note, for instance, could go in your wallet.

Building the Picture

We include a chapter on grammar in our books for two main reasons.

Firstly, some people have an aptitude for grammar and find understanding it a key tool to their learning. If you're such a person, then the grammar chapter in a phrasebook will help you build a picture of the language, as it works through all the basics.

The second reason for the grammar chapter is that it gives answers to questions you might raise as you hear or memorise some key phrases. You may find a particular word is always used when there is a question – check out the grammar heading on questions and it should explain why. This way you don't have to read the grammar chapter from start to finish, nor do you need to memorise a grammatical point. It will simply present itself to you in the course of your learning. Key grammatical points are repeated through the book.

Any Questions?

Try to learn the main question words (see page 29). As you read through different situations, you'll see these words used in the example sentences, and this will help you remember them. So if you want to hire a bicycle, turn to the Bicycles section in Getting Around (use the Contents or Index pages to find it quickly). You've already tried to memorise the word for 'where' and you'll see the word for 'bicycle'. When you come across the sentence 'Where can I hire a bicycle?', you'll recognise the key words and this will help you remember the whole phrase. If there's no category for your need, try the dictionary (the question words are repeated there too, with examples), and memorise the phrases 'Please write that down' and 'How do you say ...?' (page 61).

I've Got a Flat Tyre

Doesn't seem like the phrase you're going to need? Well, in fact it could be very useful. As are all the phrases in this book, provided you have the courage to mix and match them. We have given specific examples within each section. But the key words remain the same even when the situation changes. So while you may not be planning on any cycling during your trip, the first part of the phrase 'I've got ...' could refer to anything else, and there are plenty of words in the dictionary that, we hope, will fit your needs. So whether it's 'a ticket', 'a visa' or 'a condom', you'll be able to put the words together to convey your meaning.

Finally

Don't be concerned if you feel you can't memorise words. On the inside front and back covers are the most essential words and phrases you'll need. You could also try tagging a few pages for other key phrases, or use the notes pages to write your own reminders.

PRONUNCIATION

German pronunciation is relatively straightforward and uncomplicated. Each letter, or combination of letters, is pronounced consistently (unlike English!), that is, you pronounce them the same way each time. So, you can almost always tell how a word is pronounced by the way it's spelt.

Unlike English or French, or many other languages, which have several silent letters, German has only one: the letter h. Just as its counterpart in English, the h is sometimes silent and sometimes not, depending on its position in a word. Take the time to learn a few basic rules and you will have no trouble with the silent h. It is pronounced at the beginning of a word, eg **Hand** 'hand', or between two vowels, eg **Ahorn** 'acorn'. It is silent after a vowel and before a consonant, eg **er sieht** 'he sees', and at the end of a word. Other than the h all letters are pronounced – you pronounce the k at the start of the word **Knie** 'knee', the p at the start of **Psychologie** 'psychology', and the e at the end of **ich habe**, 'I have'.

There are some letters or letter combinations in the German alphabet that do not exist in English: these are the vowels with an umlaut (that's the two dots above a letter). Other letters you may find unfamiliar are the ß (a sharp 's') that may be replaced by ss and is pronounced as a voiceless 's', and the ch-sounds. The ch-sounds are pronounced in two ways depending on their surroundings: after a, o and u, the ch is a guttural sound like the 'ch' in the Scottish 'loch'; after i, e, ä, ö, ü, and consonants, the ch is pronounced like the initial sound you make when pronouncing the 'h' in 'huge'.

th	is always pronounced 't'
qu	is pronounced 'kv'
z	is pronounced 'ts'
w	is always pronounced 'v'

PRONUNCIATION

VOWELS

German vowels can be long or short. Although short vowels are straightforward, longer vowels can produce problems. When you pronounce the short vowel o, for example: it is said as in 'top', when it's long, the vowel still has the same quality, only longer. The spelling for long vowels is often indicated by an h after the vowel, or a doubling of the vowel oo, but not always. For i, the lengthening very often is done by writing ie.

The vowels with an umlaut are pronounced differently: ä, like the 'ai' in 'air', ö, like the 'u' in 'burn' and ü, a sound that does not exist in English but is pronounced like a 'u' as in 'soup', but with raised tongue that gives the sound the quality of an 'i' as in 'bit'.

a	short, as the 'u' in 'cut'
a, ah	long, as in 'father'
ä	short, as the 'e' in 'pet'
ä, äh	long, as in 'hair'
e	short, as in 'bet'
e, ee, eh	long, similar to the 'a' sound in 'gate', but with no 'y' sound
i	short, as in 'it'
i, ih, ie	long, as in 'see'
o	short, as in 'pot'
o, oo, oh	long, as the 'o' in 'more'
u	short, as in 'pull'
u, uu, uh	long, as in 'cool'
ö	similar to the 'er' sound in 'dirt'
ü	similar to the 'u' in 'dune', but with a raised tongue

DIPHTHONGS

ei, ai	as the 'ai' in 'aisle'
au	as the 'ow' in 'cow'
eu, äu	as the 'oy' in 'boy'

CONSONANTS

Most German consonants are similar to their English counterparts. One important difference is that **b**, **d** and **g** sound like 'p', 't' and 'k' respectively at the end of a word or syllable.

A possible source of problems might be the different pronunciation of **g**, **j** and **z** when they're at the beginning of a word. In this position, they are always pronounced the same way: **g** always as the 'g' in 'girl' and never as the 'g' in 'German'! The letter **j** is always pronounced as the 'y' in 'yes' and never as the 'j' in 'jam'! And **z** is always pronounced as the 'ts' in 'lets', never as the 'z' in 'zebra'. Many English speakers find it hard to pronounce the 'ts' sound at the beginning of a word, because they are used to it only at the end of a word. But persevere — it may spare you some misunderstandings! Remember that some words are distinguished only by the difference of this 'ts' sound: eg **sauber** 'clean' versus **Zauber** 'magic'!

b	normally the English 'b', but sometimes 'p' at the end of a word or syllable
c	as the 'ts' in 'lets', or as 'k' in foreign words
d	normally the English 'd', but sometimes 't' at the end of a word or syllable
f, ff	as the 'f' in 'feather'
g	normally the English 'g', but sometimes 'k' at the end of a word or syllable. But when a word ends in '-ig' it is 'ch'
h	as in 'harsh', silent after a vowel and before a consonant and at the end of a word
j	as the 'y' in 'yet'
l	as the 'l' in 'clear'
m, mm	as the 'm' in 'man'
n, nn	as the 'n' in 'no'
p, pp	as the 'p' in 'pan'
r	rolled at the back of the mouth, similar to the Scottish 'r'
s, ss, ß	normally as the 's' in 'sun', but as 'z' as in 'zoo' when followed by a vowel

PRONUNCIATION

t, tt	as the 't' in 'tan'
v	normally as the 'f' in 'fan', but some times as the 'v' in 'very'
w	as the 'v' in 'very'
x	as the English 'x' in 'index'
z	as the 'ts' in 'hits'

Consonantal Combinations

ch	a guttural sound like the Scottish 'loch'. But like the sound you get when pronouncing the 'h' in 'huge' after consonants and e, i, ä and ü
ng	as in 'sing', never as in 'finger' (the 'g' is not pronounced)
sch	as in 'ship'
sp	at the start of a word, the 's' sounds like the 'sh' in 'ship'
st	at the start of a word, the 's' sounds like the 'sh' in 'ship'
tion	the 't' sounds like the 'ts' in 'hits'

STRESS

Stress in German is very straightforward: the overwhelming majority of German words are stressed on the first syllable. Some prefixes are not stressed (such as **verstehen**, 'understand' which is stressed on the **stehen**); and certain foreign words, especially from French, which are stressed on the last syllable (**Organisation**; **Appetit**).

GRAMMAR

Although German grammar has a reputation for being complicated and full of exceptions, there are some straightforward rules you can learn which will help you speak the language well enough to be understood. These key rules are outlined in this chapter providing you with useful tools for building new sentences.

WORD ORDER

- In simple statements, the verb always comes second, and only one element (subject, object, adverb or adverb clause) can precede it.

  I am going to town.   **Ich gehe in die Stadt.**
                           (lit: I go in the town)

  Today, I am going to   **Heute gehe ich in die Stadt.**
  town.   (lit: today go I in the town)

- In yes/no questions the verb is placed first :

  Are you coming today?   **Kommst du heute?**
                           (lit: come you today)

- If there is a question word to introduce the question, the verb comes immediately after this:

  When are you coming?   **Wann kommst du?**
                           (lit: when come you)

- In commands the verb is normally placed at the beginning of the sentence:

  Come today!   **Komm heute!**
                           (lit: come today)

ARTICLES

Articles are the words preceding nouns which in English are 'the' (definite article) and 'a' (indefinite). In German these two articles vary according to whether they are masculine, feminine, neuter or plural, and then they vary further according to their declension. The articles are listed in a full table below, while declensions are explained on page 24.

Definite Article – 'the'

	masculine	feminine	neuter	plural
nominative	der	die	das	die
accusative	den	die	das	die
dative	dem	der	dem	den
genitive	des	der	des	der

Indefinite Article – 'a/an'

There is no plural form of ein/eine:

	masculine	feminine	neuter	plural
nom	ein	eine	ein	–
acc	einen	eine	ein	–
dat	einem	einer	einem	–
gen	eines	einer	eines	–

NOUNS

Nouns in German have three genders: masculine, feminine and neuter. Apart from nouns denoting human gender, the term 'gender' is purely grammatical. You can recognise it by the article – der (m), die (f) das (neut) – and/or adjective (if there is one). When learning each new noun, memorise both the word and its article, as there are no general rules that allow you to pick the correct gender straight off.

Here are some general hints about how to recognise gender.

Masculine Nouns

- nouns ending in **-er** that indicate a profession or the doer of an action.

  butcher **der Metzger**   teacher **der Lehrer**

- nouns ending **-ich, -ig, -ling**:

  carpet **der Teppich**   coward **der Feigling**
  vinegar **der Essig**

- abstract nouns ending **-ismus**:

  surrealism **der Surrealismus** tourism **der Tourismus**

- most nouns ending in **-en** with the exception of all infinitives used as nouns (see below):

  harbour **der Hafen**   shop **der Laden**

Feminine Nouns

- nouns derived from masculine nouns with **-er** endings to which **-in** has been added:

  player (f) **die Spielerin**   teacher (f) **die Lehrerin**

- nouns of more than one syllable ending on **-ei, -ion, -heit, -keit, -schaft, -ung**

  meaning **die Bedeutung**   opportunity **die Gelegenheit**

- most nouns ending **-e**:

  street **die Straße**   report **die Anzeige**

Neuter Nouns

- nouns ending **-lein** and **-chen** (diminutives):

  girl **das Mädchen**   little hat **das Hütchen**

- infinitives used as nouns:

  eating **das Essen**   travelling **das Reisen**

PLURAL

Forming the plural in German is not as straightforward as English. There are several forms that indicate plurality, and no hard-and-fast rules regarding their application. However, here are some guidelines that will help you.

Five Plural Groups

1. *Unchanged or with an umlaut in the plural*

   • In this group the noun is either the same in singular and plural, or it takes an umlaut but no ending. Nouns belonging to this group are mostly masculine with the endings -el, -en or -er:

finger	der Finger	fingers	die Finger
soil	der Boden	soils	die Böden
mirror	der Spiegel	mirrors	die Spiegel

   • Neuter nouns with the endings -chen, -el, -en, -er and -sel remain unchanged from singular to plural:

   | girl | das Mädchen | girls | die Mädchen |

   • The only feminine nouns in this group are:

   | mother | die Mutter | mothers | die Mütter |
   | daughter | die Tochter | daughters | die Töchter |

2. *Addition of -s in the plural*

   • Most Germanised English words belong to this group:

   | park | der Park | parks | die Parks |
   | crime thriller | der Krimi | crime thrillers | die Krimis |

GRAMMAR

- All nouns that end in a vowel, except for e, add -s in the plural:

grandmother	die Oma	grandmothers	die Omas
car	das Auto	car	die Autos
pizza	die Pizza	pizzas	die Pizzas

3. Ending in -(e)n in the plural

- Feminine and masculine nouns ending on -e add -n to create the plural:

| lady | die Dame | ladies | die Damen |
| boy | der Junge | boys | die Jungen |

- Nearly all feminine nouns, no matter what ending, also take the -(e)n plural:

| woman | die Frau | women | die Frauen |
| syllable | die Silbe | syllables | die Silben |

4. Umlaut + er in the plural

- This is the addition of -er to the singular form. Mainly monosyllabic neuter nouns belong to this group:

| picture | das Bild | pictures | die Bilder |

- If the singular noun contains an o, u or a this letter will become ö, ü or ä respectively in the plural:

| leaf | das Blatt | leaves | die Blätter |

- A few masculine words belong to this group:

god	der Gott	gods	die Götter
man	der Mann	men	die Männer
forest	der Wald	forests	die Wälder

5. Umlaut + e in the plural

• The addition of -e to the singular creates the plural. These are usually monosyllabic masculines:

| movie | der Film | movies | die Filme |
| day | der Tag | days | die Tage |

• An umlaut is sometimes added if the singular noun contains an o, u or a:

| tree | der Baum | trees | die Bäume |
| room | der Platz | rooms | die Plätze |

• Only a few monosyllabic feminines are found in this group:

| fear | die Angst | fears | die Ängste |

• No neuter nouns take the umlaut + e in the plural. However, masculines and monosyllabic neuters take -e:

| boat | das Boot | boats | die Boote |

CASES

German has four cases. Nouns, articles and adjectives all change endings according to their case.

The pattern for the four cases, in the three genders, is as follows:

	Singular Cases		
	masculine	**feminine**	**neuter**
	the/a man	*the/a woman*	*the/a book*
nom	der/ein Mann	die/eine Frau	das/ein Buch
acc	den/einen Mann	die/eine Frau	das/ein Buch
dat	dem/einem Mann	der/einer Frau	dem/einem Buch
gen	des/eines Mannes	der/einer Frau	des/eines Buches

GRAMMAR

A WORD ABOUT CASES

In English, we are able to recognise the 'role' of a noun in a sentence (that is, whether it is the subject, direct object or indirect object) by its position in the sentence and/or by the use of prepositions. However, like Latin, Russian and many other languages, German employs what are known as 'cases' to make these distinctions. Different 'case endings' (suffixes) act like labels on nouns to indicate their role and their relationship to other words in a sentence. The case endings of the other words in the sentence, for example, the articles, adjectives, adverbs or pronouns, must agree in number and gender with the case ending of the noun to which they refer.

German has only four of these cases and their application relates to grammatical usage in English. Here is a brief explanation of each case:

1. The **nominative** case refers to the subject of the verb in a sentence. It indicates **what** or **who** is doing the verb.

   The clown who stole the midget's hat gave balloons to the children. (the clown 'stole' and the clown 'gave')

2. The **accusative** case refers to the direct object. It indicates **what** or **whom** the verb refers to. Here it indicates what was 'given'.

   *The clown who stole the midget's hat gave **balloons** to the children.*

3. The **dative** case refers to the indirect object. It indicates **what** or **whom** is the indirect recipient of the verb. In English this is usually indicated by a preposition. In this case the preposition is 'to':

   *The clown who stole the midget's hat gave balloons to **the children.***

4. The **genitive** case refers to ownership or association. It indicates **whose** or **of what/of whom**.

   *The clown who stole **the midget's hat** gave balloons to the children.*

Plural

As there is no plural form of **ein/eine**, the word **kein** meaning 'no/not' is used to show the pattern.

Plural Cases

	masculine *the/men*	feminine *the/women*	neuter *the/books*
nom	di**e**/kein**e** Männer	di**e**/kein**e** Frauen	di**e**/kein**e** Bücher
acc	di**e**/kein**e** Männer	di**e**/kein**e** Frauen	di**e**/kein**e** Bücher
dat	de**n**/kein**en** Männer**n**	de**n**/kein**en** Frauen	de**n**/kein**en** Bücher**n**
gen	de**r**/kein**er** Männer	de**r**/kein**er** Frauen	de**r**/kein**er** Bücher

PRONOUNS

Personal Pronouns

In German, the mode of address varies according to the degree of intimacy between speakers. The informal **du** is used for friends, family members, and children, whereas the formal **Sie** is used with strangers and for all encounters in shops, banks etc. Sometimes it is hard to decide which form to use, especially when the person has reached a certain age (usually after 30). Although you may prefer the informal **du**, you are on the safe side using **Sie**. Older people will offer you the **du** when they think it appropriate.

STRESS

Nearly all German words are stressed on the first syllable.

However, many words which have prefixes are generally stressed on the second syllable:

ver*nunft*begabt
rational

GRAMMAR

Personal Pronouns

singular

person	nom	acc	dat	gen
I	ich	mich	mir	meiner
you (inf)	du	dich	dir	deiner
you (pol)	Sie	Sie	Ihnen	Ihrer
he	er	ihn	ihm	seiner
she	sie	sie	ihr	ihrer
it	es	es	ihm	seiner

plural

person	nom	acc	dat	gen
we	wir	uns	uns	unser
you (inf)	ihr	euch	euch	euer
you (pol)	Sie	Sie	Ihnen	Ihrer
they	sie	sie	ihnen	ihrer

The indefinite pronoun **man**, 'one', has the accusative and dative forms **einen** and **einem**.

You can eat well there.   **Man kann dort gut essen.**
                           lit: 'one can eat well there'

Reflexive Pronouns

Some German verbs always need a reflexive pronoun, for example, **sich setzen**: 'to sit down'.

'I sit down'   ich setze **mich**   lit: 'I sit myself'
'they sit down'   sie setzen **sich**   lit: 'they sit themselves'

Reflexive Pronouns

myself	**mich**	ourselves	**uns**
yourself (inf)	**dich**	yourselves (inf)	**euch**
yourself (pol)	**Sich**	yourselves (pol)	**Sich**
him/her/itself	**sich**	themselves	**sich**

GRAMMAR

Possessive Pronouns

The most common forms are:

Possessive Pronouns			
my	mein	our	unser
your (sg)	dein (inf)	your (pl)	euer (inf)
your (sg)	Ihr (pol)	your (pl)	Ihr (pol)
his/its	sein (m & neut)	their	ihr
her	ihr (f)		

The declension is given for mein only, because the endings are always the same.

Mein – 'my'				
	masculine	*feminine*	*neuter*	*plural*
nom	mein	meine	mein	meine
acc	meinen	meine	mein	meine
dat	meinem	meiner	meinem	meinen
gen	meines	meiner	meines	meiner

Demonstrative Pronouns

Dieser, 'this one' and jener, 'that one', are two common demonstrative pronouns in German. In almost all cases the definite articles, der/die/das, can be used as demonstrative pronouns – simply emphasise them.

Demonstrative Pronouns				
	masculine	*feminine*	*neuter*	*plural*
nom	dieser	diese	dieses	diese
acc	diesen	diese	dieses	diese
dat	diesem	dieser	diesem	diesen
gen	dieses	dieser	dieses	dieser

GRAMMAR

Interrogative Pronouns

Questions with an interrogative pronoun are formed the same way as in English. They start with the pronoun followed by the verb and then the rest:

Who is coming today?	Wer kommt heute?
Who did you see?	Wen hast du gesehen?

An exception to this rule is the pronoun in the genitive case which is followed by the noun it is referring to:

Whose book is this?	Wessen Buch ist das?

Interrogative Pronouns		
	who	*what*
nom	**wer**	**was**
acc	**wen**	**was**
dat	**wem**	–
gen	**wessen**	–

Note: there are no dative or genitive forms of was

ADJECTIVES
Declension of Adjectives

Adjectives also have endings that are determined both by the article before the adjective and the case of the following noun.

Strong endings mark gender and case while weak endings do not. If there is an article before the adjective, the article shows the gender and case of the noun, therefore the adjective takes weak endings that don't show gender and case:

the big man	der große Mann
the big woman	die große Frau

Weak adjective endings are the same for neuter and feminine nouns.

If there is no article the adjectives have to show gender and case and subsequently take strong endings:

| big man | **großer Mann** |
| big woman | **große Frau** |

Adjectives ending in **-abel**, **-ibel**, **-el** and in **-auer**, **-euer** drop the **-e** when declined:

| expensive **teuer** | an expensive present | **ein teures Geschenk** |
| bad **übel** | bad mood | **üble Laune** |

Adjectives that come after a noun have no declensional endings:

| the man is tall | **der Mann ist groß** |

Adjectival Endings

Weak Endings					Strong Endings			
	m	f	neut	pl		m	f	neut	pl
nom	e	e	e	en	nom	er	e	es	e
acc	en	e	e	en	acc	en	e	es	e
dat	en	en	en	en	dat	em	er	em	en
gen	en	en	en	en	gen	en	er	en	er

Comparison

All adjectives and adverbs add **-er-** before the declensional endings in the comparative and **-(e)st-** in the superlative. There is no equivalent to the English use of more/most with longer adjectives and adverbs.

small	smaller	the smallest
klein	**kleiner**	**am kleinsten**
the small woman	the smaller woman	the smallest woman
die kleine Frau	**die kleinere Frau**	**die kleinste Frau**

Common Irregular Adjectives & Adverbs:

good	gut	better	besser	best	am besten
many	viel	more	mehr	most	am meisten
glad	gern	gladder	lieber	gladdest	am liebsten
soon	bald	sooner	eher	soonest	am ehesten

When comparing two equal things by using 'as', you use wie:

> she is as tall as I am   sie ist so groß *wie* ich

When forming the comparative by using 'than', you use als:

> she is taller than I am   sie ist größer *als* ich

The comparative of the adverb follows the rules for the adjective. Most adverbs form the superlative according to the pattern am ...-sten:

> she counts the fastest   sie rechnet am schnell*sten*

DID YOU KNOW ...   German belongs to the West Germanic branch of the larger Indo-European language group. Centred in Germany, Austria and Switzerland, there are also large numbers of German speakers in the ex-Soviet republics, Romania and in France – especially in Alsace-Lorraine. The total number of German speakers in the world exceeds 100,000,000.

COMMON ENGLISH MISTAKES BY GERMAN SPEAKERS

Most Germans have learned English for a few years at school, so they at least speak rudimentary English. The most prominent feature of 'German English' is the odd pronunciation.

- A lot of people can't pronounce the 'th' and replace it with a 'z' or a 'd', so when someone says 'ze mozer' or 'de moder' they mean 'the mother'.

- The next difficulty is the pronunciation of the 'w'. While the German alphabet has the letter 'w', it is pronounced like a 'v' or an 'f', never like the English 'w'. So, 'vould you like some vater' means 'would you like some water'.

- Also, Germans tend to confuse the letters 'v' and 'w' in English:

  'Vat vere you doing last night'

  'I'm wegetarian'.

- Apart from pronunciation, German speakers have some difficulty understanding when to use verbs that end in -ing, as this form does not exist in German. As a result it is often overused.

- Prepositions can also be problematic, so you might hear 'Since a long time I haven't done that.' instead of 'I haven't done that for a long time.'

VERBS

Most German verbs are regular. The infinitive form of most German verbs ends in -en: sometimes it ends in -ln or -rn. The stem of a verb is thus found by removing the -en from verbs ending in -en (eg the stem of gehen 'to go' is geh), or the -n from verbs ending in -ln or -rn (for example, the stem of radeln 'to cycle' is radel).

The various verb forms are made by adding an ending to the stem. Finite (conjugated) verbs show person, number and tense. There are also three verb forms that cannot stand independently in a sentence (that is, without a finite verb), but are used in compound tenses such as present perfect, past perfect and future tense. They do not show person, number or tense but always have the same form: sagen 'to say' (infinitive), sagend 'saying' (present participle) and gesagt 'said' (past participle).

> ### CASE
>
> In nearly all instances, all German nouns, articles and adjectives change endings according to their case.

Regular verbs have the same vowel in their stem in all forms and take -t in the past tense and in the past participle:

to say	sagen	(infinitive)
said	sag*te*	(past tense)
said	*ge*sag*t*	(past participle)

The irregular verbs do have some regularity though. In some forms they change their stem vowel:

| to give | geben | gave | gab |
| given | gegeben | | |

Irregular verbs never take -t in the past tense, and they take -en in the past participle:

| to go | gehen | went | ging | gone | gegangen |

Present Tense

Regular Verbs (to say – sagen)

I say/I am saying	ich	sage
you say/you are saying (sg)	du	sagst
he/she/it says; he/she/it is saying	er/sie/es	sagt
we say/we are saying	wir	sagen
you say/you are saying (pl)	ihr	sagt
they say/they are saying	sie	sagen

The polite form **Sie** is identical with the **sie** 'they' form in all tenses. Verbs where the stem ends in **d**, **t**, consonant + **n** or **m** add an **-e** in the second person singular:

to talk **reden**   you talk/you are talking   **du redest**

Irregular Verbs (to eat – essen)

I eat/I am eating	ich	esse
you eat/you are eating (sg)	du	isst
he/she/it eats; he/she/it is eating	er/sie/es	isst
we eat/we are eating	wir	essen
you eat/you are eating (pl)	ihr	esst
they eat/they are eating	sie	essen

GRAMMAR

DID YOU KNOW ...   Luther – who gave his name to the Lutheran church – provided the basis for a standardised German with his landmark sixteenth-century translation of the Bible.

Auxiliary Verbs
Present tense

The auxiliary verbs **sein** 'to be', **haben** 'to have', **werden** 'to become' are used to form compound tenses such as present perfect, pluperfect and future tense.

sein – to be

I am	ich	bin	we are	wir	sind
you are (sg)	du	bist	you are (pl)	ihr	seid
he is	er	ist	they are	sie	sind
she is	sie	ist			
it is	es	ist			

haben – to have

I have	ich	habe	we have	wir	haben
you have (sg)	du	hast	you have (pl)	ihr	habt
he has	er	hat	they have	sie	haben
she has	sie	hat			
it has	es	hat			

werden – to become

I become	ich	werde	we become	wir	werden
you become (sg)	du	wirst	you become (pl)	ihr	werdet
he becomes	er	wird	they become	sie	werden
she becomes	sie	wird			
it becomes	es	wird			

GRAMMAR

KEY VERBS

The polite form Sie ('you' sg & pl, pol) is exactly the same as the sie 'they' form in all the tenses. Germans usually use the present perfect to refer to the past.

bleiben (to stay/ to remain)

	present	present perfect	future
I	bleibe	bin geblieben	werde bleiben
you (sg, inf)	bleibst	bist geblieben	wirst bleiben
he/she/it	bleibt	ist geblieben	wird bleiben
we	bleiben	sind geblieben	werden bleiben
you (pl, inf)	bleibt	seid geblieben	werdet bleiben
they/you	bleiben	sind geblieben	werden bleiben
(sg & pl, pol)			

bringen (to bring)

	present	present perfect	future
I	bringe	habe gebracht	werde bringen
you	bringst	hast gebracht	wirst bringen
he/she/it	bringt	hat gebracht	wird bringen
we	bringen	haben gebracht	werden bringen
you	bringt	habt gebracht	werdet bringen
they/you	bringen	haben gebracht	werden bringen

essen (to eat)

	present	present perfect	future
I	esse	habe gegessen	werde essen
you	isst	hast gegessen	wirst essen
he/she/it	isst	hat gegessen	wird essen
we	essen	haben gegessen	werden essen
you	esst	habt gegessen	werdet essen
they/you	essen	haben gegessen	werden essen

gehen (to go)

	present	present perfect	future
I	gehe	bin gegangen	werde gehen
you	gehst	bist gegangen	wirst gehen
he/she/it	geht	ist gegangen	wird gehen
we	gehen	sind gegangen	werden gehen
you	geht	seid gegangen	werdet gehen
they/you	gehen	sind gegangen	werden gehen

haben (to have)

	present	present perfect	future
I	habe	habe gehabt	werde haben
you	hast	hast gehabt	wirst haben
he/she/it	hat	hat gehabt	wird haben
we	haben	haben gehabt	werden haben
you	habt	habt gehabt	werdet haben
they/you	haben	haben gehabt	werden haben

kommen (to come)

	present	present perfect	future
I	komme	bin gekommen	werde kommen
you	kommst	bist gekommen	wirst kommen
he/she/it	kommt	ist gekommen	wird kommen
we	kommen	sind gekommen	werden kommen
you	kommt	seid gekommen	werdet kommen
they/you	kommen	sind gekommen	werden kommen

machen (to make/to do)

	present	present perfect	future
I	mache	habe gemacht	werde machen
you	machst	hast gemacht	wirst machen
he/she/it	macht	hat gemacht	wird machen
we	machen	haben gemacht	werden machen
you	macht	habt gemacht	werdet machen
they/you	machen	haben gemacht	werden machen

sagen (to say)

	present	present perfect	future
I	sage	habe gesagt	werde sagen
you	sagst	hast gesagt	wirst sagen
he/she/it	sagt	hat gesagt	wird sagen
we	sagen	haben gesagt	werden sagen
you	sagt	habt gesagt	werdet sagen
they/you	sagen	haben gesagt	werden sagen

sein (to be)

	present	present perfect	future
I	bin	bin gewesen	werde sein
you	bist	bist gewesen	wirst sein
he/she/it	ist	ist gewesen	wird sein
wo	sind	sind gewesen	werden sein
you	seid	seid gewesen	werdet sein
they/you	sind	sind gewesen	werden sein

GRAMMAR

verstehen (to understand)

	present	present perfect	future
I	verstehe	habe verstanden	werde verstehen
you	verstehst	hast verstanden	wirst verstehen
he/she/it	versteht	hat verstanden	wird verstehen
we	verstehen	haben verstanden	werden verstehen
you	versteht	habt verstanden	werdet verstehen
they/you	verstehen	haben verstanden	werden verstehen

werden (to become)

	present	present perfect	future
I	werde	bin geworden	werde werden
you	wirst	bist geworden	wirst werden
he/she/it	wird	ist geworden	wird werden
we	werden	sind geworden	werden werden
you	werdet	seid geworden	werdet werden
they/you	werden	sind geworden	werden werden

wissen (to know 'something')

	present	present perfect	future
I	weiß	habe gewußt	werde wissen
you	weißt	hast gewußt	wirst wissen
he/she/it	weiß	hat gewußt	wird wissen
we	wissen	haben gewußt	werden wissen
you	wißt	habt gewußt	werdet wissen
they/you	wissen	haben gewußt	werden wissen

wohnen (to live 'somewhere')

	present	present perfect	future
I	wohne	habe gewohnt	werde wohnen
you	wohnst	hast gewohnt	wirst wohnen
he/she/it	wohnt	hat gewohnt	wird wohnen
we	wohnen	haben gewohnt	werden wohnen
you	wohnt	habt gewohnt	werdet wohnen
they/you	wohnen	haben gewohnt	werden wohnen

wollen (to want)

	present	present perfect	future
I	will	habe gewollt	werde wollen
you	willst	hast gewollt	wirst wollen
he/she/it	will	hat gewollt	wird wollen
we	wollen	haben gewollt	werden wollen
you	wollt	habt gewollt	werdet wollen
they/you	wollen	haben gewollt	werden wollen

GRAMMAR

Present Perfect

The present perfect is used in spoken language when referring to the past. It is formed from the present tense of the auxiliary verbs **haben** 'to have' or **sein** 'to be' and the past participle.

The verb **haben** 'to have' is used with transitive verbs (verbs having an accusative object), reflexive and impersonal verbs and most intransitive verbs when they indicate the duration of a state.

Verbs with **haben** – to have		
I have said/eaten	ich **habe**	gesagt/gegessen
you have said/eaten	du **hast**	gesagt/gegessen
he has said/eaten	er **hat**	gesagt/gegessen
she has said/eaten	sie **hat**	gesagt/gegessen
it has said/eaten	es **hat**	gesagt/gegessen
we have said/eaten	wir **haben**	gesagt/gegessen
you have said/eaten	ihr **habt**	gesagt/gegessen
they have said/eaten	sie **haben**	gesagt/gegessen

The verb **sein** 'to be' is used with verbs of motion and verbs that indicate a transition from one state into another, and with **sein** 'to be', **bleiben** 'to stay' and **werden** 'to become'.

Verbs with **sein** to be		
I have gone/travelled	ich **bin**	gegangen/gereist
you have gone/travelled	du **bist**	gegangen/gereist
he has gone/travelled	er **ist**	gegangen/gereist
she has gone/travelled	sie **ist**	gegangen/gereist
it has gone/travelled	es **ist**	gegangen/gereist
we have gone/travelled	wir **sind**	gegangen/gereist
you have gone/travelled	ihr **seid**	gegangen/gereist
they have gone/travelled	sie **sind**	gegangen/gereist

GRAMMAR

The past participle is placed last in the clause:

> She has gone to town   Sie ist in die Stadt gegangen
> (lit: she was in the town gone)

Past

Although the most common way of talking in the past tense is to use the present perfect tense, the simple past tense is used in written language.

Regular Verbs

Regular verbs take the following endings:

Regular Verbs (to say – sagen)

I said	ich	sag**te**	we said	wir	sag**ten**
you said	du	sag**test**	you said	ihr	sag**tet**
he said	er	sag**te**	they said	sie	sag**ten**
she said	sie	sag**te**			
it said	es	sag**te**			

Irregular Verbs

There are no simple rules for the declension of irregular verbs as they can be quite different and they just have to be learnt. The verb essen 'to eat' is a typical example:

Irregular Verbs (to eat – essen)

I ate	ich	aß	we ate	wir	aßen
you ate	du	aßest	you ate	ihr	aßt
he ate	er	aß	they ate	sie	aßen
she ate	sie	aß			
it ate	es	aß			

Pluperfect

The pluperfect is formed from the past tense form of haben or
sein and the past participle. The same rules for the use of haben
or sein apply as for the present perfect. It is rarely used in southern
Germany, but you'll come across it a lot in northern Germany
where it frequently replaces the present perfect.

With 'to have' – haben			
I had said	ich	hatte	gesagt
you had said (sg)	du	hattest	gesagt
he/she/it had said	er/sie/es	hatte	gesagt
we had said	wir	hatten	gesagt
you had said (pl)	ihr	hattet	gesagt
they had said	sie	hatten	gesagt

With 'to be' – sein			
I had gone	ich	war	gegangen
you had gone (sg)	du	warst	gegangen
he/she/it had gone	er/sie/es	war	gegangen
we had gone	wir	waren	gegangen
you had gone (pl)	ihr	wart	gegangen
they had gone	sie	waren	gegangen

Future

For the future tense, you put the present tense form of werden
'to become' with the infinitive of the main verb:

    I will say   ich werde sagen

Past Tense & Past Participle

sein – to be

participle: (bin) gewesen

I was	ich	war
you were (sg)	du	warst
he/she/it was	er/sie/es	war
we were	wir	waren
you were (pl)	ihr	wart
they were	sie	waren

haben – to have

participle: (habe) gehabt

I had	ich	hatte
you had (sg)	du	hattest
he/she/it had	er/sie/es	hatte
we had	wir	hatten
you had (pl)	ihr	hattet
they had	sie	hatten

werden – to become

participle: (bin) geworden

I became	ich	wurde
you became (sg)	du	wurdest
he/she/it became	er/sie/es	wurde
we became	wir	wurden
you became (pl)	ihr	wurdet
they became	sie	wurden

GRAMMAR

Past Participle

- The past participle is needed to form the present perfect and pluperfect. The past participle of regular verbs is formed by adding ge- before and -t after the stem:

to make	machen	made	gemacht
to lay	legen	laid	gelegt
to talk	reden	talked	geredet
to kiss	küssen	kissed	geküsst
to love	lieben	loved	geliebt

- Verbs which end in -ieren and inseparable compound verbs with the prefixes be-, emp-, ent-, er-, ge-, ver- and zer- omit the ge-:

to try	probieren	tried	probiert
to hurt	verletzen	hurt	verletzt
to visit	besuchen	visited	besucht

- The past participle of separable compound verbs is formed by adding -ge- between prefix and stem and the ending -t to the stem:

to shop	einkaufen	shopped	eingekauft
to cancel	absagen	cancelled	abgesagt
to announce	durchsagen	announced	durchgesagt

- The past participle of irregular verbs is formed by adding ge- before and -en after the stem. In addition, there is often a change in the stem vowel:

to help	helfen	helped	geholfen
to go	gehen	gone	gegangen
to sleep	schlafen	slept	geschlafen

- For irregular verbs ending in -ieren, and for inseparable and separable compound verbs apply the same rules as shown above, only the ending is always -en:

to lose	verlieren	lost	verloren

Modal Verbs

The modal verbs are:

can; to be able to	können
to be allowed to; may	dürfen
to like, to want	mögen
ought to; is supposed to	sollen
to have, to must	müssen
to want to	wollen

When a modal verb is used, the main verb stays in the infinitive and at the end of a clause:

I can't come tonight   Ich *kann* heute abend nicht *kommen*

MODAL VERB TABLE

Present Tense

	können	dürfen	mögen	sollen	müssen	wollen
ich	kann	darf	mag	soll	muss	will
du	kannst	darfst	magst	sollst	musst	willst
er/sie/es	kann	darf	mag	soll	muss	will
wir	können	dürfen	mögen	sollen	müssen	wollen
ihr	könnt	dürft	mögt	sollt	müsst	wollt
sie	können	dürfen	mögen	sollen	müssen	wollen

Past Tense

ich	konnte	durfte	mochte	sollte	musste	wollte
du	konntest	durftest	mochtest	solltest	musstest	wolltest
er/sie/es	konnte	durfte	mochte	sollte	musste	wollte
wir	konnten	durften	mochten	sollten	mussten	wollten
ihr	konntet	durftet	mochtet	solltet	musstet	wolltet
sie	konnten	durften	mochten	sollten	mussten	wollten

COMMON GERMAN MISTAKES BY ENGLISH SPEAKERS

Apart from difficulties in pronunciation, here are some of the areas where English speakers can make mistakes.

Word Order

This relates especially to the position of the verb. In a main clause, the verb always comes second, even if there is an adverb at the beginning of the clause. For example, 'Today, I'm going to town' is translated as 'Heute **gehe ich** in die Stadt', and not as 'Heute, **ich gehe** in die Stadt', with the verb and subject changing positions.

Another problem is the so-called **Verbklammer**, the separating of the auxiliary from the main verb in compound tenses such as the present perfect and future tense, for example, 'Ich **bin** heute in die Stadt **gegangen**' or 'Ich **werde** heute in die Stadt **gehen**'. Here the rule is to place the conjugated auxiliary in the second position and the participle or infinitive respectively at the end of the clause. The same applies to the use of modals, for example, 'Ich **möchte** heute in die Stadt **gehen**'. However, in subordinate clauses the auxiliary and the main verb both go to the end of the clause, the main verb coming first and the conjugated auxiliary taking the last position, for example, 'Er sagte, dass sie gestern **gegangen ist**', 'He said that she went yesterday'.

Apart from the position of the verb, the word order is relatively free, at least freer than in English. This is due to the usage of three genders and the inflection of articles, adjectives and nouns. Whether a noun phrase has the function of a subject or an object does not have to be shown by the position in the clause because the endings already show it.

GRAMMAR

COMMON MISTAKES BY ENGLISH SPEAKERS

Gender
Since there are no general rules that govern the alloca-
tion of the gender to a certain noun, you have to learn
the article together with every new noun. (For the declension of articles and adjectives in the four cases,
see the Grammar chapter.)

Numbers
Another problem is the word order in numbers. In numbers above 20, the units come before the tens, for
example, 21 is **einundzwanzig**, 'one-and-twenty', 45
fünfundvierzig, 'five-and-forty' and so on.

Imperative
The imperative of regular verbs is usually formed by adding -e
(sg) or -t (pl) to the stem:

Drink! (to one person)	Trinke!
Drink! (to two people)	Trinkt!

In spoken language, however, the -e is often omitted. For the
polite form of address the pronoun is included after the verb:

Come here!	**Kommen Sie!**
	(lit. come you)

Official language often uses an infinitive for the imperative:

Please don't smoke!	**Bitte nicht rauchen!**

KEY VERBS

to be	sein
to be able	tun können
to become	werden
to bring	bringen
to buy	kaufen
to come	kommen
to cost	kosten
to depart/to leave	weggehen/verlassen
to drink	trinken
to eat	essen
to give	geben
to go	gehen
to have	haben
to know (someone)	kennen
to know (something)	wissen
to like	mögen
to live (lite)	leben
to live (somewhere)	wohnen
to love	lieben
to make	machen
to meet	treffen
to need	brauchen
to prefer	vorziehen
to return	zurückgehen
to say	sagen
to stay (remain)	bleiben
to stay (somewhere)	wohnen
to take	nehmen
to understand	verstehen
to want	wollen

GRAMMAR

NEGATION

The negation of the whole sentence is formed by the particle nicht 'not' which is placed after the finite verb:

I am going home.	Ich gehe *nach* Hause.
I am not going home.	Ich gehe *nicht nach* Hause.

If there is an object in the sentence, nicht comes after the object:

I don't love you.   Ich liebe dich *nicht*.

In sentences containing an indefinite article, ein, or no article, kein replaces nicht and the indefinite article:

I see a house.	Ich sehe *ein* Haus.
I don't see a house.	Ich sehe *kein* Haus.

Other words for negation are:

nobody   niemand
  I don't see anybody.   Ich sehe *niemand*en.

nothing/anything   nichts
  I don't see anything.   Ich sehe *nichts*.

never   nie/niemals
  I never drink alcohol.   Ich trinke *nie* Alkohol.

nowhere/anywhere   nirgends
  I don't see him anywhere.   Ich sehe ihn *nirgends*.

COMPOUND VERBS

Compound verbs follow the pattern of simple verbs. They are fomed by the addition of a prefix to the verb. This prefix may be either separable or inseparable.

Separable verbs have their main accent on the prefix, while inseparable verbs have their accent on the stem of the verb.

EIN & KEIN

Remember that although there is a plural form of the definite article **der** ('the') there is no plural form of the indefinite article **ein** ('a').

Separable

A separable prefix is found attached to its verb in the infinitive:

You have to get up.   Du musst aufstehen.

Separable Prefixes				
ab-	bei-	her-	nach-	zu-
an-	ein-	los-	vor-	zurück-
auf-	hin-	mit-	weg-	zusammen-

In the present and past tense, the prefix is separated from the stem and goes to the end of the sentence:

Everyday I get up at 6   Ich stehe jeden Tag um 6
o'clock.   Uhr auf.
Today, I got up at 6 o'clock. Ich stand heute um 6 Uhr auf.

In the present perfect and the pluperfect, however, the prefix rejoins its verb:

I got up at 6 o'clock today.   Ich bin heute um 6 Uhr
                                           aufgestanden.

Inseparable

Inseparable verbs behave like simple verbs in most cases. They keep their prefix in the present and past tense:

I'll never lose the key.   Ich verliere nie den Schlüssel.

Inseparable Prefixes						
be-	emp-	ent-	er-	ge-	ver-	zer-

The only difference is that they don't take a -ge- in the past participle:

I have lost the key.   Ich habe den Schlüssel
                                verloren.

PREPOSITIONS

The case found most frequently after a preposition in German is the dative. So one rule of thumb might be that you should use the dative if you are not sure. For those of you who want more facts, however, here are all the prepositions with their respective cases:

Prepositions with the Dative

zu	to towards	aus	out of
außer	apart from	bei	at
mit	with	nach	near
nächst	next to	seit	since
von	from	samt	together with
entgegen	against	entsprechend	according to
gegenüber	opposite	gemäß	in accordance with

Entgegen, entsprechend, gegenüber and gemäß can be placed either before or after the noun or pronoun, the rest are always placed before the noun/pronoun.

PREPOSITION MISTAKES BY ENGLISH SPEAKERS

The English preposition 'for' is **für** in German, for example, 'I have been here for three days' is translated as, **Ich war hier für drei Tage**, although it should be **Ich war drei Tage hier**.

The prepositions **an**, 'at', **in**, 'in', **auf**, 'on', **unter**, 'under', **hinter**, 'behind', **neben**, 'next to', **zwischen**, 'between' and **vor**, 'in front of' change the case of the following noun phrase depending on whether they denote a movement (accusative case) or a position (dative case):

I'm sitting down on a chair.	*Ich setze mich auf einen Stuhl. (acc)*
I'm sitting on a chair.	*Ich sitze auf einem Stuhl. (dat)*

GRAMMAR

Prepositions with the Accusative

bis	until	**durch**	through
für	for	**gegen**	against
ohne	without	**um**	around
wider	against		

Prepositions with the Genitive

(an)statt	instead of	**trotz**	in spite of
während	during	**wegen**	because of

In spoken language, the genitive use of **trotz**, **während** and **wegen** is hardly ever heard, the genitive being replaced by the dative.

Prepositions with either Accusative or Dative

an	at, on	**auf**	on
in	in	**hinter**	behind
neben	next to	**über**	above, over
vor	in front of	**zwischen**	between
unter	under		

With these prepositions, the accusative is used where motion, change of position or movement in a certain direction is implied in the sentence. The dative is used where a stationary position is implied.

Accusative:
    She sat down on the chair.   Sie setzte sich auf den Stuhl.

Dative:
    She sat on the chair.   Sie saß auf dem Stuhl.

Contracted Forms of Prepositions

The preposition and the following article are very often contracted. The most common contracted forms are:

Contracted Prepositions & Articles			
am	an dem	im	in dem
ins	in das	beim	bei dem
zur	zu der	zum	zu dem
vom	von dem		

MEETING PEOPLE

Germans can be quite reserved so don't expect a hearty welcome. When meeting someone for the first time you normally shake hands. If you know each other well enough you may exchange kisses. This is regarded as perfectly normal between women and between women and men. Men usually avoid it, giving each other a pat on the shoulder instead.

YOU SHOULD KNOW

With the following basic expressions you should be able to start and keep up a short conversation.

Hello. (good day)	Guten Tag; Hallo.
Hi.	Hallo.
Goodbye.	Auf Wiedersehen.
Bye.	Tschüss. (S)
	Ade. (inf)
Yes/No.	Ja/Nein.
Excuse me.	Entschuldigung.
May I? Do you mind?	Darf ich? Macht es Ihnen etwas aus?
Sorry. (excuse me, forgive me)	Entschuldigung.
Please.	Bitte.
Thank you.	Danke.
Many thanks.	Vielen Dank.
That's fine. You're welcome.	Bitte (sehr).

DID YOU KNOW ... In more colloquial German, the e and the u are left out. For example, you might hear g'sagt for gesagt ('said'), d' for du ('you') or Ich hab' for Ich habe ('I have').

GREETINGS

When Germans ask Wie geht es Ihnen? 'How do you do?', they expect a more or less honest answer (depending on the level of intimacy). Unlike English, 'How do you do?' is never used on its own as a form of greeting.

Good day.	Guten Tag; Grüß Gott. (S)
Good morning.	Guten Morgen.
Good afternoon.	Guten Tag.
Good evening.	Guten Abend.
Goodnight.	Gute Nacht.
How are you?	Wie geht es Ihnen/dir? (pol/inf)
Well, thanks.	Danke, gut.
Not too bad.	Es geht.
Not so good.	Nicht so gut.
And you?	Und Ihnen/dir? (pol/inf)

FORMS OF ADDRESS

As yet there is no equivalent of Ms. Frau, 'Mrs', is regarded as a respectful form of address for older women whether they are married or not. Fräulein, 'Miss', has become old-fashioned and is slowly disappearing from the spoken language.

Mrs	Frau
Mr	Herr
Miss	Fräulein
companion, friend	Freund/in
Ladies!	Meine Damen!
Gentlemen!	Meine Herren!

Often when addressing a professional person or someone of status, the person's title is used. This is especially popular in Austria where virtually everybody seems to have a title.

Doctor ...	Doktor .../Frau Doktor ...
Professor ...	Professor .../Frau Professor ...

FIRST ENCOUNTERS

What is your name?	Wie heißen Sie?;
	Wie ist Ihr Name?
My name is ...	Ich heiße ...;
	Ich bin ...;
	Mein Name ist ...
I'd like to introduce you to ...	Darf ich Ihnen ... vorstellen?
my boyfriend	meinen Freund
my daughter	meine Tochter
my daughter-in-law	meine Schwiegertochter
my girlfriend	meine Freundin
my grandchildren	meine Enkel
my grandparents	meine Großeltern
my husband	meinen Mann
my parents	meine Eltern
my parents-in-law	meine Schwiegereltern
my son	meinen Sohn
my son-in-law	meinen Schwiegersohn
my wife	meine Frau
I'm pleased to meet you.	Angenehm; Sehr erfreut.
Don't we know one another	Kennen wir uns nicht
by sight?	schon vom Sehen?
Are you Mrs Jones?	Sind Sie Frau Jones?

NATIONALITIES

A great conversation-starter in Germany is to ask someone where they come from. Unfortunately we can't list all countries here; however, you will find that many country names in German are similar in English. Remember though, that even if a word looks like the German equivalent it will have German pronunciation. (For instance, Japan: *ya-pan*). Listed here are some that differ more considerably.

MEETING PEOPLE

Where are you from?	Woher kommen Sie/ kommst du? (pol/inf)

I am from ...	Ich komme aus ...
Australia	Australien
Austria	Österreich
France	Frankreich
Germany	Deutschland
the Middle East	dem Nahen Osten
New Zealand	Neuseeland
Switzerland	der Schweiz
Great Britain	Großbritannien
the USA	den Vereinigten Staaten

AGE

How old are you?	Wie alt sind Sie/bist du? (pol/inf)
I am ... years old.	Ich bin ... Jahre alt.
I'm over 18.	Ich bin über 18 Jahre alt.
She is under age.	Sie ist minderjährig.
I was born on ...	Ich bin am ... geboren.

For numbers, see page 217.

MEETING PEOPLE

OCCUPATIONS

What (work) do you do?	Als was arbeiten Sie/ arbeitest du? (pol/inf)
What is your profession?	Was sind Sie/bist du von Beruf? (pol/inf)

I am a/an ...	Ich bin ...
accountant	Buchhalter/in
actor	Schauspieler/in
apprentice	Lehrling
architect	Architekt/in
artist	Künstler/in
baker	Bäcker/in
bricklayer	Maurer
businessperson	Geschäftsmann/ Geschäftsfrau
butcher	Metzger/in
carpenter	Schreiner/in
chemist	Apotheker/in
civil servant	Beamter/Beamtin
cook	Koch/Köchin
dentist	Zahnarzt/Zahnärztin
doctor	Arzt/Ärztin
driver	Kraftfahrer/in
electrician	Elektriker/in
employee	Angestellter/Angestellte
engineer	Ingenieur/in
factory worker	Fabrikarbeiter/in
farmer	Bauer/Bäuerin
gardener	Gärtner/in
hairdresser	Friseur/Friseuse
housewife	Hausfrau
interpreter	Dolmetscher/in
journalist	Journalist/in
lawyer	Rechtsanwalt/ Rechtsanwältin

locksmith	Schlosser
mechanic	Mechaniker/in
musician	Musiker/in
nurse	Krankenpfleger/ Krankenschwester
office worker	Büroangestellter/ Büroangestellte
painter	Maler/in
pensioner	Rentner/in
plumber	Installateur/in
postman	Briefträger/in
scientist	Wissenschaftler/in
secretary	Sekretär/in
shopkeeper	Kaufmann/Kauffrau
student	Student/in
tailor	Schneider/in
teacher	Lehrer/in
waiter	Kellner/in
worker	Arbeiter/in
writer	Schriftsteller/in

SILENT H

German has only one silent letter, **h**, and it's only silent when it's after a vowel and before a consonant, or when it's at the end of a word: eg. **Rahmen** (m) ('frame').

All other letters are pronounced. So, **k** is pronounced in **Knie** (neut) ('knee'), **p** in **Psychologie** (f) ('psychology') and **e** in **Sonne** (f) ('sun').

profession	Beruf (m)
retired	pensioniert
salary	Gehalt (neut); Lohn (m)
unemployed	arbeitslos

MEETING PEOPLE

STUDENT LIFE

Are you a student?	Bist du Student/in?
What are you studying?	Was studierst du?
I'm studying ...	Ich studiere ...
archeology	Archäologie (f)
arts	Kunst (f)
economics	Betriebswirtschaft (f)
history	Geschichte (f)

languages	Sprachen (pl)
law	Jura
literature	Literaturwissenschaft (f)
mathematics	Mathematik (f)
medicine	Medizin (f)
physics	Physik (f)
psychology	Psychologie (f)
social work	Sozialarbeit (f)
sociology	Soziologie (f)
sports	Sport (m)

What term are you in?	Im wievielten Semester bist du?
When will your finals be?	Wann hast du deine Prüfung?

MEETING PEOPLE

certificate	Schein (m)
course guidance service	Studienberatung (f)
finals	(Abschluss)Prüfungen (pl)
grant	Studienförderung (f), also called BAFÖG
hall of residents	Studentenwohnheim (neut)
lecture	Vorlesung (f)
lecturer	Dozent/in
seminar	Seminar (neut)
student card	Studentenausweis (m)
term	Semester (neut)
tuition fees	Studiengebühren (pl)

RELIGION

| What is your religion? | Was ist Ihre/deine Religion? (pol/inf) |
| I am not religious. | Ich bin nicht religiös. |

I am ...	Ich bin ...
atheist	Atheist/in
Buddhist	Buddhist/in
Catholic	katholisch
Christian	Christ/in
Hindu	Hindu
Jewish	Jude/Jüdin
Muslim	Moslem
Protestant	evangelisch

Bible	Bibel (f)
cathedral	Dom (m)
church	Kirche (f)
God	Gott (m)
mass	Messe (f)
priest	Priester (m); Pfarrer (m)
service	Gottesdienst (m)

See also Pilgrimage & Religion page 210.

MEETING PEOPLE

LANGUAGE DIFFICULTIES

Do you speak English?	Sprechen Sie Englisch?
Does anyone here speak English?	Spricht hier jemand Englisch?
I speak a little ...	Ich spreche ein bisschen...
I don't speak ...	Ich spreche kein ...
Do you understand?	Verstehen Sie mich?
I understand.	Ich verstehe.
I don't understand anything at all.	Ich verstehe überhaupt nichts.
Could you translate that for me, please?	Können Sie mir das bitte übersetzen?
Could you speak more slowly please?	Könnten Sie bitte langsamer sprechen?
Could you please write that down?	Können Sie das bitte aufschreiben?
Could you please spell it?	Können Sie das bitte buchstabieren?
How do you pronounce this word?	Wie spricht man dieses Wort aus?
Sorry? (I didn't hear.)	Bitte?
Could you repeat that?	Könnten Sie das wiederholen?
How do you say ... in German?	Was heißt ... auf Deutsch?
What does ... mean?	Was bedeutet ...?
I speak ...	Ich spreche ...
English	Englisch
French	Französisch
German	Deutsch
Italian	Italienisch
Japanese	Japanisch
Spanish	Spanisch

MEETING PEOPLE

LIKE A ROLLING STONE

NEGATIVE FEELINGS

to be frustrated	gefrustet sein
to make a pass at someone	jemanden anbaggern
to freak out	ausrasten; ausflippen
to sag	durchhängen
to get on someone's nerves	nerven
You are getting on my nerves.	Du nervst mich.
to give someone the come-on	jemanden anmachen
Don't give me the come-on!	Mach mich nicht an!
Boy, I'm really pissed off!	Mann, hab ich 'nen Frust!

blatant; gross	ultrakrass
freaked out	abgefahren
frustration	Frust (m)
lousy	abartig; ätzend
shattered; done-in	kaputt
stupid	beknackt; bescheuert; hohl
unfair	link
whacked	ausgepowert; fix und fertig

POSITIVE FEELINGS

to notice something	etwas spannen
to understand something	etwas checken; etwas raffen; etwas schnallen; durchblicken

brilliant	genial
cute	bollig; süß
galactic	galaktisch
really good	riesig; irre
super	spitze
very cool	ultracool

For more slang, see also Swear Words & Slang page 116.

FEELINGS

How are you?	Wie fühlen Sie sich? (pol)
	Wie fühlst du dich? (inf)
What's up?	Was ist los?
I (don't) like ...	... gefällt mir (nicht).

I am ...	Ich bin ...
angry	böse
grateful	dankbar
happy	glücklich
lonely	einsam
sad	traurig
sleepy	müde
tired	müde

I am right.	Ich habe recht.
I am cold.	Mir ist kalt.
I am hot.	Mir ist heiß.
I am in a hurry.	Ich habe es eilig.
I am sorry.	Es tut mir Leid.
I am (un)well.	Ich fühle mich (nicht) wohl.
I am worried.	Ich mache mir Sorgen.

USEFUL PHRASES

Sure.
  Klar!; Logisch!
Just a minute.
  Ein Moment!
It's (not) important.
  Es ist (nicht) wichtig.
It's (not) possible.
  Es ist (nicht) möglich.
Wait!
  Warten Sie mal!
Good luck!
  Viel Glück!

UMLAUTS

Vowels with umlauts (two dots) over them are pronounced differently to ordinary vowels:

ä is like the 'ai' in 'air'
ö is like the 'u' in 'burn'
ü is similar to the 'u' in 'soup'.

MEETING PEOPLE

ABBREVIATIONS

A.A.	AA
Ausw.	ID
Bhf	Station
BRD	Federal Republic of Germany (old)
DB	German Federal Railways
DDR	German Democratic Republic (old)
DJH	Youth Hostel (name of association)
DM	German Mark
EU	EU
GB	UK
HPA or HA	GPO (Main Post Office)
Hr./Fr.	Mr/Mrs
KW	Short Wave
n. Chr./v. Chr.	AD/BC
N/S	Nth/Sth
p. Adr.	c/o
S	Suburban Railway System
Str.	St/Rd/etc
U	Underground (Railway)
usw.	etc
vorm./nachm.	am/pm
z.B.	eg

GETTING AROUND

Although trains are very expensive, they are the most common form of transport for longer distances. Buses only run within cities or connect rural areas with the nearest town. An alternative to trains are the special agencies called **Mitfahrzentrale** which arrange lifts. You'll find them in all the bigger cities.

Excuse me, can you help me please?	Entschuldigen Sie, Können Sie mir bitte helfen?
What time does ... leave?	Wann fährt ... ab?
What time does ... arrive?	Wann kommt ... an?
the aeroplane	das Flugzeug
the boat	das Boot
the bus	der Bus
the train	der Zug
the tram	die Straßenbahn
the underground	die U-Bahn

FINDING YOUR WAY

Germans tends to be straightforward – if you ask someone the way and they don't know, they won't think it impolite to tell you so. On the other hand when they do give you directions, you can pretty much rely on the information given.

Where is ...?	Wo ist ...?
How do I get to ...?	Wie komme ich nach ...?
I'm looking for ...	Ich suche ...
Is it far from/near here?	Ist es weit/in der Nähe?
Can I walk there?	Kann ich zu Fuß gehen?
Can you show me (on the map)?	Können Sie es mir (auf der Karte) zeigen?
Are there other means of getting there?	Gibt es andere Möglichkeiten, dorthin zu kommen?

GETTING AROUND

DIRECTIONS

Go straight ahead.
It's two streets down.
In that direction.
As far as ...

Gehen Sie geradeaus.
Es ist zwei Straßen weiter.
In dieser Richtung.
Bis zu ...

Turn left ...
Turn right ...
   at the next corner
   at the traffic lights
   at the beginning
   at the bottom
   at the end
   at the top

Biegen Sie ... links ab.
Biegen Sie ... rechts ab.
   bei der nächsten Ecke
   bei der Ampel
   am Anfang
   unten
   am Ende
   oben

back	zurück
behind	hinter
far	weit
here	hier
in front of	vor
near	nahe
opposite	gegenüber
right there	gleich dort
there	dort

ADDRESSES

A written German address looks like this:

> Katrin Gerstner
> Hauptstr. 34
> 65143 Günzburg
> GERMANY

Str. is the abbreviation for **Straße** 'street'. You might also find **Weg** 'road', **Allee** 'alley' or **Gasse** 'lane'.

BUYING TICKETS

Excuse me, where is the ticket office?	Entschuldigung, wo ist der Fahrkartenschalter?
Where can I buy a ticket?	Wo kann ich eine Fahrkarte kaufen?
I want to go to ...	Ich möchte nach ... fahren.
Do I need to book?	Muss man einen Platz reservieren lassen?
You need to book.	Man muss einen Platz reservieren lassen.
I'd like to book a seat to ...	Ich möchte einen Platz nach ... reservieren lassen.

GETTING AROUND

I would like ...	Ich möchte ...
a one-way ticket	eine Einfachfahrkarte
a return ticket	eine Rückfahrkarte
two tickets	zwei Fahrkarten
tickets for all of us	Fahrkarten für uns alle
a family ticket	eine Familienkarte
with student concession	mit Studentenermäßigung
with child/pensioner concession	mit Kinder/Rentner-ermäßigung

Do you have special offers?	Haben Sie Sonderangebote?
It is full.	Es ist ausgebucht.
Is it completely full?	Ist es ganz ausgebucht?
1st class	erste Klasse
2nd class	zweite Klasse

CUSTOMS

Do I have to declare this?	Muss ich das verzollen?
How much alcohol can I import duty-free?	Wie viel Alkohol darf ich zollfrei einführen?
Do I have to declare gifts?	Muss ich Geschenke verzollen?
customs	Zoll (m)
customs declaration	Zollerklärung (f)
customs regulation	Zollbestimmung (f)
duty-free	zollfrei

THEY MAY SAY ...

Haben Sie etwas zu verzollen?
  Do you have anything to declare?

Bitte füllen Sie eine Zollerklärung aus.
  Please fill out a customs declaration.

AIR

Domestic flights are usually very expensive, but you can sometimes find special offers. In many cases the rule is: the sooner you book, the cheaper the ticket. For travelling abroad, however, flights are faster and only slightly more expensive than trains.

Is there a flight to ...?	Gibt es einen Flug nach ...?
When is the next flight to ...?	Wann ist der nächste Flug nach ...?
Is there a stopover?	Gibt es eine Zwischenlandung?
Is there a connecting flight to ...?	Habe ich Anschluss nach ...?
How long does the flight take?	Wie lange dauert der Flug?
What is the flight number?	Welche Flugnummer ist es?
What time do I have to check in?	Um wie viel Uhr muss ich einchecken?
You must check in at ...	Sie müssen um ... einchecken.
Can I take this as hand luggage?	Kann ich das als Handgepäck mitnehmen?
What's the free luggage allowance?	Wie viel Gepäck ist frei?
What does excess luggage cost?	Was kostet das Übergepäck?
How much is the airport tax?	Wie hoch ist die Flughafengebühr?
I've nothing to declare.	Ich habe nichts zu verzollen.
Do I have to pay duty on this?	Muss ich das verzollen?
This is a present.	Das ist ein Geschenk.
Is the x-ray film-safe?	Wird das Röntgen meinen Film beschädigen?
Where will the baggage arrive?	Wo kommt das Gepäck an?
My baggage is missing.	Mein Gepäck ist weg.

GETTING AROUND

I want to reconfirm my flight.	Ich möchte meinen Flug rückbestätigen.
I have to cancel my flight.	Ich muss meinen Flug stornieren.
Which gate do I have to go to?	Zu welchem Flugsteig muss ich gehen?

aeroplane	**Flugzeug** (neut)
airport tax	**Flughafengebühr** (f)
airsickness	**Luftkrankheit** (f)
aisle seat	**Platz am Gang** (m)
boarding pass	**Bordkarte** (f)
crew	**Besatzung** (f)
customs	**Zoll** (m)
destination	**Zielflughafen** (m)
duty-free goods	**zollfreie Waren** (pl)
to embark	**einsteigen**
emergency landing	**Notlandung** (f)
excess baggage	**Übergepäck** (neut)
landing	**Landung** (f)
life jacket	**Schwimmweste** (f)
return flight	**Rückflug** (m)
seat belt	**Gurt** (m)
stopover	**Zwischenlandung** (f)
takeoff	**Abflug** (m)
window seat	**Fensterplatz** (m)

DID YOU KNOW ...   If you have an accident or any sort of mishap on a train or at a train station in Berlin, you are better off contacting the **Bahnpolizei** rather than the ordinary police (**Polizei**). You'll find them at ground level of Zoo Station.

BUS

Where is the bus/tram stop?	Wo ist die Bushaltestelle/ Straßenbahnhaltestelle?
Where do buses for ... stop?	Wo halten die Busse nach ...?
Which bus goes to ...?	Welcher Bus fährt nach ...?
Does this bus go to ...?	Fährt dieser Bus nach ...?
Is there a bus to ...?	Gibt es einen Bus nach ...?
How often do buses pass by?	Wie oft fahren Busse vorbei?
When is the last bus to ...?	Wann fährt der letzte Bus nach ...?
Could you let me know when we get to ...?	Könnten Sie mir bitte Bescheid geben, wenn wir in ... ankommen?
I want to get off!	Ich möchte aussteigen!
What time is the ... bus?	Wann fährt der ... Bus?
Do you have daily/weekly tickets?	Gibt es eine Tageskarte/ Wochenkarte?
Do I have to change for ...?	Muss ich nach ... umsteigen?
Where do I have to change?	Wo muss ich umsteigen?

THEY MAY SAY ...

Der Zug fährt vom Bahnsteig ... ab.
The train leaves from platform ...

Der Zug hat Verspätung/fällt aus.
The train is delayed/cancelled.

Er hat ... Stunden Verspätung.
There is a delay of ... hours.

Passagiere müssen umsteigen.
Passengers must change trains

Passagiere müssen auf einen anderen Bahnsteig gehen.
Passengers must change platforms.

conductor	Schaffner/in
direction	Richtung (f)
driver	Fahrer/in
first	erste
last	letzte
next	nächste/r/s
route	Strecke (f)
terminus	Endstation (f)

CURDLED

Qu is always pronounced as 'kv' in German: **Quark** ('curdled cheese') is pronounced 'kvark'.

TRAIN

There are two extra rapid trains: the older IC (Intercity) and the ultra-modern ICE (Intercityexpress). They only stop in major cities and have special fares. Normal speed trains service the smaller cities. For the IC you have to pay a supplement in addition to the normal ticket, for the ICE there are special tickets. It's always worth asking for special offers, for example, the Schönes Wochenendticket for weekend trips, or cheaper fares for groups/families.

Where is the station?	Wo ist der Bahnhof?
When is there a slow train (express) to ...?	Wann fährt ein Personenzug (Schnellzug) nach ...?
Can I reserve a seat?	Kann ich einen Platz reservieren lassen?
Is this the right platform for ...?	Fährt der Zug nach ... auf diesem Bahnsteig ab?
Is this the train to ...?	Ist das der Zug nach ...?
Does this train go via ...?	Fährt dieser Zug über ...?
Does this train stop at ...?	Hält dieser Zug in ...?
Is the train from ... late?	Hat der Zug aus ... Verspätung?
How long will it be delayed?	Wie viel Verspätung wird er haben?

Useful Words

carriage	Waggon (m)
compartment	Abteil (neut)
connection	Anschlusszug (m)
couchette	Liegeplatz (m)
dining car	Speisewagen (m)
express train	Schnellzug (m)
fast train	Eilzug (m)
goods station	Güterbahnhof (m)
guard	Schaffner (m)
left-luggage office	Gepäckaufbewahrung (f)
left-luggage withdrawals	Gepäckausgabe (f)
local train	Nahverkehrszug (m)
luggage locker	Schließfach (neut)
platform/track	Gleis (neut)
porter	Gepäckträger (m)
sleeping car	Schlafwagen (m)
slow train	Personenzug (m)
suburban train	Vorortzug (m); S-Bahn (f)
supplement	Zuschlag (m)
supplementary fares payable	zuschlagpflichtig
waiting room	Wartesaal (m)

METRO

There are very few ticket offices in metro stations. Most are equipped with ticket machines which display the fare when you select a destination.

Where can I buy a ticket?	Wo kann ich eine Fahrkarte kaufen?
How much does a ticket to ... cost?	Wie viel kostet eine Fahrkarte nach ...?
Is there a daily/weekly ticket?	Gibt es eine Tagesfahrkarte/ eine Wochenfahrkarte?

Can you change a 10 DM note?	Können Sie mir 10 Mark wechseln?
Which line takes me to ...?	Welche Linie fährt nach ...?
What is the next station?	Wie heißt der nächste Bahnhof?

TAXI

Taking a taxi is quite a luxury in Germany. On top of the fare the drivers expect a tip, usually the fare rounded up to the nearest DM. You can either book a taxi by telephone or go to a taxi rank.

Where is the nearest taxi rank?	Wo ist der nächste Taxistand?
Are you free?	Sind Sie frei?
Can you take me to ...?	Können Sie mich zu ... bringen?

Please take me ...	Bringen Sie mich bitte ...
to a cheap hotel	zu einem billigen Hotel
to this hotel/street	zu diesem Hotel/dieser Straße
to the city centre	zur Stadtmitte
to the airport	zum Flughafen
to the railway station	zum Bahnhof
to a doctor	zu einem Arzt

Can you show me on the map?	Können Sie mir das auf der Karte zeigen?
How much is it to go to ...?	Was kostet es bis ...?
Keep the change.	Der Rest ist für Sie; Stimmt so.

DID YOU KNOW ...	Germans like to refer to their country as the land of Dichter und Denker ('poets and philosophers'), due to its rich cultural heritage.

Instructions

Here is fine, thank you.	Halten Sie bitte hier.
Please stop at the next corner.	Halten Sie bitte an der nächsten Ecke.
Please stop here!	Bitte halten Sie hier!
Continue!	Weiter!
The next street to the left/right.	Biegen Sie an der nächsten Ecke links/rechts ab.
Stop here!	Halten Sie hier!
Please slow down.	Fahren Sie bitte langsamer.
Please wait here.	Bitte warten Sie hier.
Please switch the meter on!	Schalten Sie bitte den Taxameter ein!

CAR

Highways in Germany are free and there's no speed limit. In Switzerland, you must buy a Vignette at the border. In Austria the government has imposed tolls on the once-free highways and you have to buy a Pickerl. On Germany's cross-country roads there is a speed limit of 100 km/h unless otherwise stated; in cities and villages the speed limit is 50 km/h. Exceeding the speed limit can be very costly, especially in Switzerland where if you exceed it by more than 20 km/h, the police can withdraw your Führerschein, 'driver's licence'.

Car Hire

Where can I hire a car?	Wo kann ich ein Auto mieten?
I want to hire a car.	Ich möchte ein Auto mieten.
How much is it per day/week?	Wie viel kostet es pro Tag/Woche?
Does that include insurance/mileage?	Ist die Versicherung/das Kilometergeld inbegriffen?
How much deposit do I have to pay?	Wie viel muss ich bei Ihnen hinterlegen?
Will there be someone when I bring the car back?	Ist jemand da, wenn ich das Auto zurückbringe?

Parking

Can I park here?	Kann ich hier parken?
How long can I park here?	Wie lange kann ich hier parken?
Is there a parking lot nearby?	Ist hier in der Nähe ein Parkplatz?
Is the parking lot open all night?	Ist der Parkplatz die ganze Nacht geöffnet?
Is there a parking attendant?	Ist der Parkplatz bewacht?
Is it safe to park here?	Ist es sicher hier zu parken?
How much do I have to pay?	Wie viel kostet das?

At the Petrol Station

Nearly all petrol stations in Germany are self-service. There are numbers written on the petrol pump which you cite when paying inside the petrol station. The bigger petrol stations are also little supermarkets where you can get all the usual things you need – including alcohol – even on Sundays!

Where's the next petrol station?	Wo ist die nächste Tankstelle?
I want ... litres of petrol (gas).	Geben Sie mir ... Liter Benzin.
Please check the oil and water.	Bitte sehen Sie nach Öl und Wasser.
A road map, please.	Eine Straßenkarte, bitte.
Does this road lead to ...?	Führt diese Straße nach ...?

air (for tyres)	**Luft** (f)
diesel	**Diesel** (m)
leaded fuel	**verbleites Benzin** (neut)
oil	**Öl** (neut)
petrol	**Benzin** (neut)
petrol can	**Benzinkanister** (m)
unleaded fuel	**bleifreies Benzin** (neut)

Car Problems

I need a mechanic.	Ich brauche einen Mechaniker.
What make is it?	Welche Marke ist es?
The battery is flat.	Die Batterie ist leer.
The radiator is leaking.	Der Kühler ist undicht.
I have a flat tyre.	Ich habe eine Reifenpanne.
It's overheating.	Er ist heißgelaufen.
It's not working.	Es funktioniert nicht.
It's not starting.	Es springt nicht an.
The engine misses.	Der Motor stottert.
Could you tow the car, please?	Könnten Sie das Auto bitte abschleppen?
Where can I get it fixed?	Wo kann ich das reparieren lassen?
When will it be ready?	Wann ist es fertig?
Where will I get the spare parts from?	Woher bekomme ich die Ersatzteile?
Can I continue to drive the car?	Kann ich das Auto noch fahren?

Useful Words

battery	Batterie (f)
boot	Kofferraum (m)
brake fluid	Bremsflüssigkeit (f)
brakes	Bremsen (pl)
breakdown service	Abschleppdienst (m)
carburettor	Vergaser (m)
cylinder	Zylinder (m)
distributor	Verteiler (m)
engine/motor	Motor (m)
exhaust	Auspuff (m)
fan belt	Keilriemen (m)
fuse	Sicherung (f)
gear	Gang (m)
generator	Lichtmaschine (f)
heating	Heizung (f)
high beam	Fernlicht (neut)
ignition	Zündung (f)
ignition key	Zündschlüssel (m)
indicator	Blinker (m)
jack	Wagenheber (m)
lights	Scheinwerfer (m)
puncture	Reifenpanne (f)
radiator	Kühler (m)
to recharge	aufladen
screwdriver	Schraubenzieher (m)
service	Kundendienst (m)
spare tyre	Reservereifen (m)
spare parts	Ersatzteile (pl)
spark plug	Zündkerze (f)
tools	Werkzeug (neut)
to tow	abschleppen
tyre	Reifen (m)
windscreen	Windschutzscheibe (f)
windscreen wiper	Scheibenwischer (m)

BICYCLE

It is not compulsory to wear a helmet in Germany.

Where can I hire a bike?	Wo kann ich ein Fahrrad mieten?
I want to hire a bike.	Ich möchte ein Fahrrad mieten.
How much is it per day/week?	Wie viel kostet es pro Tag/Woche?
Where's a good bike repair shop?	Wo ist eine gute Fahrradreparaturwerkstatt?
How many gears does this bike have?	Wie viele Gänge hat dieses Fahrrad?
Can you repair the bike by tomorrow?	Können Sie das Fahrrad bis morgen reparieren?
I've got a flat tyre.	Ich habe einen Platten.
Is this road OK for bikes?	Kann man auf diesem Weg radfahren?
Is there a cycling track?	Gibt es einen Fahrradweg?

bicycle	**Fahrrad** (neut)
bike chain	**Schloss** (neut)
chain	**Kette** (f)
frame	**Rahmen** (m)
front light	**Vorderlicht** (neut)
gears	**Gangschaltung** (f)
handlebars	**Lenker** (m)
inner tube	**Schlauch** (m)
pedal	**Pedal** (neut)
pump	**Luftpumpe** (f)
rear light	**Rücklicht** (neut)
seat	**Sattel** (m)
spokes	**Speichen** (pl)
tyre	**Mantel** (m)
tyres	**Reifen** (pl)

GETTING AROUND

Accidents

I've had an accident.	Ich hatte einen Unfall.
Please call the police.	Bitte rufen Sie die Polizei.
Please call an ambulance.	Bitte rufen Sie einen Krankenwagen.
I need bandages.	Ich brauche Verbandszeug.
Could you give me a lift?	Können Sie mich mitnehmen?
Could you send a mechanic?	Können Sie mir einen Mechaniker schicken?
Where is your car insured?	Wo ist Ihr Wagen versichert?
I need a witness.	Ich brauche einen Zeugen.
I had the right of way.	Ich hatte Vorfahrt.
Will you give me your name and address, please?	Bitte geben Sie mir Ihren Namen und Ihre Adresse.

CROSSWORD – GETTING AROUND

Across
3. Where trains gather
4. It sparks, but it's not much use as a plug
6. Not far
7. Infamous for their economy class
9. To the rear

Down
1. Beats walking when you've got wheels
2. What turbulence can cause
3. Vital engine ingredient
5. Not over here, but over ...
8. Buckle up with this

Answers on page 290.

ACCOMMODATION

FINDING ACCOMMODATION

Unfortunately there is no backpacker accommodation in Germany. The cheapest type of accommodation you will find is the youth hostels. For these you'll need an International Youth Hostel Card. Some accommodation highlights include the Hostels along the Rhine and Moselle Rivers, in Rothenburg and Nuremberg. In the country, some Pensionen 'pensions' and Gasthöfe 'inns/guesthouses' offer rooms at reasonable prices. For phrases on camping, see page 168.

SIGNS	
ZIMMER FREI	ROOMS AVAILABLE
VOLL/ BESETZT	FULL/ NO VACANCIES

Can you recommend a good hotel?	Können Sie mir ein gutes Hotel empfehlen?
Can you recommend a cheap hotel?	Können Sie mir ein billiges Hotel empfehlen?
I'm looking for ...	Ich suche ...
Where is ...?	Wo ist ...?
a cheap hotel	ein billiges Hotel
a good hotel	ein gutes Hotel
a nearby hotel	ein Hotel in der Nähe
a clean hotel	ein sauberes Hotel
What is the address?	Wie ist die Adresse?
Could you write the address, please?	Könnten Sie bitte die Adresse aufschreiben?

ACCOMMODATION

BOOKING AHEAD

I'd like to book a room please.	Ich möchte ein Zimmer reservieren.
Do you have any rooms available?	Haben Sie noch Zimmer frei?
I will be arriving at (two o'clock).	Ich komme um (zwei Uhr) an.
My name is ...	Mein Name ist ...
How much is it per night/ person?	Wie viel kostet es pro Nacht/ Person?

CHECKING IN

I'd like ...	Ich möchte ...
a single room	ein Einzelzimmer
a double room	ein Doppelzimmer
a room with a bathroom	ein Zimmer mit Bad
to share a dorm	einen Schlafsaal teilen
a bed	ein Bett

I want a room with a ...	Ich möchte ein Zimmer mit ...
bathroom	Bad
phone	Telefon
shower	Dusche
television	Fernseher
toilet	Toilette
view	Aussicht

I'm not sure how long I'm staying.	Ich weiß nicht, wie lange ich bleibe.

I'm going to stay for ...	Ich bleibe ...
one day	eine Nacht
two days	zwei Nächte
one week	eine Woche
two weeks	zwei Wochen

Is there a reduction for
students/children?
   Gibt es Ermäßigung
   für Studenten/Kinder?
Does it include breakfast?
   Ist Frühstück
   inbegriffen?

Can I see the room?
   Kann ich das
   Zimmer sehen?
Are there any others?
   Haben Sie noch
   andere?
Is there anything cheaper?
   Gibt es etwas
   Billigeres?

Where is the bathroom?
   Wo ist das Bad?
Can I see the bathroom?
   Kann ich das Bad
   sehen?

Is there hot water all day?
   Gibt es den ganzen
   Tag warmes Wasser?
Is there a lift?
   Gibt es einen Aufzug?

THEY MAY SAY ...

Können Sie sich
ausweisen?
   Do you have
   identification?

Ihren Mitgliedsausweis,
bitte.
   Your membership
   card, please.

Entschuldigung, wir
haben keine
Zimmer frei.
   Sorry, we're full.

Wie lange bleiben Sie?
   How long will you
   be staying?

Wie viele Nächte?
   How many nights?

Es kostet ... pro Nacht/
pro Person.
   It's ... per day/
   per person.

ACCOMMODATION

It's fine, I'll take it.
Do I have to hire bedlinen
Do you require a deposit?

Can I pay by credit card?

Es ist gut, ich nehme es.
Muss ich Bettwäsche mieten?
Brauchen Sie eine
   Anzahlung?
Nehmen Sie Kreditkarten?

REQUESTS & QUERIES

Do you have a safe where I can leave my valuables?	Haben Sie einen Safe, in dem ich meine Wertsachen lassen kann?
Is there somewhere to wash clothes?	Kann man irgendwo Wäsche waschen?
Can I use the kitchen?	Kann ich die Küche benutzen?
Can I use the telephone?	Kann ich das Telefon benutzen?
When's breakfast?	Wann gibt es Frühstück?
Is the hotel open all night?	Ist das Hotel die ganze Nacht geöffnet?
Please wake me up at ...	Bitte wecken Sie mich um ...
Please change the sheets.	Wechseln Sie bitte die Bettwäsche.
I've locked myself out of my room.	Ich habe mich aus meinem Zimmer ausgesperrt.

COMPLAINTS

I don't like this room.	Das Zimmer gefällt mir nicht.
It's too ...	Es ist zu ...
small	klein
noisy	laut
dark	dunkel
expensive	teuer
The room needs to be cleaned.	Mein Zimmer ist nicht gemacht.
There aren't any towels.	Es gibt keine Handtücher.
The heating doesn't work.	Die Heizung funktioniert nicht.
The washbasin is blocked.	Das Waschbecken ist verstopft.
The tap drips.	Der Wasserhahn tropft.

ACCOMMODATION

The key doesn't fit.	Der Schlüssel passt nicht.
Could you fix that, please?	Könnten Sie das bitte in Ordnung bringen?
I can't open/close the window.	Ich kann das Fenster nicht aufmachen/zumachen.
The toilet won't flush.	Die Spülung in der Toilette funktioniert nicht.

CHECKING OUT

When is checkout time?	Wann muss ich auschecken?
I am/We are leaving now.	Ich reise/Wir reisen jetzt ab.
I would like to pay the bill.	Kann ich bitte die Rechnung haben?
Can I pay by credit card?	Kann ich mit Kreditkarte bezahlen?

ACCOMMODATION

USEFUL WORDS

ACCOMMODATION

air-conditioned	mit Klimaanlage
balcony	Balkon (m)
bath	Bad (neut)
bed	Bett (neut)
bill	Rechnung (f)
blanket	Wolldecke (f)
candle	Kerze (f)
chair	Stuhl (m)
clean	sauber
cold water	kaltes Wasser
cupboard	Schrank (m)
dark	dunkel
dirty	schmutzig
double bed	Doppelbett (neut)
electricity	Elektrizität (f)
excluding ...	außer; ausgenommen ...
fan	Ventilator (m)
hot water	warmes Wasser
included	inbegriffen
key	Schlüssel (m)
lift/elevator	Lift (m); Aufzug (m)
light bulb	Glühbirne (f)
lock	Schloss (neut)
mattress	Matratze (f)
mirror	Spiegel (m)
padlock	Vorhängeschloss (neut)
pillow	Kissen (neut)
quiet	ruhig
room	Zimmer (neut)
room number	Zimmernummer (f)
sheet	Bettlaken (neut)
shower	Dusche (f)
soap	Seife (f)
suitcase	Koffer (m)

surname	Nachname (m)
swimming pool	Schwimmbad (neut)
table	Tisch (m)
toilet	Toilette (f)
toilet paper	Toilettenpapier (neut)
towel	Handtuch (neut)
water	Wasser (neut)
window	Fenster (neut)

PAPERWORK

address	**Adresse** (f)
age	**Alter** (neut)
birth certificate	**Geburtsurkunde** (f)
border	**Grenze** (f)
car owner's title; registration	**(Kraft)fahrzeugbrief** (m)
customs	**Zoll** (m)
date of birth	**Geburtsdatum** (neut)
driver's licence	**Führerschein** (m)
identification	**Ausweispapiere** (pl)
immigration	**Einwanderung** (f)
marital status	**Familienstand** (m)
name	**Name** (m)
nationality	**Nationalität** (f)
passport	**(Reise)pass** (m)
passport number	**Passnummer** (f)
place of birth	**Geburtsort** (m)
profession	**Beruf** (m)
religion	**Religion** (f)
sex	**Geschlecht** (neut)
visa	**Visum** (neut)

ACCOMMODATION

ACCOMMODATION

RENTING

To rent a house or apartment, you can either go to an agency or look in the local newspaper on Saturdays and Wednesdays. If you want to rent a furnished place, it's easier to find furnished apartments than houses.

Rental ads list all the rooms in an apartment/house thus: 2 ZKB means two rooms (Z is for Zimmer, 'room'), kitchen (K is for Küche, 'kitchen'), bathroom (B is for Bad, 'bath'). When you find an advertisement that suits you, you either phone (as soon as possible) to arrange a meeting or you write to the newspaper if a code has been provided instead of a telephone number.

Students looking for rental accommodation are best served through the students' union, ASTA. Their staff can help you find a room in a student hostel.

When you find your rental place, you'll have to pay two or three months' rent as deposit. If you obtained it through an agency, you'll have to pay an additional sum. The fee shouldn't be higher than two months' rent.

I'm looking for an apartment.	Ich suche eine Wohnung.
I've seen your ad in the paper.	Ich habe Ihre Anzeige in der Zeitung gesehen.
How much is the rent?	Wie hoch ist die Miete?
I'm very interested in the flat.	Ich bin sehr interessiert an der Wohnung.
Is heating included in the rent?	Ist das Kaltmiete oder Warmmiete?
How many rooms does the apartment have?	Wie viele Zimmer hat die Wohnung?
When can I have a look at it?	Wann kann ich sie mir anschauen?
How much is the deposit?	Wie hoch ist die Kaution?
Are pets allowed?	Darf ich Haustiere halten?

Useful Words

apartment	Wohnung (f)
attic	Dachboden (m)
balcony	Balkon (m)
bedroom	Schlafzimmer (neut)
cellar	Keller (m)
central heating	Zentralheizung (f)
coal heating	Kohleheizung (f)
deposit	Kaution (f)
dining room	Esszimmer (neut)
flat in a new building	Neubauwohnung (f)
flat in an old building	Altbauwohnung (f)
floor heating	Fußbodenheizung (f)
furnished	möbliert
garden	Garten (m)
gas heating	Gasheizung (f)
house	Haus (neut)
housing advertisements	Wohnungsanzeigen (pl)
kid's room	Kinderzimmer (neut)
kitchen	Küche (f)
landlady	Vermieterin (f)
landlord	Vermieter (m)
lease	Mietvertrag (m)
living room	Wohnzimmer (neut)

ACCOMMODATION

DID YOU KNOW ...

In more colloquial German, the definite article ('the' in English) is sometimes placed before a person's name. For example:

Was macht die Gertrude?
What is Gertrude doing?

Wo geht der Hans hin?
Where is Hans going?

lodger	Untermieter (m)
oil heating	Ölheizung (f)
patio	Terrasse (f)
rent	Miete (f)
rent increase	Mieterhöhung (f)
renting out	Vermietung (f)
residential area	Wohnviertel (neut)
roof garden	Dachterrasse (f)
semi-detached house	Doppelhaus (neut)
tenant	Mieter/in
toilet	Toilette (f)
unfurnished	unmöbliert

ACCOMMODATION

AROUND TOWN

LOOKING FOR ...

I'm looking for ...	Ich suche ...
a bank	eine Bank
the city centre	die Innenstadt
the ... embassy	die ... Botschaft
my hotel	mein Hotel
the market	den Markt
the police	die Polizei
the post office	das Postamt
a public toilet	eine öffentliche Toilette
the telephone centre	die Telefonzentrale
the tourist information office	das Fremdenverkehrsbüro

AT THE BANK

The currency in Germany is the Deutsche Mark (DM). In Austria it's the Österreichische Schilling (AS) and in Switzerland, the Schweizer Franken (Sfr). The Euro complements these currencies and may eventually replace them.

I want to exchange some money.	Ich möchte Geld umtauschen.
I want to change some travellers cheques.	Ich möchte Reiseschecks einlösen.
What is the exchange rate?	Wie ist der Wechselkurs?
How much do I get for ...?	Wie viel bekomme ich für ...?
I need some small change too, please.	Bitte geben Sie mir auch etwas Kleingeld.
Can I have money transferred here from my bank?	Kann ich Geld aus meiner Bank überweisen lassen?
When will it arrive?	Wann wird es ankommen?
Has my money arrived yet?	Ist mein Geld schon angekommen?
I want to draw money from my bank account.	Ich möchte von meinem Bankkonto Geld abheben.

Useful Words

amount	Betrag (m)
ATM card	Scheckkarte (f)
bank account	Bankkonto (neut)
banknote	Banknote (f); Geldschein (m)
bank statement	Kontoauszug (m)
cash	bar/Bargeld (neut)
cashier	Kassierer/in
coin/s	Münze/n (f/pl)
commission	Gebühr (f)
credit	Kredit (m)
credit card	Kreditkarte (f)
currency	Währung (f)
exchange of money	Geldwechsel (m)
exchange office	Wechselstube (f)
exchange rate	Wechselkurs (m)
loose/small change	Kleingeld (neut)
to pay	bezahlen
to pay (into account)	einzahlen
to raise a loan	Kredit aufnehmen
receipt	Quittung (f)
saving book	Sparbuch (neut)
signature	Unterschrift (f)
transfer	Überweisung (f)

DID YOU KNOW ... In central Berlin street numbers usually run sequentially up one side of the street and down the other, with the exception of one or two. Number guides appear on most corner street signs, however, to help you. Be aware, too, that a long street may change names several times.

AROUND TOWN

AT THE POST OFFICE

I would like to send ...	Ich möchte ... senden.
an aerogram	einen Luftpostleichtbrief
a fax	ein Fax
a letter	einen Brief
a parcel	ein Paket
a postcard	eine Postkarte
a telegram	ein Telegramm

How much does it cost to send this to ...?	Wie viel kostet es, das nach ... zu senden?
How much is the postage?	Wie viel kostet das Porto?
I would like some stamps.	Ich möchte Briefmarken kaufen.
Have you got any special-issue stamps?	Haben Sie Sondermarken?
Five of each, please.	Von jedem fünf Stück, bitte.
I want to register this letter, please.	Ich möchte diesen Brief bitte per Einschreiben schicken.
How long does a letter to ... take?	Wie lange braucht ein Brief nach ...?
I would like to have my mail forwarded.	Ich möchte meine Post nachsenden lassen.
This is my new address.	Hier ist meine neue Adresse.

address	Adresse (f)
airmail	Luftpost (f)
cash on delivery	Nachnahme (f)
counter	Schalter (m)
customs declaration	Zollerklärung (f)
declaration of value	Wertangabe (f)
destination	Bestimmungsort (m)
dispatch note	Paketkarte (f)
envelope	Umschlag (m)
mailbox	Briefkasten (m)
parcel	Paket (neut)
poste restante	postlagernd
postman	Briefträger (m)
post office box	Postfach (neut)
registered mail	per Einschreiben
sender	Absender (m)
stamp	Briefmarke (f)
stamp machine	Briefmarkenautomat (m)
surface mail	gewöhnliche Post

STREET LIFE

What's this?	Was ist das?
What's happening?	Was ist los?
What's he/she doing?	Was macht er/sie?
What do you charge?	Wie viel verlangen Sie?
How much is it?	Was kostet das?
Can I have one, please?	Kann ich bitte eins haben?

People

band	Band (f)
busker	Straßenmusikant/in
fortune teller	Wahrsager/in
magician	Zauberer (m)
street vendor	Straßenverkäufer/in

Things

crafts	Kunsthandwerk (neut)
earring/s	Ohrring/e (m/pl)
festival	Festival (neut)
fleamarket	Flohmarkt (m)
happening	Happening (neut)
meeting point	Treffpunkt (m)
painting	Bild (neut)
pedestrian zone	Fußgängerzone (f)
poster	Poster (neut)
scarf	Schal (m)
street demonstration	Straßendemonstration (f)
T-shirt	T-Shirt (neut)

AROUND TOWN

TELEPHONE

The cheapest time to make local and long-distance calls is in the middle of the night. However, if you make a phone call after 6 pm or, even better, after 10 pm, it is still cheaper than the standard rate. On Sundays and holidays there is a reduced fare all day long. All German phone books have a full list of prices on page 18. Although you can use coins with older public telephones most phones now only take phone cards. You can buy cards at post offices, kiosks and Telekom shops.

Where can I make a phone call?	Wo kann ich telefonieren?
I want to make a long-distance call to ...	Bitte ein Ferngespräch nach ...
Your call is in box 10.	Ihr Gespräch ist in Kabine zehn.
What is the area code for Berlin?	Wie ist die Vorwahl von Berlin?
The number is ...	Die Nummer ist ...
I want to speak for three minutes.	Ich möchte drei Minuten lang sprechen.
How much does a three-minute call cost?	Wie viel kostet ein drei-minutiges Gespräch?
How much does each extra minute cost?	Wie viel kostet jede zusätzliche Minute?
I would like to speak to Mrs Schmidt.	Ich möchte Frau Schmidt sprechen.
This is ...	Hier ist ...
Hold the line, please.	Bleiben Sie bitte am Apparat.
There is no reply.	Es meldet sich niemand.
It's engaged.	Es ist besetzt.
I've been cut off.	Ich bin unterbrochen worden.

area code	Vorwahl (f)
card phone	Kartentelefon (neut)
directory enquiries	Telefonauskunft (f)
pay phone	Münztelefon (neut)
phone book	Telefonbuch (neut)
phone box	Telefonzelle (f)
phonecard	Telefonkarte (f)
switchboard	Telefonzentrale (f)
telephone	Telefon (neut)

SIGHTSEEING

At the tourist information offices, usually located in the city centres, you can get maps, hotel addresses and tips on places worth visiting.

Do you have a guidebook/ street map?	Haben Sie einen Reiseführer/ Stadtplan?
What are the main attractions?	Welche sind die Hauptsehenswürdigkeiten?
Is there an organised sight-seeing tour?	Gibt es eine organisierte Stadtbesichtigung?
What time will it be?	Um wie viel Uhr findet sie statt?
What is that?	Was ist das?
How old is it?	Wie alt ist das?
Which ... is that by?	Von welchem/welcher ... ist das?
architect	Architekt/in
painter	Maler/in
sculptor	Bildhauer/in
Can I take photographs?	Darf ich fotografieren?
What time does it open/close?	Wann macht es auf/zu?

AROUND TOWN

AROUND TOWN

What is the name of ...?	Wie heißt ...?
this street	diese Straße
this suburb	dieser Vorort

art gallery	Kunstgalerie (f)
beach	Strand (m)
birthplace of ...	Geburtshaus (neut) von ...
botanic garden	botanischer Garten (m)
castle	Schloss (neut)
cathedral	Dom (m)
cemetery	Friedhof (m)
church	Kirche (f)
concert hall	Konzerthalle (f)
fair	Messe (f)
fountain	Brunnen (m)
harbour	Hafen (m)
main square	Hauptplatz (m)

SIGNS

NOTAUSGANG	EMERGENCY EXIT
EINGANG	ENTRANCE
AUSGANG	EXIT
EINTRITT FREI	FREE ADMISSION
HEISS/KALT	HOT/COLD
KEIN ZUTRITT	NO ENTRY
RAUCHEN VERBOTEN	NO SMOKING
OFFEN/GESCHLOSSEN	OPEN/CLOSED
VERBOTEN	PROHIBITED
RESERVIERT	RESERVED
TELEFON	TELEPHONE
TOILETTEN (WC)	TOILETS

monastery	Kloster (neut)
monument	Denkmal (neut)
mosque	Moschee (f)
museum	Museum (neut)
old part of the city	Altstadt (f)
opera house	Opernhaus (neut)
palace	Palast (m)
ruins	Ruinen (pl)
stadium	Stadion (neut)
statues	Statuen (pl)
synagogue	Synagoge (f)
temple	Tempel (m)
tomb/grave	Grab (neut)
tower	Turm (m)
university	Universität (f)
zoo	Zoo (m); Tiergarten (m)

AROUND TOWN

For directions, see Getting Around, page 66.

CROSSWORD – AROUND TOWN

Across
3. Where letters get stamped
6. Royal home
7. Where stallholders haggle with shoppers
8. Not private
10. Metallic units of currency

Down
1. Commemorative statue, obelisk, building
2. Sculptures of bodies
4. Vital for calling home
5. Cross between a market and public holiday
9. Around

Answers on page 290.

AROUND TOWN

GOING OUT

WHERE TO GO

What's there to do in the evenings?	Was kann man abends unternehmen?
Are there any discos?	Gibt es hier Discos?
Is there a concert on tonight?	Gibt es heute abend ein Konzert?
What band is playing tonight?	Was für eine Band spielt heute?
What time should I arrive?	Um wie viel Uhr soll ich kommen?
What time does the disco close?	Um wie viel Uhr macht die Disco zu?
Is there a door charge?	Muss man Eintritt bezahlen?
How much is it to get in?	Wie viel kostet der Eintritt?
Which is the best night?	Welcher Abend ist der beste?
Can I reserve a ticket?	Kann ich eine Karte vorbestellen?
Are there reduced tickets for students?	Gibt es Studentenermäßigung?

bouncer	Türsteher (m)
cinema	Kino (neut)
concert	Konzert (neut)
dance music	Tanzmusik (f)
dancing	tanzen
disco/nightclub	Disco (f)
party	Party (f)
performance	Aufführung (f)
program	Programm (neut)
sold out	ausverkauft
standing room	Stehplatz (m)
theatre	Theater (neut)

See also Music, Cinema and Theatre in Interests page 119.

GOING OUT

THEATRE & CONCERTS

Would you like to go to a concert?	Möchten Sie zu einem Konzert gehen?
Are there places where you can hear local folk music?	Kann man hier irgendwo typische Volksmusik hören?
Who's playing?	Wer spielt?
I've never heard of this band.	Ich habe noch nie etwas von dieser Band gehört.
Are they any good?	Sind sie gut?
What kind of music do they play?	Was für eine Musik machen sie?
How much are the tickets?	Wie viel kosten die Karten?
What time does the concert start?	Um wie viel Uhr fängt das Konzert an?
Where shall we sit?	Wo wollen wir sitzen?
Shall we go closer to the stage?	Wollen wir näher an die Bühne gehen?
What a fantastic concert!	Was für ein tolles Konzert!
It's awfully loud!	Es ist sehr laut!

DID YOU KNOW ...

To find out what's going on in Berlin, look for *Metropolis* which is an English-language magazine, or *Berlin Magazine* which is bilingual. Some German-language entertainment guides are *Berlin Programm*, *Zitty* and *Tip*.

They all have details on concerts, theatre, clubs, gallery exhibits, events, movies, etc.

I'm going deaf!
Where can I buy discounted tickets?
Are there any tickets left for tomorrow?
Can I get the tickets at the door?

I'd like a seat ...
  in the stalls
  in the dress circle
  in the upper circle
  in the middle
  in a box

Ich werde taub!
Wo bekomme ich verbilligte Karten?
Gibt es noch Karten für morgen?
Gibt es eine Abendkasse?

Ich hätte gern einen Platz ...
  im Parkett
  im ersten Rang
  im zweiten Rang
  in der Mitte
  in einer Loge

GOING OUT

ARRANGING TO MEET

When should we meet?	Wann wollen wir uns treffen?
Where should we meet?	Wo wollen wir uns treffen?
Would ... o'clock be OK?	Würde dir ... Uhr passen?
What about ...?	Wie wär's mit ...?
That's fine.	Das ist gut.

Shall we have dinner together?	Wollen wir zusammen abendessen?
Shall we go dancing?	Wollen wir tanzen gehen?
Shall we go for a walk?	Wie wär's mit einem Spaziergang?

Will you visit me?	Besuchst du mich mal?
You are always welcome!	Du bist immer willkommen!
Why don't you drop in?	Warum schaust du nicht mal vorbei?

Can you pick me up?	Kannst du mich abholen?
I can pick you up.	Ich kann dich abholen.
We can take a taxi.	Wir können ein Taxi nehmen.

Where is the ...?	Wo ist ...?
cinema	das Kino
disco	die Disco
park	der Park
pub	die Kneipe
restaurant	das Restaurant

Afterwards

It was nice talking to you.	Es war nett, mit dir zu sprechen.
Can we meet again?	Wollen wir uns wieder treffen?
I have to get going now.	Ich muss jetzt gehen.

I had a great day/evening.	Es war ein schöner Tag/Abend.
Hope to see you again soon.	Ich hoffe, dich bald wiederzusehen.
Next time it's on me.	Das nächste Mal lade ich dich ein.
I'll give you a call.	Ich rufe dich an.
See you soon.	Bis bald.
We must do this again some time.	Wir müssen das unbedingt noch mal machen.

DATING & ROMANCE

Would you like to do something ...?	Hast du Lust ... was zu unternehmen?
tomorrow	morgen
tonight	heute Abend
on the weekend	am Wochenende
Where would you like to go?	Wo möchtest du hingehen?
I'd like to see you again.	Ich möchte dich wieder sehen.
Can we meet again?	Wollen wir uns wieder sehen?
I'd rather not.	Lieber nicht.
I'd like to.	Gerne.
That would be nice.	Das wäre schön.

CLASSIC PICK-UP LINES

Do you have a boyfriend/ girlfriend?	Hast du einen Freund/eine Freundin?
Can I buy you a drink?	Darf ich dich zu einem Drink einladen?
Would you like to dance?	Möchtest du mit mir tanzen?

Getting Closer

You're very nice.	Du bist sehr nett.
I like you very much.	Ich mag dich sehr.
Do you like me, too?	Magst du mich auch?
You're very pretty.	Du bist sehr hübsch.
You look great.	Du schaust toll aus.
I'm interested in you.	Ich interessiere mich für dich.
You're great.	Du bist toll.
What would you like to drink?	Was möchtest du trinken?
You're a great dancer!	Du tanzt wirklich gut!
You're very sexy.	Du bist sehr sexy.
May I kiss you?	Darf ich dich küssen?
Will you take me home?	Kannst du mich nach Hause bringen?
Do you want to come inside for a while?	Möchtest du kurz reinkommen?
Can I call you?	Kann ich dich anrufen?
I'll call you tomorrow.	Ich rufe dich morgen an.

Du bist sehr nett.

GOING OUT

CLASSIC REJECTIONS

I don't think it would be a good idea.	Ich glaube nicht, dass das gut wäre.
No thanks.	Nein, danke.
Get lost!	Hau bloß ab!

Making Love

Your place or mine?	Zu dir oder zu mir?
You have a great body.	Du hast einen schönen Körper.
Let's go to bed.	Gehen wir ins Bett.
I (don't) want to sleep with you.	Ich möchte (nicht) mit dir schlafen.
Not yet.	Noch nicht.
Give me some time.	Gib mir noch etwas Zeit.

Safe Sex

Do you have a condom?
  Hast du ein Kondom?
  Hast du einen Gummi?
I don't do it without a condom.
  Ich mache es nicht
  ohne Gummi.
Do you take any contraceptives?
  Verhütest du?
I'm on the pill.
  Ich nehme die Pille.
I have a diaphragm.
  Ich habe ein Pessar.
I have my period.
  Ich habe meine Tage.
  Ich habe meine Periode.

STAY NICE

Remember to use the appropriate form of 'you' when addressing someone. The polite **Sie** is used with strangers and superiors and **du** is used with friends, family, colleagues and children.

If you are unsure what to use, try **Sie**. People will let you know if they prefer you to use **du**.

GOING OUT

INTIMATE GERMAN

Touch my ...	Streichle ...
breast	meine Brüste
nipples	meine Brustwarzen
bum	meinen Po
hips	meine Hüften
penis	meinen Penis
cock	meinen Schwanz
vagina	meine Vagina
back	meinen Rücken

Kiss me.	Küss mich.
Touch me.	Streichle mich.
Caress me.	Sei zärtlich.
Fuck me!	Fick mich!

That's great!	Das ist gut!
Go on.	Mach weiter.
Stop it.	Hör auf.
Did you enjoy it?	Hat es dir gefallen?

After Sex

That was great.	Das war toll.
Can I stay over?	Kann ich bei dir übernachten?
You can't sleep here tonight.	Du kannst heute Abend nicht hier bleiben.
Would you like a cigarette?	Möchtest du eine rauchen?
When can I see you again?	Wann kann ich dich wieder sehen?
I'll call you.	Ich rufe dich an.

GOING OUT

Love

I've fallen in love with you.	Ich habe mich in dich verliebt.
I love you.	Ich liebe dich.
Do you love me?	Liebst du mich?
I must see you again.	Ich muss dich wieder sehen.
I'll always love you.	Ich werde dich immer lieben.
I'll never forget you.	Ich werde dich nie vergessen.
Let's move in together.	Wollen wir zusammenziehen?
Will you marry me?	Willst du mich heiraten?

Breaking Up

When you break up with somebody, it can sometimes be messy.
If the expressions given here aren't strong enough for your needs,
see also Swear Words & Slang page 116.

I have to leave tomorrow.	Ich muss morgen los.
I'll miss you.	Ich werde dich vermissen.
I'll come and visit you.	Ich komme dich besuchen.
I really want to keep in touch.	Ich möchte wirklich mit dir in Kontakt bleiben.
I want to remain friends.	Können wir Freunde bleiben?
I don't think it's working out.	Ich glaube nicht, dass es klappt.
I want to end the relationship.	Ich möchte Schluss machen.
I don't love you.	Ich liebe dich nicht.
I don't love you any more.	Ich liebe dich nicht mehr.

ARGUING

I didn't say that!	Das habe ich nicht gesagt!
Say that again!	Sag das nochmal!
Don't be so impertinent!	Sei nicht so unverschämt!
I didn't mean to be rude.	Ich wollte nicht gemein sein.
You are stupid!	Du bist doof!
Will you listen to me?	Hör mir bitte zu!
May I finish the sentence?	Darf ich bitte ausreden?
Don't interrupt me!	Unterbrich mich nicht!
I don't want to talk about it now.	Ich möchte jetzt nicht darüber sprechen.
Leave me alone.	Lass mich in Ruhe.
We'll talk about it later.	Wir sprechen später darüber.

I have never loved you.	Ich habe dich nie geliebt.
You'd better go now.	Du gehst jetzt besser.
Go away.	Geh weg.
Leave me alone.	Lass mich allein.
I want to be alone.	Ich möchte allein sein.
I don't ever want to see you again.	Ich will dich nie mehr wieder sehen.
Piss off!	Verpiss dich!

QUESTIONS

Are you married?	Sind Sie verheiratet? (pol); Bist du verheiratet? (inf)
How long have you been married?	Wie lange sind Sie verheiratet? (pol); Wie lange bist du verheiratet? (inf)
Do you have a partner?	Haben Sie einen Partner? (pol); Hast du einen Partner? (inf)
Do you have a boyfriend/ girlfriend?	Haben Sie einen Freund/eine Freundin? (pol)
Is your husband/wife here?	Ist Ihr Mann/Ihre Frau hier? (pol)
How many children do you have?	Wie viele Kinder haben Sie? (pol); Wie vele Kinder hast du? (inf)
Do you have any brothers or sisters?	Haben Sie noch Geschwister? (pol)

ANSWERS

I am single.	Ich bin unverheiratet.
I am married.	Ich bin verheiratet.
I am divorced.	Ich bin geschieden.
I live with my partner.	Ich lebe mit meinem Partner zusammen.
I have a boyfriend/girlfriend.	Ich habe einen Freund/ eine Freundin.
I don't have any children.	Ich habe keine Kinder.
I have a son/daughter.	Ich habe einen Sohn/ eine Tochter.

FAMILY MEMBERS

aunt	**Tante** (f)
brother	**Bruder** (m)
children	**Kinder** (pl)
cousin	**Cousin/e**
daughter	**Tochter** (f)
family	**Familie** (f)
father	**Vater** (m)
grandchildren	**Enkel** (pl)
granddaughter	**Enkelin** (f)
grandfather	**Großvater** (m); **Opa** (m)
grandmother	**Großmutter** (f); **Oma** (f)
grandson	**Enkel** (m)
husband	**Ehemann** (m)
mother	**Mutter** (f)
nephew	**Neffe** (m)
niece	**Nichte** (f)
parents	**Eltern** (pl)
sister	**Schwester** (f)
sisters and brothers	**Geschwister** (pl)
son	**Sohn** (m)
wife	**Ehefrau** (f)
uncle	**Onkel** (m)

FAMILY

DID YOU KNOW ...	The word **Aas**, which literally means 'animal carcass', can be used as a term of abuse:
	feiges Aas coward
	blödes Aas stupid guy
	Strangely enough, it can also be used as a compliment:
	goldiges Aas lovable girl
	schlaues Aas shrewd guy

FAMILY

TALKING WITH CHILDREN

Do you have brothers and sisters?	Hast du Geschwister?
How old are you?	Wie alt bist du?
Are you going to school?	Gehst du zur Schule?
Are you going to playschool?	Gehst du zum Kindergarten?
Do you like school/ playschool?	Gefällt es dir in der Schule/ im Kindergarten?
Do you have any pets?	Hast du ein Haustier?
What pets do you like best?	Welches Haustier magst du am liebsten?
Do you have many friends?	Hast du viele Freunde?
Would you like to play with me?	Möchtest du mit mir spielen?
Do you know hide and seek?	Kennst du das Versteckspiel?

FAMILY

TALKING WITH PARENTS

What a cute baby!	Ist das ein süßes Baby!
How old is it?	Wie alt ist es?
Is it a boy or a girl?	Ist es ein Junge oder ein Mädchen?
Can he/she sit up already?	Kann er/sie schon alleine sitzen?
May I hold he/she for a minute?	Darf ich ihn/sie kurz halten?
Does he/she sleep through the night?	Schläft er/sie durch?
Do you have other children?	Haben Sie noch mehr Kinder?
How old are they?	Wie alt sind sie?
Do they get along well?	Verstehen sie sich gut?
Do they fight a lot?	Streiten sie oft?

PETS

Do you have a pet?	Haben Sie ein Haustier?
Does it create a lot of work?	Macht es viel Arbeit?
Does it need a lot of exercise?	Braucht es viel Bewegung?

bird	Vogel (m)
budgie	Wellensittich (m)
canary	Kanarienvogel (m)
cat	Katze (f)
dog	Hund (m)
guinea pig	Meerschweinchen (neut)
hamster	Hamster (m)
parrot	Papagei (m)
rabbit	Kaninchen (neut)
turtle	Schildkröte (f)

COMMON INTERESTS

How long have you been here?	Seit wann bist du hier?
I have been here for ...	Ich bin seit ... hier.
Do you like it here?	Gefällt es dir hier?
I like it here.	Es gefällt mir hier.
Have you been to ... yet?	Warst du schon in ...?
Shall we go together?	Sollen wir zusammen hingehen?

Do you like ...?	Magst du ...?
arts	Kunst (f)
literature	Literatur (f)
music	Musik (f)
sports	Sport (m)
travelling	Reisen (neut)

I'd like to see ...	Ich würde gerne ... sehen.
castles	Burgen; Schlösser
churches	Kirchen
museums	Museen
old buildings	alte Gebäude
typical pubs	typische Kneipen
typical restaurants	typische Restaurants

STAYING IN TOUCH

Tomorrow is my last day here.	Morgen ist mein letzter Tag hier.
Let's swap addresses.	Tauschen wir unsere Adressen aus?
Do you have a pen and paper?	Hast du Stift und Papier?
What's your address?	Wie ist deine Adresse?
Here's my address.	Hier ist meine Adresse.
Do you have an email address?	Hast du eine E-Mail-Adresse?

Do you have access to a fax machine?	Hast du Zugang zu einem Faxgerät?
I'll write you a letter as soon as I get home.	Ich schreibe dir, sobald ich zu Hause bin.
I'll send you copies of the photos.	Ich schicke dir Abzüge von den Bildern.
Don't forget to write!	Vergiss nicht zu schreiben!
Keep in touch!	Lass von dir hören!
I'm not very good at writing letters.	Ich bin kein guter Briefschreiber.
I'll call you.	Ich rufe dich an.
What's your phone number?	Wie ist deine Telefonnummer?
Call me.	Ruf mich an.

SWEAR WORDS & SLANG

Some of the expressions below are quite strong, so be careful not to use them when the recipient is stronger than you!

Das ist doch zum Kotzen! Das ist total beschissen!	What a balls-up!
Du kannst mich mal!	Kiss my arse!
Herrgott nochmal! Verdammt nochmal! Herrschaftszeiten!	Damn it all!
So ein Mist!	Damn it!
Herrgottsak(rament)!	Good Lord!
Jetzt hab ich aber die Schnauze voll!	Now I'm really pissed off!
Motz mich nicht an!	Get off my back!
Sauerei!	Disgusting!
Scheißdreck!	Fuck!
Schweinerei!	What a disgrace!

INTERESTS

Writing Letters

You may like to write a few words in German when you are trying to keep in touch with friends. Here are some useful words and phrases.

Dear ...	*Lieber .../Liebe ...*
I'm sorry it's taken me so long to write.	*Es tut mir leid, dass es so lange gedauert hat, bis ich dir schreibe.*
It was great to meet you.	*Es war schön, dich zu treffen.*
Thank you so much for your hospitality.	*Vielen Dank für deine Gastfreundschaft.*
I miss you.	*Ich vermisse dich.*
I had a fantastic time in Germany.	*Ich hatte eine tolle Zeit in Deutschland.*
I hope to visit Germany again soon.	*Ich hoffe, dass ich bald wieder nach Deutschland fahren kann.*
Say 'hi' to Stefan and Maria for me!	*Grüße auch Stefan und Maria von mir!*
I'd love to see you.	*Ich würde dich so gerne wieder sehen.*

Finishing Off

Write soon!	*Schreibe bald zurück!*
With love/Regards, ...	*Alles Liebe, dein/e ...*

INTERESTS

ART
Seeing Art

Where is the gallery district?	Wo sind die Galerien?
Whose works are there?	Wer stellt dort aus?
Where can I see the work of ...?	Wo kann ich die Arbeiten von ... sehen?

architecture	Architektur (f)
art	Kunst (f)
art collection	Kunstsammlung (f)
art dealer	Kunsthändler/in
art gallery	Kunstgalerie (f)
artist	Künstler/in
art lover	Kunstfreund (m)
art print	Kunstdruck (m)
arts & crafts	Kunstgewerbe (neut)
computer/technological art	Computerkunst (f)
graphic arts	Grafik (f)
modern art	moderne Kunst (f)
movement	Bewegung (f)
multimedia	Multimedia (neut)
painting	Gemälde (neut)
performance art	Performance (f)
sculpture	Skulptur (f)
studio	Atelier (neut)
style	Stil (m)
technique	Technik (f)
work of art	Kunstwerk (neut)
to paint in oils	mit Ölfarben malen
to paint in watercolors	in Aquarell malen

Where can I buy ...?	Wo kann ich ... kaufen?
brush/es	Pinsel/- (m/pl)
paint/s	Farbe/n (f/pl)
paper	Papier (neut)
oil-based paint	Ölfarbe (f)

INTERESTS

MUSIC

Germany does not have many international stars. Possibly the best known groups are the Scorpions and Kraftwerk. Famous within Germany is BAP, a group from Cologne that sing in their own dialect. Other stars include Udo Lindenberg, Nina Hagen, Herbert Grönemeyer, Pe Werner and Jule Neigel.

What sort of music do you like?	Welche Musik gefällt Dir?
Do you like ...?	Magst du ...?
blues	Blues (m)
classical music	klassische Musik (f)
contemporary music	zeitgenössische Musik (f)
dance music	Tanzmusik (f)
disco	Discomusik (f)
folk music	Volksmusik (f)
hard rock	Hardrock (m)
hip hop	Hip-Hop (m)
jazz	Jazz (m)
pop	Popmusik (f)
rap	Rap (m)
reggae	Reggae (m)
rock	Rockmusik (f)
techno	Techno (neut/m)
Where can I hear live music?	Wo gibt es Livemusik?
Are there any open-air performances?	Gibt es Openairkonzerte?
Where can I buy this music?	Wo kann ich diese Musik kaufen?

INTERESTS

DID YOU KNOW ... The word Trott comes from the slow, loping gait of horses. When referring to people it means someone who does the same old daily routine; the same old thing.

Playing Music

| Do you play an instrument? | Spielst du ein Instrument? |

I play ...

Ich spiele ...

bass	Bass (m)
cello	Cello (neut)
double bass	Kontrabass (m)
flute	Flöte (f)
guitar	Gitarre (f)
organ	Orgel (f)
percussions	Schlagzeug (neut)
piano	Klavier (neut)
saxophone	Saxofon (neut)
trumpet	Trompete (f)
violin	Geige (f)

| I sing. | Ich singe. |
| I play in a band. | Ich spiele in einer Band. |

CINEMA & THEATRE

German cinema isn't known for its great productions, and very few locally produced movies are known in other countries. Most movies come from the USA or Britain, making it hard for the low-budget German movies to compete.

Well-known German films include *Die Blechtrommel* by Volker Schlöndorff, *Das Boot* by Wolfgang Petersen, *Schtonk* by Helmut Dietl and *Nosferatu* by Werner Herzog. There are also some young directors who've made good films, including Wim Wenders with *Himmel über Berlin*, Doris Dörrie with *Männer*, Sönke Wortmann with *Der bewegte Mann,* and Detlev Buck with *Wir können auch anders*.

Famous German actors include Armin Müller-Stahl, Jürgen Prochnow, Götz George, Till Schweiger, Heiner Lauterbach, Katja Riemann, Uwe Ochsenknecht, Hannah Schygulla, Klaus Kinski and, of course, Marlene Dietrich. Also well-known are Klaus

INTERESTS

INTERESTS

Maria Brandauer and Arnold Schwarzenegger from Austria and
Bruno Ganz from Switzerland.

In some cities, cinemas offer reduced rates on Mondays or for
afternoon shows. Some cinemas have discounted rates for students,
but you have to show your student card.

In major cities, there are often cinemas showing films in their
original versions with or without German subtitles. Look for the
letters OmU (Original mit Untertiteln), OF (Originalfassung)
or OV (Original Version).

What's on at the cinema/ theatre tonight?	Was gibt es heute im Kino/ Theater?
Where can I see a/an ...?	Wo kann ich ... sehen?
action movie	einen Actionfilm
adventure movie	einen Abenteuerfilm
afternoon show	eine Nachmittags- vorstellung
black comedy	eine schwarze Komödie
children's movie	einen Kinderfilm
comedy	eine Komödie
drama	ein Schauspiel
evening show	eine Abendvorstellung
film noir	einen Film-noire
late show	eine Spätvorstellung
love story	eine Liebesgeschichte
matinée	eine Matinee
thriller	einen Thriller
How much are tickets?	Wie viel kosten die Karten?
Are there any tickets for ...?	Gibt es noch Karten für ...?
Sorry, we're sold out.	Es ist leider ausverkauft.
Are there any cheaper seats?	Gibt es billigere Plätze?
Does it have English subtitles?	Hat es englische Untertitel?
Are those seats taken?	Sind diese Plätze noch frei?
Is there a discount for ...?	Gibt es eine Ermäßigung für ...?
children	Kinder
students	Studenten
pensioners	Rentner
advance booking office	Kartenvorverkauf (m)
intermission	Pause (f)
opera glasses	Opernglas (neut)
opera house	Opernhaus (neut)
opera singer	Opernsänger/in
theatre	Theater (neut)

INTERESTS

Talking About Cinema & Theatre

Did you like ...?	Hat dir ... gefallen?
the concert	das Konzert
the film	der Film
the performance	die Aufführung
the play	das Stück

I liked it very much.	Es hat mir sehr gut gefallen.
I didn't like it.	Es hat mir nicht gefallen.

I thought it was ...	Ich fand es ...
boring	langweilig
excellent	ausgezeichnet
good	gut
interesting	interessant

Who is your favourite director?	Wer ist dein Lieblingsregisseur?
What sort of films do you like?	Was für Filme gefallen dir?
Have you seen ...?	Hast du schon ... gesehen?
Do you know the latest film by ...?	Kennst du den neuesten Film von ...?
Who is your favourite actor?	Wer ist dein Lieblingsschauspieler?

INTERESTS

DID YOU KNOW ...	Bavaria produces and consumes the most beer in Germany. In fact Munich's unofficial coat-of-arms shows a monk with a bible in his right hand and a large glass of beer in his left. The Augustiner monks actually introduced beer to the people of Munich in 1328.

INTERESTS

LITERATURE

Who is your favourite author?	Wer ist dein Lieblingsschriftsteller?
What kind of books do you read?	Was für Bücher liest du?
Do you read in other languages?	Liest du auch fremdsprachige Bücher?
Can you recommend a book?	Kannst du mir ein Buch empfehlen?

I like ...	Ich lese gerne ...
the classics	Klassiker
comics	Comics
contemporary literature	Gegenwartsliteratur
crime (detective) novels	Krimis
erotic literature	erotische Literatur
fantasy literature	Fantasyromane
fiction	Prosaromane
nonfiction	Sachbücher
novels	Romane
poetry	Poesie/Gedichte/Lyrik
science fiction	Sciencefiction
short stories	Kurzgeschichten
travel writing	Reiseberichte

Have you read ...?	Hast du ... gelesen?
What did you think of it?	Hat es dir gefallen?

I thought it was ...	Ich fand es ...
badly/well written	schlecht/gut geschrieben
boring	langweilig
entertaining	unterhaltsam
interesting	interessant
badly/well translated	schlecht/gut übersetzt

author	Autor/in; Schriftsteller/in
bookshop	Buchladen (m)
hardback	ein gebundenes Buch
library	Bücherei (f); Bibliothek (f)
novella	Novelle (f)
paperback	Taschenbuch (neut)
reading	Lesung (f)
second-hand bookshop	Antiquariat (neut)

HOBBIES

Do you have any hobbies?	Hast du ein Hobby?
What are your hobbies?	Was für Hobbys hast du?
My hobbies are ...	Meine Hobbys sind ...
collecting stamps	Briefmarkensammeln
going for walks	Spazierengehen
going to the cinema	ins Kino gehen
going to the theatre	ins Theater gehen
handicrafts	Handarbeiten
meeting people	Leute treffen
painting	Malen
playing games	Spiele spielen
playing sports	Sport
reading	Lesen
travelling	Reisen
I like to play computer games.	Ich spiele gerne Computerspiele.
I like to surf the 'Net.	Ich surfe gern im Internet.
I'm interested in video games.	Ich interessiere mich für Videospiele.
Me too.	Ich auch.
Do you know this one?	Kennst du das schon?

TALKING WITH OTHER TRAVELLERS

Have you been to ... yet?	Waren Sie schon in ...?
Yes, I have been there.	Ja, da war ich schon.
No, I haven't been there.	Nein, da war ich noch nicht.
Can you recommend it?	Können Sie es empfehlen?
When are you going on holidays?	Wann fahren Sie in Urlaub?
Do you prefer travelling by bus, car or train?	Reisen Sie lieber mit dem Bus, dem Auto oder dem Zug?
I like flying best.	Am liebsten fliege ich.

STARS
Astronomy

astronaut	Austronaut/in
astronautics	Raumfahrt (f)
astronomer	Astronom/in
astronomy	Astronomie (f)
astrophysics	Astrophysik (f)
constellation	Sternbild (neut)
cosmology	Kosmologie (f)
cosmonaut	Kosmonaut/in
cosmos	Kosmos (m)
earth	Erde (f)
galaxy	Galaxie (f)
Mars	Mars (m)
moon	Mond (m)
planet	Planet (m)
planetarium	Planetarium (neut)
space program	Raumfahrtprogramm (neut)
star	Stern (m)
sun	Sonne (f)
telescope	Teleskop (neut)
universe	Universum (neut)
Venus	Venus (f)

INTERESTS

Astrology

astrology	Astrologie (f)
horoscope	Horoskop (neut)
star sign	Sternzeichen (neut)

What is your birthdate?	Wann hast du Geburtstag?
What time/year?	Welche Uhrzeit/welches Jahr?
What is your ascendant?	Was ist dein Aszendent?
What is your star sign?	Was für ein Sternzeichen bist du?

I am a...   Ich bin...

Capricorn	Steinbock
Aquarius	Wassermann
Pisces	Fisch
Aries	Widder
Taurus	Stier
Gemini	Zwilling
Cancer	Krebs
Leo	Löwe
Virgo	Jungfrau
Libra	Waage
Scorpio	Skorpion
Sagittarius	Schütze

FUTURE SHOCK

Remember that to form the future tense you use the present tense of **werden** ('to become') plus the infinitive of the main verb. See page 42 for the present tense of **werden**.

INTERESTS

CROSSWORD - INTERESTS

INTERESTS

Across
5. Tourists tour as travellers ...
6. Nearest star
7. Sweetly trilling wind instrument
8. Zodiac sign of the bull
10. Collective name for disco, techno and polka

Down
1. A person skilled in painting or sculpture, for example
2. The truth is stranger than this
3. Works of beauty (or significant ugliness)
4. The product of an artist
9. Characteristic manner of expression

Answers on page 290.

POLITICS

Germany is a federal democracy consisting of 11 old **Bundes-länder** (states) and 5 new **Bundesländer** of the former GDR (East Germany), with elections held every four years. The main parties are:

CDU (Christlich Demokratische Union):

This conservative party was founded in 1945. From 1949 until 1969 the **CDU**, together with the **CSU** (see below), formed the government. They were in opposition until 1982 when they returned to power under the leadership of Helmut Kohl. In 1998, after 16 years of Kohl as chancellor, **CDU** lost the election to **SPD**. Among its more well-known members are Adenauer, Erhard, and Kiesinger.

CSU (Christlich Soziale Union):

This party was also founded after WWII. The **CSU** exists only in Bavaria, but its policy is very similar to the **CDU**'s. The **CDU** and the **CSU** are also called **Unionsparteien**. Members include Strauß and Waigel.

SPD (Sozialdemokratische Partei Deutschlands):

This is the oldest party in Germany, founded in 1869. Over its history it has changed from a workers' party to a party for the middle class. After winning the election in 1998, **SPD** formed the government in coalition with **Bündnis 90; die Grünen**. Members include Brandt, Schmidt, Lafontaine and Schröder.

FDP (Freie Demokratische Partei):

Founded in 1948, the **FDP** is the smallest party in parliament, but by forming coalitions with either the **CDU**, **CSU** or the **SPD**, it has often participated in forming the government. Members include Genscher, Lambsdorff and Kinkel.

Bündnis 90; die Grünen:

The Green party was founded in 1980, but before that year smaller groups had already been represented in local parliaments. After the reunification of Germany the Bündnis 90 party, which had been fighting the regime in the former GDR and largely contributed to the nonviolent fall of Honecker, joined the Green party. The best known member is Joschka Fischer.

PDS (Partei des Demokratischen Sozialismus):

This left-wing party is a leftover of the former GDR and, due to the problems resulting from the reunification, is getting more votes every year. Its most famous member is Gregor Gysi.

Die Republikaner: Founded 1983, this is an extreme right party. Its most well-known member is Schönhuber.

Apart from the above there are many small parties which are not represented in parliament because of the so-called 5% regulation. This means that parties need a minimum of 5% of votes to get a seat in parliament. This is supposed to prevent governments from forming coalitions with a large number of small parties with diverging interests. Only German citizens who are 18 or over can vote.

DID YOU KNOW ... Be warned! Insulting someone in public in Germany could land you with a fine. Insulting any uniformed official will cost you DM3000. Giving another driver the finger will cost you about DM1200. And just because you may be a tourist, you are not exempt from this law.

Useful Words

authority of state	Staatsgewalt (f)
constituency	Wahlkreis (m)
constitution	Verfassung (f)
election	Wahl (f)
electorate	Wähler (pl)/Wählerschaft (f)
eligible to vote	wahlberechtigt
first-past-the-post	Mehrheitswahlrecht (neut)
fundamental right	Grundrecht (neut)
demand	Forderung (f)
Germany's federal parliament	der Bundestag
government coalition	Regierungskoalition (f)
legislation	Wahlperiode (f)
majority	Mehrheit (f)
member of parliament	Abgeordneter/Abgeordnete
national debt	Staatsverschuldung (f)
opinion poll	Meinungsumfrage (f)
parliament	Parlament (neut)
policy/politics	Politik (f)
politician	Politiker/in

president
   Präsident (m)
prime minister
   Bundeskanzler (m)
proportional representation
   Verhältniswahlrecht (neut)
referendum
   Volksentscheid (m)
state
   Staat (m)
term of office
   Wahlperiode (f)
type of state
   Staatsform (f)
to vote
   wählen

HARD G

When the letter g is at the beginning of a word it is always hard as in 'girl', never as in 'gentle' and j is as the 'y' in 'yes'.

When the letters b, d and g are at the end of a word or syllable, they sound more like 'p', 't' and 'k' respectively. But when a word ends in -ig the g sounds like 'ch'.

SOCIAL ISSUES

ENVIRONMENT

Environmental consciousness has increased in Germany since the 1970s, as this relatively small country with a dense population faced serious problems concerning the environment. As a result, the Green Party gained influence and entered parliament.

Garbage sorting is widely carried out. Nearly every city has bins for organic waste (normally brown), others for plastic, aluminium and other recyclable materials (normally yellow), others for paper (normally green or blue), and black bins for the rest. Glass has to be brought to bottle banks that are found all over town. This may seem confusing to first-timers, but foreigners are advised to learn the system because using the wrong bin will incur a fine.

SOCIAL ISSUES

But the Germans who love their cars and, even more, speeding on the freeways, still have a lot to learn. Exhaust fumes from cars continue to cause damage to health and the environment. A proposal for a bill to reduce the speed limit to 130 km/h was rejected and even led to the foundation of a 'car-driver party' with the slogan **Freie Fahrt für freie Bürger!**, 'Unrestricted driving for free citizens!'

Is there a nuclear power station around here?	Ist hier in der Nähe ein Atomkraftwerk?
Does ... have a recycling program?	Hat ... ein Recyclingprogramm?
Does ... have a pollution problem?	Hat ... ein Umweltproblem?
Are there any ... here?	Gibt es hier ...?
protected parks	geschützte Parks
protected forests	geschützte Wälder
protected species	geschützte Tierarten
air pollution	**Luftverschmutzung** (f)
deforestation	**Abholzung** (f)
destruction of the rain forests	**Zerstörung der Regenwälder** (f)
exhaust fumes	**(Auto) Abgase** (pl)
garbage/rubbish bin	**Mülltonne** (f)
garbage/rubbish tip	**Müllkippe** (f)
global warming	**globale Erwärmung** (f)
incinerating plant	**Müllverbrennungsanlage** (f)
nature reserve	**Naturreservat** (neut)
nuclear energy	**Atomenergie** (f)
nuclear power station	**Atomkraftwerk** (neut)
nuclear testing	**Atomtests** (pl)
nuclear waste	**Atommüll** (m)
ozone smog	**Ozonsmog** (m)
pollution	**Umweltverschmutzung** (f)

SOCIAL ISSUES

recycling	Recycling (neut); Wiederverwertung (f)
smog	Smog (m)
solar energy	Solarenergie (f)
sorting garbage	Mülltrennung (f)
toxic waste	Giftmüll (m)
waste	Abfall (m)

SOCIAL ISSUES

Germany has one of the best social welfare systems in the world. However, this high welfare standard is expensive and the government is finding it increasingly hard to raise the necessary funds. Following Germany's reunification, the unemployment rate went up to 10% and the costs of social benefits exploded. As a result, the state has been trying to save money by reducing the benefits.

abortion	Abtreibung (f)
alcoholic	Alkoholiker/in
asylum	Obdachlosenunterkunft (f); Asylheim (neut)
asylum seeker	Asylbewerber/in
bum	Penner (m) (derogatory)
citizenship	Staatsbürgerschaft (f)
class system	Klassensystem (neut)
crime-fighting	Verbrechensbekämpfung (f)
discrimination	Diskriminierung (f)
dole	Stempelgeld (neut)
equality	Gleichberechtigung (f)
euthanasia	Euthanasie (f)
homeless people	Obdachlose (pl)
human rights	Menschenrechte (pl)
immigration	Einwanderung (f)
inequality	Ungleichheit (f)
job market	Arbeitsmarkt (m)
marches	Demonstrationen (pl); Demos (abbr)

political exiles	politische Flüchtlinge (pl)
protest	Protest (m)
social security	Sozialunterstützung (f)
street kids	Straßenkinder (pl)
strike	Streik (m)
to be on strike	streiken
tax	Steuer (f)
unemployment	Arbeitslosigkeit (f)
unemployment benefits (the dole)	Arbeitslosengeld (neut)
I'm unemployed.	Ich bin arbeitslos.
welfare	Sozialhilfe (f)
welfare state	Sozialstaat (m)

DRUGS

All drugs are illegal in Germany. You may, however, find yourself in a position where the issue is being discussed, and the following phrases may help you understand the conversation, but if referring to your own interests, use discretion.

Do you smoke?	Rauchst du?
Do you take drugs?	Nimmst du Drogen?
Do you smoke marijuana?	Rauchst du Haschisch?;
	Kiffst du? (colloquial)
I don't do it anymore.	Ich mache das nicht mehr.
I'm clean.	Ich bin clean; sauber.
I'm not interested.	Ich bin nicht interessiert.
I don't take drugs.	Ich nehme keine Drogen.
I need help.	Ich brauche Hilfe.
Do you sell syringes?	Verkaufen Sie Spritzen?
Do you have a methadone program in this country?	Gibt es hier ein Methadonprogramm?
Can I register?	Kann ich mich dafür anmelden?

THEY MAY SAY ...

Möchtest du ein bisschen Gras?
Do you want some marijuana?

Bist du an etwas Kokain interessiert?
Are you interested in some cocaine?

Ich habe etwas Haschisch.
I've got some hash.

Das ist wirklich ein gutes Geschäft.
It's a really good deal.

Das ist echt gute Qualität.
It's good stuff.

addiction	Abhängigkeit (f)
cocaine	Kokain (neut); Koks (neut)
cold turkey	cold turkey; Entzugserscheinung (f)
dealer	Dealer (m); Drogenhändler (m)
dope	Dope (neut); Stoff (m)
drug addict	Drogenabhängiger/ Drogenabhängige; Fixer (m)
drug counselling service	Drogenberatungsstelle (f)
ecstacy	Ecstasy; E (f)
heroin	Heroin (neut)
joint	Joint (m); Tüte (f)
methadone	Methadon (neut)
overdose	Überdosis (f)
pure	rein
to be hooked on heroin	an der Nadel hängen
to roll a joint	einen Joint drehen

Opening hours are a hot issue in Germany. Despite trade union protests, opening hours have been extended. The bigger shops are open from 9 am to 8 pm. Smaller shops might only open until 6 pm, and many close between 1 and 3 pm and on Wednesday afternoons. On Saturdays shops close at 2 pm except for the first Saturday of every month when they are open until 4 pm. On Sundays all shops are closed.

LOOKING FOR ...

Where can I get ...?   Wo bekomme ich ...?

Where is the ...?   Wo ist ...?
   bakery   die Bäckerei
   bookshop   die Buchhandlung
   butcher   die Metzgerei
   camera/photo shop   das Fotogeschäft
   clothing store   das Bekleidungsgeschäft
   delicatessen   der Feinkostladen
   department store   das Kaufhaus
   drugstore   der Drogeriemarkt
   drycleaner   die chemische Reinigung
   flower shop   der Blumenladen
   grocery   der Lebensmittelladen
   hairdresser   der Friseur
   laundry   die Wäscherei
   market   der Markt
   newsagency/   der Zeitungshändler/
     stationer's   der Schreibwarenladen
   optometrist   der Optiker
   perfumery   die Parfümerie
   pharmacy   die Apotheke
   shoeshop   das Schuhgeschäft
   souvenir shop   der Souvenirladen

SHOPPING

supermarket	der Supermarkt
tailor	der Schneider
travel agency	das Reisebüro
vegetable shop	der Gemüseladen

MAKING A PURCHASE

I would like to buy ...	Ich möchte ... kaufen.
How much is it?	Wie viel kostet es?
Do you have others?	Haben Sie noch andere?
I don't like it.	Es gefällt mir nicht.
Can I change it?	Kann ich es umtauschen?
Can I look at it?	Könnten Sie es mir zeigen?
I'm just looking.	Ich sehe mich nur um.
Can you write down the price?	Könnten Sie den Preis aufschreiben?
Do you accept credit cards?	Nehmen Sie Kreditkarten?
Could you lower the price?	Könnten Sie den Preis reduzieren?
I don't have much money.	Ich habe nur wenig Geld.

THEY MAY SAY ...

Kann ich Ihnen helfen?
Can I help you?

Möchten Sie das anprobieren?
Would you like to try it on?

Sonst noch etwas?
Anything else?

Soll ich es Ihnen einwickeln?
Would you like it wrapped?

Entschuldigung, das ist das einzige.
Sorry, this is the only one.

Wie viel/wie viele möchten Sie?
How much/many do you want?

SHOPPING

BARGAINING

bargain
  Schnäppchen (neut)
to bargain
  feilschen
flea-market
  Flohmarkt (m)
reduced price
  herabgesetzter Preis (m)
second-hand shop
  Secondhandshop (m)
special offer
  Sonderangebot (neut)
I'll take it for ... DM.
  Ich nehme es für ... DM.

ARTHUR OR MARTHA

Although there are no hard and fast rules to help you recognise the gender of every German noun, there are a few patterns that can make them easier to determine. See Gender, page 21, for an explanation.

ESSENTIAL GROCERIES

batteries	**Batterien** (pl)
bread	**Brot** (neut)
butter	**Butter** (f)
cheese	**Käse** (m)
chocolate	**Schokolade** (f)
coffee/tea	**Kaffee** (m)/**Tee** (m)
ham	**Schinken** (m)
matches	**Streichhölzer** (pl)
milk	**Milch** (f)
mineral water	**Mineralwasser**
(without bubbles)	(**ohne Kohlensäure**) (neut)
fruit	**Früchte** (pl); **Obst** (neut)
shampoo	**Shampoo** (neut)
soap	**Seife** (f)
sugar	**Zucker** (m)
toilet paper	**Toilettenpapier** (neut)
toothpaste	**Zahnpasta** (f)
washing powder	**Waschpulver** (neut)
yoghurt	**Jogurt** (m)

SHOPPING

SOUVENIRS

beer stein/mug	**Bierkrug** (m)
cuckoo clock	**Kuckucksuhr** (f)
earrings	**Ohrringe** (pl)
embroidery	**Stickerei** (f)
handicraft	**Kunsthandwerk** (neut)
necklace	**Halskette** (f)
porcelain	**Porzellan** (neut)
ring	**Ring** (m)

CLOTHING

It doesn't fit.	**Es passt nicht.**
Do you have it in size ...?	**Haben Sie das in Größe ... ?**
I need one size smaller/larger.	**Ich brauche eine Größe kleiner/größer.**

It is too ...	**Es ist zu ...**
big/small	**groß/klein**
short/long	**kurz/lang**
tight/loose	**eng/weit**

belt	**Gürtel** (m)
bra	**Büstenhalter** (m); **BH** (m)
button	**Knopf** (m)
clothing	**Kleidung** (f)
coat	**Mantel** (m)
collar	**Kragen** (m)
dress	**Kleid** (neut)
jacket	**Jacke** (f)
jumper; sweater	**Pullover** (m); **Pulli** (m)
raincoat	**Regenmantel** (m)
panties	**Unterhose** (f); **Slip** (m)
scarf	**Halstuch** (neut)
shirt	**Hemd** (neut)
shoes	**Schuhe** (pl)

skirt	**Rock** (m)
trousers	**Hose** (f)
T-shirt	**T-Shirt** (neut)
long-sleeved	**langärmelig**
short-sleeved	**kurzärmelig**
without sleeves	**ärmellos**
zipper	**Reißverschluss** (m)

Fashion Terms

on sale	Sonderangebot (neut)
factory sale	Fabrikverkauf (m)
latest collection	aktuelle Kollektion (f)
all the rage	der letzte Schrei

SIGNS

RÄUMUNGSVERKAUF	CLEARANCE SALE
WINTERSCHLUSSVERKAUF	WINTER SALE
SOMMERSCHLUSSVERKAUF	SUMMER SALE

MATERIALS

brass	Messing (neut)
cotton	Baumwolle (f)
gold	Gold (neut)
handmade	handgearbeitet
leather	Leder (neut)
linen	Leinen (neut)
satin	Satin (m)
silk	Seide (f)
silver	Silber (neut)
velvet	Samt (m)
viscose	Viskose (f)
wool	Wolle (f)

COLOURS

black	schwarz	orange	orange
blue	blau	pink	rosa
brown	braun	purple	lila
dark	dunkel	red	rot
green	grün	turquoise	türkis
grey	grau	white	weiß
light	hell	yellow	gelb

SHOPPING

TOILETRIES

comb	Kamm (m)
conditioner	Spülung (f)
condoms	Kondome (pl)
deodorant	Deodorant (neut)
hairbrush	Haarbürste (f)
mirror	Spiegel (m)
moisturising cream	Feuchtigkeitscreme (f)
nail polish	Nagellack (m)
nail polish remover	Nagellackentferner (m)
powder	Puder (m)
razor	Rasierapparat (m)
sanitary napkins	Damenbinden (pl)
shampoo	Shampoo (neut)
shaving cream	Rasiercreme (f)
soap	Seife (f)
sunblock cream	Sonnenschutzmittel (neut)
tampons	Tampons (pl)
tissues	Papiertücher (pl)
toilet paper	Toilettenpapier (neut)
toothbrush	Zahnbürste (f)
toothpaste	Zahnpasta (f)
tweezers	Pinzette (f)

Often in more colloquial German (and almost always in spoken German) you'll notice the omission of consonants. For example, you might hear is' for ist ('is'), mei' for mein ('my') or scho' for schon ('already').

STAND ON THE CABLE

aus einer Mücke einen Elefanten machen
to make a mountain out of a molehill
lit: to make an elephant out of a mosquito

aus dem letzten Loch pfeifen
to be at the end of one's tether
lit: to whistle out of the last hole

ein Brett vor dem Kopf haben
to be as thick as two short planks
lit: to have a plank of wood in front of one's head

auf der Leitung stehen
to be slow on the uptake
lit: to stand on the cable

zwei Fliegen mit einer Klappe schlagen
to kill two birds with one stone
lit: to kill two flies with one swat

den Löffel abgeben
to kick the bucket
lit: to give away the spoon

alles auf eine Karte setzen
to put all your eggs in one basket
lit: to bet everything on one card

eine Frau anbaggern
to chat up
lit: to dig at a woman

den Teufel werde ich tun
never in a month of Sundays
lit: I'll do the devil

jemanden auf den Arm nehmen
to pull someone's leg
lit: to take somebody on the arm

SHOPPING

FOR THE BABY

What size would fit a six month-old baby?	Welche Größe brauche ich für ein sechs Monate altes Kind?
Is it cotton?	Ist es aus Baumwolle?
Do you have summer hats?	Haben Sie Sommerhüte?
Is it for a boy or a girl?	Ist es für einen Jungen oder für ein Mädchen?

baby bottle	Fläschen (neut)
baby lotion	Wickelcreme (f)
dummy/pacifier	Schnuller (m)
feeding cup	Schnabeltasse (f)
hat	Hut (m)
mash (purée)	Brei (m); Babynahrung (f)
nappies	Windeln (pl)
socks	Söckchen (pl)
sunblock cream	Sonnenschutzcreme (f)
teat	Sauger (m)
underwear	Unterwäsche (pl)

STATIONERY & PUBLICATIONS

crayons	Buntstifte (pl)
envelope	Briefumschlag (m)
ink	Tinte (f)
map	Karte (f)
newspaper	Zeitung (f)
newspaper in English	Zeitung auf Englisch
novels in English	Romane auf Englisch
paper	Papier (neut)
pen (ballpoint)	Kugelschreiber (m)
pencil	Bleistift (m)
rubber	Radiergummi (m)
scissors	Schere (f)
writing paper	Briefpapier (neut)

PHOTOGRAPHY

I'd like to have this film developed.	Bitte entwickeln Sie diesen Film.
When will the photos be ready?	Wann werden die Fotos fertig sein?
I'd like a film for this camera.	Ich möchte einen Film für diese Kamera.
B&W (film)	Schwarzweißfilm (m)
battery	Batterie (f)
camera	Kamera (f); Fotoapparat (m)
colour film	Farbfilm (m)
colour slide film	Farbfilm für Dias
enlargement	Vergrößerung (f)
film	Film (m)
flash	Blitz (m)
lens	Objektiv (neut)
light meter	Belichtungsmesser (m)
print	Abzug (m)
slide	Dia (neut)

SMOKING

A packet of cigarettes, please.	Eine Schachtel Zigaretten bitte.
Are these cigarettes strong/ mild?	Sind diese Zigaretten stark/ leicht?
Do you have a light?	Haben Sie Feuer?
Please don't smoke.	Rauchen verboten.
Could I have one of yours?	Kann ich eine Zigarette von Ihnen/dir haben?
I'm trying to give up.	Ich versuche aufzuhören.
Do you smoke?	Rauchen Sie?/Rauchst du?
I don't smoke (anymore).	Ich rauche nicht (mehr).

SIGNS

| BITTE RAUCHEN SIE NICHT | PLEASE DON'T SMOKE |

cigarette papers	Zigarettenpapiere (pl)
cigarettes	Zigaretten (pl)
filtered	mit Filter
lighter	Feuerzeug (neut)
matches	Streichhölzer (pl)
menthol	Menthol (neut)
pipe	Pfeife (f)
tobacco (pipe)	Tabak; Pfeifentabak (m)

SIZES & COMPARISONS

a little bit	ein bisschen
also	auch
big	groß
enough	genug
heavy	schwer
light	leicht
many	viele
more	mehr
less (not so much/many)	nicht so viel/viele
small	klein
too much/many	zu viel/viele

SHOPPING

CROSSWORD – SHOPPING

Across

3. Vermilion
4. Emporium of many wares
7. Calorific brown sugary foodstuff
8. Chain or cord with beads or jewels
9. To argue over price

Down

1. Downmarket market
2. Azure
5. Where pills and ointments are sold
6. Matching feet coverings

Answers on page 290.

FOOD

Germans love a big breakfast. Wherever you stay in German-speaking areas, breakfast will almost always be included as part of the price. Even at cheap hotels you may get ham, sausage, herrings, boiled eggs, bread rolls and fresh fruit, as well as coffee, milk and fruit juice. Some Germans have a 'second breakfast' (zweites Frühstück) mid-morning, which can be a smaller version of the earlier breakfast, only sometimes with beer; or it may be just a morning tea with cakes and coffee.

Traditionally lunch is the biggest meal, with dinner more like a small breakfast – some eating places, in fact, have a main menu for lunch and a smaller one for the evening. However, at most restaurants (called Restaurant or Gaststätte) you can get a large dinner if you want.

German food tends to be filling, with lots of meat, especially pork and chicken. Offal is quite common. Pickled vegetables like Sauerkraut (pickled cabbage), rather than fresh vegetables, are very popular. And of course sausage – you'll see lots of snack bars (called Imbiss or Schnellimbiss) selling only sausages.

Some areas, especially southern Germany and Austria, are renowned for their cakes and pastries – you are probably already familiar with apple strudel (Apfelstrudel) and Black Forest cake (Schwarzwälder Kirschtorte). Vienna has been called the café capital of the world, with an unbelievable array of elegant establishments to visit for coffee and cake.

Pubs (Kneipen) are popular and similar to those in England or Australia. They generally sell snacks and light food.

Restaurants often have a menu displayed outside. Many offer a good-value set menu (Gedeck or Tagesmenü). Inside, you don't usually have to wait to be seated, and it is common in less expensive restaurants for other people to sit at your table too. The bill at the end of a meal always includes tax and service charges; however, it is customary to leave a small tip (about 5%) if the service has been good.

Menus always start with Vorspeisen, 'starters', often followed by small dishes which are called Für den kleinen Hunger or kleine Gerichte. Kalte Speisen 'cold dishes' come next followed by Hauptgerichte 'main courses'. Children's dishes are called Für unsere kleinen Gäste or Kinderteller. 'Desserts' are called Nachspeisen.

For regional specialities, see Varieties of German page 219.

FOOD

BREAKFAST (FRÜHSTÜCK)

apricot jam	Aprikosenmarmelade (f)
blueberry jam	Heidelbeermarmelade (f)
boiled eggs	gekochte Eier (pl)
cereal	Müsli (neut)
fried eggs	Spiegeleier (pl)
fruit juice	Fruchtsaft (m)
ham	Schinken (m)
hard-boiled	hartgekocht
honey	Honig (m)
jam	Marmelade (f)
marmelade	Orangenmarmelade (f)
porridge	Haferbrei (m)
sausage	Wurst (f)
scrambled eggs	Rühreier (pl)
soft-boiled	weichgekocht
strawberry jam	Erdbeermarmelade (f)

DID YOU KNOW ... If you see a sign that says **Stammtisch** on a restaurant table in Germany, don't sit there. This means that it is reserved for regulars.

VEGETARIAN MEALS (FÜR VEGETARIER)

Do you serve vegetarian meals?	Haben Sie auch vegetarische Kost?
I am a vegetarian.	Ich bin Vegetarier/in.
I'm a vegan.	Ich bin Makrobiotiker/in.

I don't eat ...	Ich esse ...
chicken	kein Hühnchen
fish	keinen Fisch
meat	kein Fleisch
pork	kein Schweinefleisch

EATING OUT

I'm looking for ...	Ich suche ...
a cheap restaurant	ein preiswertes Restaurant
a typical restaurant	ein typisches Restaurant
a restaurant with good home-cooking	ein Restaurant mit gutbürgerlicher Küche
a restaurant with international cooking	ein Restaurant mit internationaler Küche

I'd like to have ...	Ich möchte bitte ...
breakfast	frühstücken
lunch	mittagessen
dinner	abendessen

I'd like to reserve a table for four people at 8 pm.	Ich möchte für acht Uhr einen Tisch für vier Personen reservieren.
Table for ..., please.	Einen Tisch für ..., bitte.
Is this table free?	Ist dieser Tisch frei?
Can I see the menu please?	Kann ich bitte die Speisekarte haben?
What do you recommend?	Was empfehlen Sie?

FOOD

FOOD

Are there any specialities from this region?	Gibt es etwas typisches aus der Region?
I'd like the set lunch.	Ich hätte gern das Tagesmenü.
What does it include?	Was enthält das?
The bill, please.	Die Rechnung, bitte.

ashtray	Aschenbecher (m)
bill	Rechnung (f)
bottle	Flasche (f)
bowl	Schüssel (f)
cup	Tasse (f)
cutlery	Besteck (neut)
dessert	Nachspeise (f)
drink	Getränk (neut)
fork	Gabel (f)
fresh	frisch
glass	Glas (neut)
knife	Messer (m)
milk jug	Milchkännchen (neut)
napkin; serviette	Serviette (f)
plate	Teller (m)
spicy	würzig
spoon	Löffel (m)
stale	alt
sweet	süß

tablecloth
   Tischdecke (f)

teaspoon
   Teelöffel (m)

toothpick
   Zahnstocher (m)

tray
   Tablett (neut)

waiter
   Kellner/in

SOFTLY SOFTLY

Remember that s can be like the 'sh' sound in 'shop':

when sch-, sp- and st- are at the start of a word, the s sounds like a 'sh'

MENU DECODER

Aal	eel	Brombeere	blackberry
Ananas	pineapple	Brot	bread
Apfel	apple	Brötchen	roll
Apfelsine	orange	Brühwürfel	stock cube
Apfelstrudel	apple strudel	Butter	butter
Aprikose	apricot	Cremespeise	mousse
Artischocke	artichoke	Dattel	date
Austern	oysters	Dorsch	cod
Banane	banana	Eintopf; Ragout	stew
Barsch	perch	Eis	ice cream
Bauernsuppe	'farmer's soup' (cabbage & sausage)	englisch	rare
		Ente	duck
		Erbse	pea
Beefsteak	steak	Erbsensuppe	pea soup
belegtes Brot	open sandwich	Erdbeere	strawberry
Berliner	jam doughnut	Erdnuss	peanut
Birne	pear	Essig	vinegar
Blaukraut	red cabbage	Fasan	pheasant
Blumenkohl	cauliflower	Filet	fillet; tenderloin
Blutwurst	blood sausage	Fisch	fish
Bockwurst	pork sausage	Fischgerichte	fish dishes
Bohnen	beans	Fleischbrühe	bouillon
Brathuhn	roast chicken	Fleischsülze	aspic
Bratwurst	fried pork sausage	Forelle	trout
Brokkoli	broccoli	Frankfurter Kranz	sponge cake with rum, butter cream and cherries (Frankfurt)
		Frikadelle	meatball
		Frühlingssuppe	vegetable soup
		Gans	goose
		Garnele	shrimp; prawn
		Gebäck	pastries
		gebacken	baked
		gebraten	cooked (fried, roasted, grilled or baked)
		gedämpft	steamed
		Geflügel	poultry
		gefüllt	stuffed

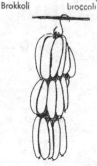

FOOD

FOOD

MENU DECODER

gekocht	boiled	Heilbutt	halibut
gekochte Eier	boiled eggs	Hering	herring
Gemüse	vegetables	Himbeere	raspberry
Gemüsesuppe	vegetable soup	Hirsch	stag
gepökelt	salted	Holsteiner	veal with fried
geräuchert	smoked	Schnitzel	egg, accompanied by seafood
geräucherte Forelle	smoked trout		
geräucherter Aal	smoked eel	Honig	honey
geräucherter Schinken	gammon	Hühnerbrust	chicken breast
		Hühnersuppe	chicken soup
geschmort	braised; stewed	Hummer	lobster
Getränk	drink	Kabeljau	cod
getrocknet	dried	Kalbfleisch	veal
Grapefruit	grapefruit	Kaninchen	rabbit
Graupensuppe	barley soup	Kapern	capers
grüner Salat	salad	Karotte	carrot
Grünkohl mit Pinkel	kale (cabbage) with sausages (Bremen)	Karpfen	carp
		Kartoffel	potato
		Bratkartoffeln	fried potatoes
Gurke	cucumber; gherkins	Kartoffelbrei	mashed potatoes
gut durchgebraten	well-done	Kartoffelsalat	potato salad
		Käse	cheese
Hackbraten	meatloaf	Keule	leg
Hackfleisch	minced meat	Kieler Sprotten	small smoked herring
Haferbrei	porridge		
Hähnchen	chicken	Kirsche	cherry
Backhähnchen	fried chicken	kleine/ kalte Gerichte	small/cold dishes
Brathuhn	roast chicken		
hartgekocht	hard-boiled	Knoblauch	garlic
Hase	hare	Kohl	cabbage
Haselnuss	hazelnut	Kohlroulade	cabbage leaves stuffed with minced meat
Hasenpfeffer	hare stew with mushrooms and onions		
		Kompott	stewed fruit
Haxe	leg	Königsberger	meatballs in a
Hecht	pike	Klopse	sour-cream-and-caper-sauce
Heidelbeere; Blaubeere	blueberry		

MENU DECODER

Königstorte	rum-flavoured fruit cake
Kopfsalat	lettuce
Koteletts	chops
Krabbe	crab
Kräuter	herbs
Krebs	shellfish
Kuchen	cake
Kümmel	caraway (seeds)
Kürbis	pumpkin
Kutteln	tripe
Labskaus	thick meat-and-potato stew
Lachs	salmon
Lamm	lamb
Languste	crayfish
Lauch	leak
Leber	liver
Leberwurst	liver sausage
Leipziger Allerlei	mixed vegetable stew (Leipzig)
Lende	loin
Linsen mit Spätzle	lentil stew with noodles and sausages (Stuttgart)
Linsensuppe	lentil soup
Lorbeerblätter	bay leaves
Lübecker Marzipan	marzipan (Lübeck)
Mais	sweetcorn
Makrele	mackerel
Mandarine	tangerine
Mandel	almond
Marmelade	jam
Meeresfrüchte	seafood
Mehl	flour
Milch	milk
Muschel	clam; mussel
Müsli	cereal
Nachspeise	dessert

Nelken	cloves
Niere	kidney
Nudeln	noodles
Obstsalat	fruit salad

Ochsenschwanz-suppe	oxtail soup
ohne	without
Orangen-marmelade	marmelade
Paprika	capsicum (pepper)
Petersilie	parsley
Pfälzer Saumagen	stuffed stomach of pork
Pfannkuchen	pancake
Pfeffer	pepper
Pfirsich	peach
Pflaume	plum
Pilz	mushroom
Preiselbeere	cranberry
Pute	turkey
Ragout; Eintopf	stew
Räucherlachs	smoked salmon
Reh	venison
Reis	rice
Rhabarber	rhubarb
Rheinischer Sauerbraten mit Kartoffelklößen	roasted marinated meat, slightly sour, often served with potato dumpling.

MENU DECODER

FOOD

Rindfleisch	beef	Spargel	asparagus
roh	raw (uncooked)	Spekulatius	almond biscuits
Rollmops	pickled herrings	Spiegeleier	fried eggs
Rosenkohl	Brussel sprouts	Spinat	spinach
Rosinen	raisins	Stachelbeere	gooseberry
rote Beete; rote Rübe	beetroot	süß	sweet
		Suppe	soup
rote Johannisbeere	red currant	Teigwaren	pasta
		Tintenfisch	cuttlefish
Rotkohl	red cabbage	Toast	toast
Roulade	beef olive	Tomate	tomato
Rührei	scrambled eggs	Tomatenketchup	tomato sauce
Russische Eier	eggs with mayonnaise	Tomatensuppe	tomato soup
		Torte	layer cake
Salz	salt	Truthahn	turkey
Schellfisch	haddock	Tunfisch	tuna
Schinken	ham	Wachtel	quail
Schlachtplatte	selection of pork and sausage	Walnuss	walnut
		Wasser	water
Schmorbraten	beef pot roast	weichgekocht	soft-boiled
Schnitten	cold cuts and vegetables	Wein	wine
		Weinberg- schnecken	snails
Schnittlauch	chives		
Scholle	plaice	Weintraube	grape
schwarze Johannisbeere	black currant	Weißwurst	veal sausage
		Wiener Art	the (Vienna) style
Schwarzwälder Kirschtorte	Black Forest cake (chocolate layer cake filled with cream and cherries)	Wiener Schnitzel	crumbed veal
		Wild	game
		Wildschwein	wild boar
		Wurst	sausage
		Wurstplatte	cold cuts
		würzig	spicy
		Zahnstocher	toothpick
Schweinebraten	roast pork	Zimt	cinnamon
Schweinefleisch	pork	Zunge	tongue
Schweinshaxen	crispy leg of pork served with dumplings	Zwetsche	damson
		Zwieback	rusk
		Zwiebel	onion
Seezunge	sole	Zwiebelsuppe	onion soup
Sellerie	celery	Zwiebelwurst	liver-and-onion sausage
Senf	mustard		

APPETISERS & SNACKS (VORSPEISEN)

belegtes Brot (neut)	open sandwich
Brezen (f)	pretzel
Fleischsülze (f)	aspic
geräucherter Aal (m)	smoked eel
geräucherte Forelle (f)	smoked trout
geräucherter Schinken (m)	gammon
kleine/kalte Gerichte (pl)	small/cold dishes
Pfannkuchen (m)	pancake
Pilz (m)	mushroom

Räucherlachs (m)
  smoked salmon
Rollmops (m)
  pickled herrings
Russische Eier (pl)
  eggs with mayonnaise
Schnitten (pl)
  cold cuts and vegetables
Weinbergschnecken (pl)
  escargots (snails)
Wurst (f)
  sausage
    Wurstplatte (f)
      cold cuts
    Blutwurst (f)
      blood sausage
    Bockwurst (f)
      pork sausage
    Bratwurst (f)
      fried pork sausage
    Leberwurst (f)
      liver sausage
    Weißwurst (f)
      veal sausage
    Zwiebelwurst (f)
      liver-and onion sausage

FOOD

FOOD

SOUPS (SUPPEN)

Bauernsuppe (f)	'farmer's soup' (cabbage & sausage)
Erbsensuppe (f)	pea soup
Fleischbrühe (f)	bouillon
Gemüsesuppe (f); Frühlingssuppe (f)	vegetable soup
Graupensuppe (f)	barley soup
Hühnersuppe (f)	chicken soup
Linsensuppe (f)	lentil soup
Ochsenschwanzsuppe (f)	oxtail soup
Tomatensuppe (f)	tomato soup
Zwiebelsuppe (f)	onion soup

MEAT DISHES (FLEISCHGERICHTE)

Beefsteak (neut)	steak
Brathuhn (neut)	roast chicken
Eintopf (m); Ragout (neut)	stew
Frikadelle (f)	meatball
Hackbraten (m)	meatloaf
Hasenpfeffer (m)	hare stew with mushrooms and onions
Holsteiner Schnitzel (neut)	veal schnitzel with fried egg, accompanied by seafood
Kohlroulade (f)	cabbage leaves stuffed with minced meat
Königsberger Klopse (pl)	meatballs in a sour-cream-and-caper sauce
Koteletts (pl)	chops
Labskaus (m)	thick meat-and-potato stew
Roulade (f)	beef olive
Schlachtplatte (f)	selection of pork and sausage
Schmorbraten (m)	beef pot roast
Schweinebraten (m)	roast pork
Wiener Schnitzel (neut)	crumbed veal

DESSERT & PASTRIES (NACHSPEISEN & KUCHEN)

Apfelstrudel (m)	apple strudel
Berliner (m)	jam doughnut
Cremespeise (f)	mousse
Eis (neut)	ice cream
Gebäck (neut)	pastries
Kompott (neut)	stewed fruit
Königstorte (f)	rum-flavoured fruit cake
Kuchen (m)	cake
ein Stück Kuchen	a piece of cake
Nürnberger Lebkuchen;	cakes with chocolate, nuts,
Aachener Printen	fruit peel, honey and spices
Obstsalat (m)	fruit salad
Schwarzwälder Kirschtorte (f)	Black Forest cake (chocolate layer cake filled with cream and cherries)
Spekulatius (m)	almond biscuits
Torte (f)	layer cake

FOOD

METHODS OF COOKING

baked	gebacken
boiled	gekocht
braised	geschmort
cooked (any way)	gebraten
rare	englisch
salted	gepökelt
smoked	geräuchert
steamed	gedämpft
stewed	geschmort
stuffed	gefüllt
in the (Vienna) style	(Wiener) Art
well done	gut durchgebraten
with	mit
without	ohne

FOOD

STAPLES

bread	Brot (neut)		noodles	Nudeln (pl)
butter	Butter (f)		pasta	Teigwaren (pl)
cheese	Käse (m)		rice	Reis (m)
croissant	Croissant (neut);		roll	Brötchen (neut)
	Hörnchen (neut)		rusk	Zwieback (m)
flour	Mehl (neut)		toast	Toast (m)

CONDIMENTS, HERBS & SPICES (GEWÜRZE)

bay leaves	Lorbeerblätter (pl)
capers	Kapern (pl)
caraway (seeds)	Kümmel (m)
chives	Schnittlauch (m)
cinnamon	Zimt (m)
cloves	Nelken (pl)
garlic	Knoblauch (m)
herbs	Kräuter (pl)
mustard	Senf (m)
parsley	Petersilie (f)
pepper	Pfeffer (m)
raisins	Rosinen (pl)
salt	Salz (neut)
stock cube	Brühwürfel (m)
tomato sauce	Tomatenketchup (neut)
vinegar	Essig (m)

SELF CATERING

Are there cooking facilities?	Gibt es hier eine Kochgelegenheit?
Is cutlery/crockery provided?	Gibt es Besteck/Geschirr?
Is there a food-store nearby?	Gibt es hier einen Laden, wo ich Essen einkaufen kann?
self catering	selbst Kochen

AT THE MARKET
Meat (Fleisch)

beef	Rindfleisch (neut)
fillet; tenderloin	Filet (neut)
game	Wild (neut)
hare	Hase (m)
kidney	Niere (f)
leg	Haxe (f); Keule (f)
liver	Leber (f)
loin	Lende (f)
minced meat	Hackfleisch (neut)
pork	Schweinefleisch (neut)
stag	Hirsch (m)
tongue	Zunge (f)
tripe	Kutteln (pl)
veal	Kalbfleisch (neut)
venison	Reh (neut)
wild boar	Wildschwein (neut)

FOOD

Poultry (Geflügel)

chicken	Hähnchen (neut)
chicken breast	Hühnerbrust (f)
fried chicken	Backhähnchen (neut)
roast chicken	Brathuhn (neut)
duck	Ente (f)
goose	Gans (f)
pheasant	Fasan (m)
quail	Wachtel (f)
turkey	Truthahn (m); Pute (f)

DID YOU KNOW ... In bars you usually don't pay for your drinks when you order them. A tab is kept and you pay on leaving.

FOOD

Seafood (Meeresfrüchte)

carp	Karpfen (m)
clam; mussel	Muschel (f)
cod	Dorsch (m)
cod fish	Kabeljau (m)
crab	Krabbe (f)
crayfish	Languste (f)
cuttlefisch	Tintenfisch (m)
eel	Aal (m)
fish	Fisch (m)
fish dishes	Fischgerichte (pl)
haddock	Schellfisch (m)
halibut	Heilbutt (m)
herring	Hering (m)
lobster	Hummer (m)
mackerel	Makrele (f)
oysters	Austern (pl)
perch	Barsch (m)
pike	Hecht (m)
plaice	Scholle (f)
salmon	Lachs (m)
shellfish	Krebs (m)
shrimp; prawn	Garnele (f)
sole	Seezunge (f)
trout	Forelle (f)
tuna	Tunfisch (m)

Vegetables (Gemüse)

artichoke	Artischocke (f)
asparagus	Spargel (m)
beans	Bohnen (pl)
beetroot	Rote Beete (f); Rote Rübe (f)
broccoli	Brokkoli (m)
Brussel sprouts	Rosenkohl (m)

cabbage	Kohl (m)
capsicum (peppers)	Paprika (f)
carrot	Karotte (f)
cauliflower	Blumenkohl (m)
celery	Sellerie (m)
cucumber; gherkins	Gurke (f)
garlic	Knoblauch (m)
leek	Lauch (m)
lettuce	Kopfsalat (m)
mushroom	Pilz (m)
onion	Zwiebel (f)
pea	Erbse (f)
potato	Kartoffel (f)
fried potatoes	Bratkartoffeln (pl)
mashed potatoes	Kartoffelbrei (m)
potato salad	Kartoffelsalat (m)
pumpkin	Kürbis (m)
red cabbage	Rotkohl (m); Blaukraut (neut)
salad	grüner Salat (m)
spinach	Spinat (m)
sweetcorn	Mais (m)
tomato	Tomate (f)

Fruit & Nuts (Früchte & Nüsse)

almond	Mandel (f)
apple	Apfel (m)
apricot	Aprikose (f)
banana	Banane (f)
blackberry	Brombeere (f)
black currant	schwarze Johannisbeere (f)
blueberry	Blaubeere (f); Heidelbeere (f)
cherry	Kirsche (f)
cranberry	Preiselbeere (f)
damson	Zwetsche (f)
date	Dattel (f)

FOOD

FOOD

gooseberry	Stachelbeere (f)
grape	Weintraube (f)
grapefruit	Grapefruit (f)
hazelnut	Haselnuss (f)
orange	Apfelsine (f); Orange (f)
peach	Pfirsich (m)
peanut	Erdnuss (f)
pear	Birne (f)
pineapple	Ananas (f)
plum	Pflaume (f)
raspberry	Himbeere (f)
red currant	rote Johannisbeere (f)
rhubarb	Rhabarber (m)
strawberry	Erdbeere (f)
tangerine	Mandarine (f)
walnut	Walnuss (f)

DRINKS
Non-alcoholic Drinks

coffee	Kaffee (m)
Vienna coffee (black, topped with whipped cream)	Einspänner (m)
fruit juice	Fruchtsaft (m)
apple juice	Apfelsaft (m)
orange juice	Orangensaft (m)
juice and soda water	Saftschorle (f)
milkshake	Milchshake (neut)
mineral water	Mineralwasser (neut)
peppermint tea	Pfefferminztee (m)
tea	Tee (m)
water	Wasser (neut)
with/without ...	mit/ohne ...
cream	Sahne (f)
milk	Milch (f)
sugar	Zucker (m)

In the Bar

Do you serve food?	Haben Sie auch etwas zum Essen?
I'm drunk.	Ich bin blau (lit: I'm blue); Ich bin betrunken
a bag of crisps/chips	eine Tüte Chips
peanuts	Erdnüsse (pl)

Alcoholic Drinks

apple brandy	Apfelschnaps (m)
apple cider	Apfelwein (m)
beer	Bier (neut)
lager	Helles (neut); Pils (neut)
dark	Dunkles (neut)
draught beer	Bier vom Fass (neut)

FOOD

WINE APPRECIATION

May I see the wine list?	Kann ich die Weinkarte sehen?
May I try the wine?	Kann ich den Wein probieren?
Which is a good year?	Welcher Jahrgang ist gut?

full-bodied	gehaltvoll	taste	Geschmack (m)
grapes	Trauben (pl)	nose	Bouquet (neut)
harvest	Lese (f)	vineyards	Weingärten (pl)
late harvest	Spätlese (f)	vintage	Weinlese (f);
light	leicht		Jahrgang (m)
oak barrels	Eichenfässer (pl)	wine tasting	Weinprobe (f)

made with wheat	Weißbier (neut);
	Weizenbier (neut)
malt beer	Malzbier (neut)
brandy	Weinbrand (m)
champagne	Sekt (m)
kirsch	Kirschwasser (neut)
spirit made from grain	Schnaps (m)
wine	Wein (m)
chilled	gekühlt
dry	trocken
mulled wine	Glühwein (m)
red wine	Rotwein (m)
rosé	Rosé (m)
sparkling	prickelnd
sweet	süß
white wine	Weißwein (m)
with ice	mit Eis (neut)

For more on wine and beer, see Varieties of German page 219.

IN THE COUNTRY

WEATHER

What is the weather forecast?	Wie ist die Wettervorhersage?
Will It rain/snow?	Wird es regnen/schneien?
How long has it been raining?	Wie lange regnet es schon?
Do you think it will brighten up today?	Glauben Sie, dass es sich heute noch aufklärt?
What's the maximum temperature today?	Wie viel Grad hat es heute?
What's the weather like?	Wie ist das Wetter?
The weather is going to change.	Das Wetter wird sich ändern.
There will be a thunderstorm tonight.	Heute Nacht wird es ein Gewitter geben.
The weather is ... today.	Das Wetter ist heute ...

Will it be ... tomorrow?	Wird es morgen ... sein?
cloudy	wolkig
cold	kalt
fine	schön
foggy	neblig
frosty	frostig
hot	heiß
muggy	schwül
stormy	stürmisch
warm	warm
windy	windig

DID YOU KNOW ... Weather in Germany is very variable but the most reliable weather is from May to October. This, of course, coincides with the peak tourist season.

Useful Words

air	Luft (f)
climate	Klima (neut)
dawn	Morgendämmerung (f)
dusk	Abenddämmerung (f)
fog	Nebel (m)
frost	Frost (m)
hail	Hagel (m)
heat	Hitze (f)
ice	Eis (neut)
lightning	Blitz (m)
moon	Mond (m)
rain	Regen (m)
shower	Regenschauer (m)
slippery	glatt
snow	Schnee (m)
storm	Sturm (m)
sun	Sonne (f)
sunrise	Sonnenaufgang (m)
sunset	Sonnenuntergang (m)
temperature	Temperatur (f)
thunder	Donner (m)
wind	Wind (m)

CAMPING

Camping is very popular in Germany. There are lots of official campsites of varying standards. In more remote areas you might ask farmers for permission to camp on their land, but in general it is illegal to camp anywhere other than on an official campsite.

Am I allowed to camp here?	Kann ich hier zelten?
Is there a campsite nearby?	Gibt es in der Nähe einen Campingplatz?
Do you have room for a large tent and a car?	Haben Sie noch Platz für ein großes Zelt und ein Auto?

How much do you charge ...?	Wie viel berechnen Sie ...?
per night	pro Nacht
per person	pro Person
for a tent	für ein Zelt
for a car	für ein Auto
for a caravan	für einen Wohnwagen
for a campervan	für ein Wohnmobil
Do you have hot showers?	Haben Sie Warmwasserduschen?
Do you have cooking facilities?	Haben Sie Kochmöglichkeiten?
Is there electricity?	Gibt es einen Stromanschluss?
Where can I get butane gas?	Wo bekomme ich Butangas?
I'm staying for ... nights.	Ich bleibe ... Nächte.
Is the water drinkable?	Kann man das Wasser trinken?
airbed	Luftmatratze (f)
axe	Axt (f)
camping stove	Kocher (m)
can	Kanister (m)
can opener	Dosenöffner (m)
cooker	Herd (m)
cutlery	Besteck (neut)
fee	Benutzungsgebühr (f)
firewood	Brennholz (neut)
foam mattress	Isomatte (f)
frying pan	Bratpfanne (f)
fuel	Brennstoff (m)
gas cartridge	Gaskartusche (f)
hammock	Hängematte (f)
to hire	mieten
kettle	Kessel (m)
matches	Streichhölzer (pl)
notice of departure	Abmeldung (f)

IN THE COUNTRY

penknife	**Taschenmesser** (neut)
petrol	**Benzin** (neut)
pot	**Topf** (m)
sanitary facilities	**sanitäre Einrichtungen** (pl)
sleeping bag	**Schlafsack** (m)
spade	**Spaten** (m)
spirit	**Spiritus** (m)
tent	**Zelt** (neut)
tent pegs	**Heringe** (pl); **Zeltpflöcke** (pl)
toilet paper	**Klopapier** (neut)
torch (flashlight)	**Taschenlampe** (f)

HIKING & MOUNTAINEERING

Germany, Austria and Switzerland offer great trekking at all levels. Lonely Planet's *Trekking in Switzerland* details a broad selection of suggested walks in that country.

I want to hire a tent.	Ich möchte ein Zelt mieten.
Is it waterproof?	Ist es wasserdicht?
Do I need a guide?	Brauche ich einen Führer?
Where can I find a mountain guide?	Wo finde ich einen Bergführer?
What does the price for this trip include?	Was beinhaltet der Preis für diese Tour?
Where do we meet?	Wo treffen wir uns?
Is there a walking map for this area?	Gibt es eine Wanderkarte für dieses Gebiet?
How many hours per day will we walk?	Wie viele Stunden am Tag werden wir laufen?
Is it a difficult tour?	Ist es eine schwierige Tour?
Are there any serviced mountain huts along the route?	Gibt es auf der Strecke bewirtschaftete Berghütten?
Is it possible to stay there overnight?	Kann man dort übernachten?
Do I have to make a reservation?	Muss ich reservieren?
Is the trail steep?	Ist der Weg steil?
Where are we on this map?	Wo sind wir auf dieser Karte?
I'm lost.	Ich habe mich verlaufen.
Where does this path go to?	Wo führt dieser Pfad hin?
Is this the trail to ...?	Führt dieser Pfad nach ...?
Which trail goes to ...?	Welcher Pfad führt nach ...?
Can you show me the way to ...?	Können Sie mir den Weg nach ... zeigen?
How many hours to ...?	Wie viele Stunden sind es nach ...?

IN THE COUNTRY

Do I need to bring (a/an) ...?	Muss ich ... mitbringen?
altitude metre	einen Höhenmeter
backpack	einen Rucksack
crampons	Steigeisen
gaiters	Gamaschen
gloves	Handschuhe
ice axe	einen Eispickel
map	eine Landkarte
rope	ein Seil
strap (for a pack)	einen Packriemen
sun cream	eine Sonnencreme
thermos	eine Thermosflasche
trekking shoes	Trekkingstiefel
water bottle	eine Feldflasche

Useful Words

avalanche
Lawine (f)
cable car
Seilbahn (f)
crossing
Übergang (m)
hut
Hütte (f)
mountain hut
Berghütte (f)
mountaineering
Bergsteigen (neut)
path; track
Pfad (m)
shortcut
Abkürzung (f)
signpost
Wegweiser (m)
snowfield
Schneefeld (neut)

ADJECTIVES

When adjectives are not placed before a noun, they do not show case and have no declensional endings:

Der Mann ist groß.
The man is tall.

When the adjectives are placed before a noun, however, they do show case and have declensional endings:

Der große Mann.
The tall man.

See page 29 for an explanation.

AT THE BEACH

awning	Sonnensegel (neut)
beach	Strand (m)
beach towel	Badetuch (neut)
bucket	Eimer (m)
crab	Krebs (m)
current	Strömung (f)
dangerous	gefährlich
heat stroke	Sonnenstich (m)
high tide	Flut (f)
jelly fish	Qualle (f)
lake	See (m)
life guard	Badewächter (m)
low tide	Ebbe (f)
pollution	Verschmutzung (f)
river	Fluss (m); Strom (m)
rocky beach	Felsküste (f)
sandy beach	Sandstrand (m)
sea	Meer (neut)
seaweed	Algen (pl)
shark	Hai (m)
shovel	Schaufel (f)
sunburn	Sonnenbrand (m)
sun-tan oil	Sonnenöl (neut)
wave	Welle (f)

IN THE COUNTRY

Is this a public beach?	Ist das ein öffentlicher Strand?
Are there dangerous currents?	Gibt es hier gefährliche Strömungen?
What time is the tide coming in?	Wann ist Flut?
Where can I rent a sun-shade?	Wo kann ich einen Sonnenschirm mieten?
Can we swim here?	Können wir hier baden?

For phrases on Aquatic Sports see page 185.

GEOGRAPHICAL TERMS

bay	Bucht (f)
cape	Kap (neut)
cave	Höhle (f)
desert	Wüste (f)
glacier	Gletscher (m)
gorge	Schlucht (f)
gulf	Golf (m)
hill	Hügel (m)
island	Insel (f)
landslide	Erdrutsch (m)
marsh	Sumpf (m)
mountain	Berg (m)
mountain range	Gebirgszug (m); Gebirgskette (f)
ocean	Ozean (m)
pass	Pass (m)
peak	Gipfel (m)
peninsula	Halbinsel (f)
plain	Ebene (f)
plateau	Hochebene (f)
rapids	Stromschnellen (pl)
ridge	Grat (m)
river	Fluss (m)
rock	Fels (m)
saddle	Joch (neut); Sattel (m)
scree; talus	Geröll (neut)
sea	Meer (neut); See (f)
slope	Hang (m)
spring	Quelle (f)
stone	Stein (m)
stream	Bach (m)
tide	Gezeiten (pl)
valley	Tal (neut)
waterfall	Wasserfall (m)
wave	Welle (f)

DIRECTIONS

north	Norden (m); nördlich
south	Süden (m); südlich
east	Osten (m); östlich
west	Westen (m); westlich

FAUNA

What's that animal called?   Wie heißt dieses Tier?

Farm Animals & Insects

ant	Ameise (f)	frog	Frosch (m)
bee	Biene (f)	hen	Henne (f)
butterfly	Schmetterling (m)	hornet	Hornisse (f)
chicken	Huhn (neut)	horse	Pferd (neut)
cow	Kuh (f)	mouse	Maus (f)
dog	Hund (m)	ox	Ochse (m)
donkey	Esel (m)	pig	Schwein (neut)
duck	Ente (f)	sheep	Schaf (neut)
gnat	Schnake (f)	snail	Schnecke (f)
goat	Ziege (f)	spider	Spinne (f)
goose	Gans (f)	wasp	Wespe (f)
fly	Fliege (f)		

IN THE COUNTRY

DID YOU KNOW ... There are about 2600 campsites in Germany. They are graded from good to excellent. All campsites have at least toilet and washing facilities. Some are positively luxurious by camping standards with shops and swimming pools too.

IN THE COUNTRY

Wildlife

Are there any nature reserves around here?	Gibt es hier Naturschutzgebiete?
Is there ...?	Gibt es dort ...?
Is it dangerous?	Ist es gefährlich?

badger	Dachs (m)
bear	Bär (m)
boar	Wildschwein (neut)
chamois	Gämse (f)
deer	Reh (neut); Hirsch (m)
fox	Fuchs (m)
lynx	Luchs (m)
marmot	Murmeltier (neut)
snake	Schlange (f)
wolf	Wolf (m)

Birds

What is that bird called?	Wie heißt dieser Vogel?

blackbird	Amsel (f)
cuckoo	Kuckuck (m)
eagle	Adler (m)
hawk	Habicht (m)
kingfisher	Eisvogel (m)
lark	Lerche (f)
nightingale	Nachtigall (f)
owl	Eule (f)
parrot	Papagei (m)
pigeon	Taube (f)
robin	Rotkehlchen (neut)
seagull	Möwe (f)
sparrow	Spatz (m)
stork	Storch (m)

V OR W?

The letter w is pronounced as 'v' in German. So, Wo ('where') is pronounced 'voh'.

The letter z in German is always pronounced as 'ts' at the beginning of a word. So a word like Zauber ('magic') is pronounced 'tsowber'.

Fish

Is fishing allowed here?   Darf man hier angeln?

eel   Aal (m)
fish   Fisch (m)
herring   Hering (m)
perch   Barsch (m)
pike   Hecht (m)
trout   Forelle (f)

FLORA

ash tree   Esche (f)
beech   Buche (f)
blueberry   Heidelbeere (f)
buttercup   Hahnenfuß (m)
chestnut   Kastanie (f)
cowslip   Schlüsselblume (f)
daffodil   Osterglocke (f)
edelweiss   Edelweiß (neut)
gentian   Enzian (m)
geranium   Geranie (f)
heather   Heidekraut (neut)
larch   Lärche (f)
maple   Ahorn (m)
pasque flower; anemone   Anemone (f)
pine tree   Kiefer (f)
pussy willow   Palmkätzchen (neut)
red spruce   Fichte (f)
rose   Rose (f)
silver fur   Weißtanne (f)
snowdrop   Schneeglöckchen (neut)
sweet chestnut tree   Kastanienbaum (m)
tulip   Tulpe (f)
weeping willow   Trauerweide (f)

IN THE COUNTRY

CROSSWORD - IN THE COUNTRY

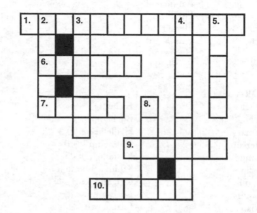

Across
1. Event at dawn
6. Silvery fish often eaten pickled
7. Level expanse of land
9. Useful for cooking when camping
10. Sonic result of lightning

Down
2. Castrated bovine
3. General direction of Arctic Ocean
4. River of ice
5. Ground-level cloud
8. It's leaf graces the Canadian flag

Answers on page 290.

TYPES OF SPORT

The national sport of Germany is soccer (Fußball). Tens of thousands of fans watch the games of their favourite clubs every weekend. The best known clubs are Bayern München, Borussia Dortmund, Borussia Mönchengladbach and VFB Stuttgart. Renowned players are Jürgen Klinsmann, Oliver Bierhoff, Lothar Matthäus and, one of the sport's greatest players, Franz Beckenbauer (Kaiser Franz). Another popular sport is, of course, tennis with favourites Steffi Graf, Anke Huber, Boris Becker and Michael Stich.

badminton	Badminton (neut)
badminton court	Badmintonfeld (neut)
badminton racket	Badmintonschläger (m)
basketball	Basketball (m)
curling	Eisstockschießen (neut)
cycling	Radsport (m)
diving	Tauchen (neut)
fencing	Fechten (neut)
figure skating	Eiskunstlauf (m)
to skate	Eis laufen
fishing	Fischen (neut)
bait	Köder (m)
fishing rod	Angel (f)
golf	Golf (neut)
gymnastics	Gymnastik (f)
handball	Handball (m)
hang-gliding	Drachenfliegen (neut)
ice hockey	Eishockey (neut)
ice rink	Eisstadion (neut)
ice skating	Eis laufen (neut)
kayaking	Kajak fahren (neut)

parachuting	Fallschirmspringen (neut)
paragliding	Gleitschirmfliegen (neut)
rafting	Rafting (neut)
rowing	Rudern (neut)
oarsman	Ruderer (m)
cox	Steuermann (m)
sailing	Segeln (neut)
shooting	Schießsport (m)
clay-pigeon shooting	Tontaubenschießen (neut)
target	Zielscheibe (f)
shuttlecock	Federball (m)
speed skating	Eisschnelllauf (m)
table tennis/ping pong	Tischtennis (neut)
table-tennis bat	Tischtennisschläger (m)
table-tennis table	Tischtennisplatte (f)
volleyball	Volleyball (m)
wrestling	Ringkampf (m);
	Ringen (neut)

For Hiking & Mountaineering, see In the Country page 171.

TALKING ABOUT SPORT

Do you like sport?	Mögen Sie Sport?
Yes, very much.	Ja, sehr gerne.
No, not at all.	Nein, überhaupt nicht.
I like watching rather than participating.	Ich sehe lieber zu als selbst mitzumachen.
Do you play ...?	Spielen Sie ...?
Are you good?	Sind Sie gut?
I'm a beginner.	Ich bin Anfänger.
Where is ...?	Wo ist ...?
the nearest swimming pool	das nächste Schwimmbad
the nearest gym	das nächste Fitnesscenter
the nearest tennis court	der nächste Tennisplatz

ACTIVITIES

What is the charge per ...?
    day
    game
    hour

Wie viel kostet es pro ...?
    Tag
    Spiel
    Stunde

ACTIVITIES

SOCCER

Which is your favourite football team?	Welcher ist dein Lieblingsfußballverein?
Are you going to the match?	Gehst du zum Spiel?
Who is playing?	Wer spielt?
Against who?	Gegen wen?
Do you have a ticket?	Hast du eine Karte?

goal	Tor (neut)
football	Fußball (m)
football boot	Fußballschuh (m)
football league championship	Fußballmeisterschaft (f)
football match	Fußballspiel (neut)
football pitch	Fußballplatz (m)
football team	Fußballmannschaft (f)
foul	Foul (neut)
referee	Schiedsrichter (m)
soccer	Fußball (m)

TENNIS & SQUASH

Is there a tennis court here?	Gibt es hier einen Tennisplatz?
Do I have to be a member to play here?	Muss ich Mitglied sein, um hier spielen zu können?
Can I borrow a racket?	Kann ich einen Schläger ausleihen?
I'm looking for a tennis/ squash partner.	Ich suche jemanden, der mit mir Tennis/Squash spielt.
What level are you at?	Wie gut spielst du?
I'm a beginner.	Ich bin Anfänger/in.
I'm quite good.	Ich spiele ganz gut.
I'm advanced.	Ich bin Fortgeschrittener/ Fortgeschrittene.

ACTIVITIES

Whose turn is it to serve?	Wer hat den Aufschlag?
The ball was on the line.	Der Ball war auf der Linie.
The ball was out!	Der Ball war im Aus!
No, it wasn't!	Nein, war er nicht!

net	Netz (neut)
out	Aus (neut)
squash	Squash (neut)
squash racket	Squashschlager (m)
tennis	Tennis (neut)
tennis court	Tennisplatz (m)
tennis racket	Tennisschläger (m)
timeout	Auszeit (f)

HORSE RIDING

Is there a riding stable in this town?	Gibt es in dieser Stadt einen Reitstall?
Can I take riding lessons?	Kann ich Reitstunden nehmen?
Can I borrow the equipment?	Kann ich mir die Ausrüstung ausleihen?

Useful Words

American style	Westernreiten (neut)
bridle	Zaumzeug (neut)
bridle-path	Reitweg (m)
dressage	Dressurreiten (neut)
English style	englischer Stil
horse	Pferd (neut)
horse riding	Reiten (neut)
horse show	Reitturnier (neut)
pony	Pony (neut)
riding breeches	Reithose (f)
riding crop	Reitgerte (f)
riding lessons	Reitunterricht (m)

ACTIVITIES

riding school	Reitschule (f)
riding stable	Reitstall (m)
saddle	Sattel (m)
show jumping	Springreiten (neut)
to put a bridle on a horse	ein Pferd aufzäumen
to ride out	ausreiten

SKIING

Where can I take a skiing course?	Wo kann ich einen Skikurs machen?
Can I hire the gear?	Kann ich die Ausrüstung mieten?
I want a ski pass for one week.	Ich möchte einen Skipass für eine Woche.

ski	Ski (pl)
ski binding	Skibindung (f)
ski boot	Skischuh (m)
ski goggles	Skibrille (f)
ski instructor	Skilehrer/in
ski lift	Skilift (m)
ski run	Skipiste (f)
ski stick	Skistock (m)
ski wax	Skiwachs (neut)
toboggan	Schlitten (m)
to ski	Ski fahren; Ski laufen

DID YOU KNOW ... The most extensive area for downhill and cross-country skiing is in the Bavarian Alps. The Black Forest and the Harz Mountains are good if you want to avoid the glitz, glamour and high prices.

ACTIVITIES

AQUATIC SPORTS

SIGNS	
FÜR NICHTSCHWIMMER VERBOTEN.	FOR SWIMMERS ONLY
NICHT VON DER SEITE SPRINGEN!	NO JUMPING IN

Can we swim here?	Kann man hier schwimmen?
Is there ...?	Gibt es ...?
a public beach	einen öffentlichen Strand
an indoor swimming pool	ein Hallenbad
an outdoor swimming pool	ein Freibad
a lake	einen See
Do you feel like going for a swim?	Möchten Sie vielleicht schwimmen gehen?
That'd be great!	Das wäre toll!
Not now, thank you.	Jetzt lieber nicht.
Do I have to wear a swimming cap?	Muss ich eine Badekappe tragen?
bath towel	Badetuch (neut)
flipper	Flossen (pl)
nonswimmer	Nichtschwimmer/in
pool attendant	Bademeister (m)
pool for nonswimmers	Nichtschwimmerbecken (neut)
pool for swimmers	Schwimmbecken (neut)
swimmer	Schwimmer/in
swimming cap	Badekappe (f)
swimming costume	Badeanzug (m)
swimming trunks	Badehose (f)

ACTIVITIES

GAMES

Despite television, Germans love to play games. Every year an independent jury votes for the 'game of the year', chosen from all games released in that year. Some of the most popular board games are quite old but still widely played, for example **Mensch ärgere dich nicht**, 'Don't get angry', or **Malefiz**. Other popular board games are **Backgammon**, **Schach**, 'chess', or **Halma**. The most popular card games for adults are **Skat** (mainly in the north) and **Schafkopf** (mainly in the south), both of which are quite complicated and also played in competitions.

Do you like to play games?
    Spielen Sie gerne Spiele?

Do you know the rules of the game?
    Kennen Sie die Spielregeln?

Would you like to play ...?	Möchten Sie ... spielen?
bridge	Bridge
cards	ein Kartenspiel; Karten
checkers	Dame
chess	Schach
computer games	Computerspiele
dominoes	Domino

THEY MAY SAY ...

Wer ist dran?
    Who's next?

Sie sind an der Reihe.
    It's your turn.

Sie müssen aussetzen.
    You have to sit out.

Wie sind die Regeln?
    What are the rules?

Gibt es eine Anleitung auf Englisch?
    Are there English instructions?

Sie haben gemogelt.
    You've cheated.

Das stimmt nicht!
    That's not true!

Ich spiele nicht mehr mit.
    I'm not playing anymore.

Sie haben verloren.
    You've lost.

ACTIVITIES

a game of dice	ein Würfelspiel
nine men's morris	Mühle
pool	Billard
snooker	Snooker

board	Spielbrett (neut)
deck of cards	Spielkarten (pl)
dice	Würfel (m)
figure	Spielfigur (f)

TELEVISION

Germany has both public and, since 1985, private TV stations. The three public stations (**die öffentlich-rechtlichen Rundfunk-anstalten**) don't have commercials in-between films and they're funded through licence fees levied on every TV/radio owner (about DM 25 per month). These first two are broadcast throughout Germany:

(1) **die Arbeitsgemeinschaft der öffentlich-rechtlichen Rundfunkanstalten (ARD)**, also called **das erste deutsche Fernsehen**

(2) **das zweite deutsche Fernsehen (ZDF)**

(3) **die dritten Programme** (third channels), are broadcast in their own regions; **Bayern 3**, **Hessen 3** or **West 3**.

The private stations (**die Privaten**), on the other hand, rely on commercials and are thus free to the public. They tend to offer mainstream programs while the public stations' content is more intellectual and news is presented more objectively.

Programs

Germany's most popular soap opera is *Lindenstraße*, shown on the **ARD** on Sunday at 6.40 pm. Millions follow the adventures of this street's residents, and those who miss out on an episode can look up the program's homepage on the Internet!

ACTIVITIES

On Tuesday night, *Boulevard Bio* is a good cooking show hosted by Alfred Biolek whose videos, CDs and recipe books are widely available.

Crime series are usually shown on Friday on the ZDF, including the popular *Derrick* and *Der Alte*.

Arte, a joint French-German TV station has mostly cultural programs.

Popular talkshow hosts include Thomas Gottschalk and Harald Schmidt.

The German music channel is VIVA.

In addition, there's an overwhelming number of US programs, all dubbed into German of course. You'll probably find it strange to hear your favourite TV hero talking in an odd language. But believe it or not, a dubbed David Hasselhoff or Melanie Griffith sound great.

Switzerland has three channels: Schweiz (Swiss German), französische Schweiz (Swiss French) and italienische Schweiz (Swiss Italian). Austria has two channels, the ORF 1 and the ORF 2.

Do you mind if I turn the TV on?	Haben Sie etwas dagegen, wenn ich den Fernseher anmache?
Turn the TV off!	Schalten Sie den Fernseher aus!
Where's the remote control?	Wo ist die Fernbedienung?
Which channel is ... on?	In welchem Programm kommt ...?
What time does ... start?	Um wie viel Uhr fängt ... an?
I'd like to watch this film.	Ich möchte gerne diesen Film ansehen.
What's on TV today?	Was kommt heute im Fernsehen?
What a bad program!	Was für ein schlechtes Programm!
Not another ad!	Schon wieder Werbung!

ACTIVITIES

When does the film start?	Wann fängt der Film an?
I like that program, too.	Das sehe ich mir auch gerne an.
I'm really interested in that.	Das interessiert mich sehr.

comedy	**Komödie** (f)
documentary	**Dokumentarfilm** (m)
feature film	**Spielfilm** (m)
game show	**Unterhaltungsshow** (f)
love story	**Liebesfilm** (m)
news	**Nachrichten** (pl)
remote control	**Fernbedienung** (f)
serial	**Serie** (f)
sport	**Sportschau** (f)
thriller	**Krimi** (m)
tragedy	**Tragödie** (f)
TV	**Fernseher** (m)
TV ad	**Fernsehwerbung** (f)
TV guide	**Fernsehzeitung** (f)
to watch TV	**fernsehen**

VIDEO

Watching videos is increasingly popular in Germany especially since going to the cinema has become quite expensive.

Where can I hire videos?	Wo kann ich Videos ausleihen?
Do I have to be a member?	Muss ich Mitglied sein?
Do you have ... on video?	Haben Sie ... auf Video?
Can I reserve it?	Kann ich es reservieren?
How long can I rent this video for?	Wie lange kann ich dieses Video ausleihen?
How much is it until tomorrow?	Wie viel kostet es bis morgen?

FESTIVALS & HOLIDAYS

RELIGIOUS FESTIVALS

Germans are notorious for their many holidays, a lot of them religious. Here are some of the major ones, together with some common sayings for these occasions.

Weihnachten (Christmas Eve)

This is the most important celebration in Germany. Unlike in English-speaking countries, the main Christmas celebration is on Christmas Eve. Families gather around a Christmas tree (**Weihnachtsbaum** or **Christbaum**), sing Christmas carols (**Weihnachtslieder**) and read out the Christmas story (**Weihnachtsgeschichte**). Then the presents are opened and everybody wishes the others a merry Christmas (**Fröhliche Weihnachten**). After traditional dishes of stuffed goose (**Weihnachtsgans**) or Christmas carp (**Weihnachtskarpfen**), a lot of people go to midnight Mass (**Christmette**).

Adventszeit (Advent)

The period that covers the four Sundays before Christmas is celebrated by lighting candles of the Advent wreath (**Adventskranz**). Every Sunday one candle is lit, until all four are burning. In addition, children get an Advent calendar (**Adventskalender**) on the first of December. This is a calendar with 24 small doors that open (one each day) to reveal either pictures (angels, candles etc) or a small piece of chocolate.

Nikolaustag (St Nicholas' Day, 6 December)

On the eve of the 5th or the 6th of December, Santa Claus visits the children, bringing them either small presents and nuts (if they have been well behaved) or a rod (if they haven't).

Silvester (New Year's Eve, 31 December)
Celebrated with parties, lots of alcohol and fireworks when the new year is ushered in. People go out on the streets with a glass of champagne to watch the fireworks, kiss everybody and wish them a happy new year (Ein gutes neues Jahr). Another custom on New Year's Eve, known as Bleigießen, is to melt small lumps of lead and throw them into cold water, then try to tell fortunes from the resulting shapes.

Heilige Drei Könige
(The Three Kings, 6 January)
In Catholic areas children dress up as the three wise men and go from house to house, singing songs and asking for donations for charities. They then write signs on the door frames to bring good luck to the households.

Ostern (Easter)
On Easter Sunday, children look for eggs (Ostereier) (either hard-boiled, coloured or chocolate) that have been hidden by the Easter bunny (Osterhase). Traditional pastries such as the Osterlamm (a cake in the shape of a lamb) and the Osterkranz (a sort of bread made of sweet dough) are enjoyed. People exchange the greeting Frohe Ostern, 'Happy Easter'.

Erntedankfest (Harvest festival)
At the beginning of October the altars of churches are decorated with the harvest (fruits, cereals but also bread and vegetables) and given away to the poor after the mass.

DID YOU KNOW ... At the Oktoberfest you can only be served beer in a 1L glass called a Maß (neut).

NON-RELIGIOUS HOLIDAYS

Karneval (north Germany) or Fasching (south Germany)
The carnival starts at 11 o'clock on 11 November and lasts until Ash Wednesday (Aschermittwoch). The main celebrations focus on the last week. People shout Helau! and Alaaf!

Oktoberfest (Volksfest) (end of September to early October).
This is Germany's biggest festival, which starts with a procession of beer brewers and their traditional horses and carts. The opening's highlight is the tapping of the first beer barrel by the mayor of Munich who then shouts O'zapft is! 'The barrel is tapped'. The Oktoberfest is famous for the huge beer tents and the large amount of beer that is consumed. Cheers! (Prost!) is heard often as are drinking songs:

Ein Prosit der Gemütlichkeit!	lit: cheers on the friendliness!
Eins, zwei, drei, gsuffa!	lit: one, two, three, sculled!

Kirchweihen.
These annual fairs, held mostly in rural regions in autumn, celebrate the consecration of a church. They include small beer tents and some merry-go-rounds.

Muttertag (Mother's Day)
Celebrated, as in other countries, on the second Sunday of May. Mothers receive presents while the children and husbands are on their best behaviour in an attempt to make up for the rest of the year!

Der Erste Mai (May Day)
The international labour holiday is celebrated with parades and demonstrations. Participation is declining, though, and most people just enjoy the holiday.

Maibäume (Maypole)
The erection of a Maypole in spring, either of tall fir or birch, is a 400-year-old tradition. The Maypole is decorated with colourful ribbons, and in rural regions a dance around the Maypole is held on the first of May.

Tag der Einheit (Reunification Day, 3 October)
This relatively new holiday came into existence when the two Germanies reunified in 1990.

Geburtstag (Birthdays)
If someone is celebrating their birthday, you wish them **Alles Gute zum Geburtstag.**

PLACES

Where is ...?	Wo ist ...?
a doctor	ein Arzt
the hospital	das Krankenhaus
the chemist	die Apotheke
the dentist	der Zahnarzt

AT THE DOCTOR

I am sick.	Ich bin krank.
My friend is sick.	Mein/e Freund/in ist krank.
It hurts here.	Es tut hier weh.
Do I need a prescription for this?	Brauche ich dafür ein Rezept?
Could you give me a prescription for this medicine?	Könnten Sie mir dieses Medikament verschreiben?

AILMENTS

I have (a/an) ...	Ich habe ...
allergy	eine Allergie
anaemia	Anämie
blister	eine Blase
cold	eine Erkältung
constipation	Verstopfung
cough	Husten
diarrhoea	Durchfall
fever	Fieber
headache	Kopfschmerzen
indigestion	eine Magenverstimmung
infection	eine Infektion
influenza	eine Grippe
injury	eine Verletzung
lice	Läuse

low/high blood pressure	niedriger/hoher Blutdruck
nausea	Übelkeit
pain	Schmerzen
sore throat	Halsschmerzen
sprain	eine Muskelzerrung
sunburn	einen Sonnenbrand
venereal disease	eine Geschlechtskrankheit
worms	Würmer

HEALTH

THE DOCTOR MAY SAY ...

Was fehlt Ihnen?	What's the matter?
Haben Sie Schmerzen?	Do you feel any pain?
Wo tut es weh?	Where does it hurt?
Haben Sie Fieber?	Do you have a temperature?
Wie lange sind Sie schon krank?	How long have you been ill?
Hatten Sie das schon einmal?	Have you had this before?
Nehmen Sie regelmäßig Medikamente?	Are you on medication?
Rauchen Sie?	Do you smoke?
Trinken Sie?	Do you drink?
Sind Sie gegen bestimmte Stoffe allergisch?	Are you allergic to anything?
Haben Sie Ihre Periode?	Are you menstruating?
Sind Sie schwanger?	Are you pregnant?
Machen Sie sich bitte frei.	Please get undressed.
Atmen Sie tief ein und aus.	Breathe deeply.
Öffnen Sie den Mund.	Open your mouth.
Zeigen Sie Ihre Zunge.	Put out your tongue.
Husten Sie.	Cough.
Tut das weh?	Does that hurt?

WOMEN'S HEALTH

I think I'm pregnant.	Ich glaube, ich bin schwanger.
I'm on the pill.	Ich nehme die Pille.
I'd like to see a female doctor.	Ich möchte eine Ärztin sprechen.
Is there a female doctor here?	Gibt es hier eine Ärztin?
I've got my period.	Ich habe meine Tage.
I haven't had my period for ... months.	Ich habe seit ... Monaten meine Periode nicht gehabt.
I've got a lump in my breast.	Ich habe einen Knoten in meiner Brust.
Can I have the pill for the day after?	Kann ich die Pille für danach haben?

abortion	Abtreibung (f)
breast	Brust (f)
cervix	Gebärmutterhals (m)
cramps	Krampf (m)
cystisis	Blasenkatarr (m)
diaphragm	Pessar (neut)
IUD	Spirale (f)
mammogram	Mammographie (f)
menstruation	Menstruation (f); Periode (f)
miscarriage	Fehlgeburt (f)
nipple	Brustwarze (f)
pregnant	schwanger
smear	Abstrich (m)
thrush	Pilzkrankheit (f)
uterus	Gebärmutter (f)
vagina	Scheide (f)

EU & ÄU

In German, **eu** and **äu** are pronounced as 'oy', the same as in the English 'boy'.

HEALTH

HEALTH

SPECIAL HEALTH NEEDS

I'm on a special diet.	Ich mache eine besondere Diät.
I'm on regular medication (for ...)	Ich nehme regelmäßig Medikamente (gegen ...)
asthma	Asthma
diabetes	Zuckerkrankheit
high blood pressure	Bluthochdruck
I'm allergic to ...	Ich bin allergisch gegen ...
antibiotics	Antibiotika
penicillin	Penizillin
dairy products	Milchprodukte
bees	Bienen
pollen	Pollen
I'm ...	Ich bin ...
addicted to ...	abhängig von ...
asthmatic	Asthmatiker/in
epileptic	Epileptiker/in
deaf	taub
paralysed	gelähmt
Is there a wheelchair access?	Gibt es eine Rollstuhlrampe?
Is there a discount for the handicapped?	Gibt es eine Ermäßigung für Behinderte?
I've got a pass for handicapped persons.	Ich habe einen Behindertenausweis.

DID YOU KNOW ... The word **etwas** ('something; anything; some; any') is sometimes shortened to **was**:

Ich will dir was sagen.
I'll tell you something.

ALTERNATIVE TREATMENTS

Is there a homoeopathic doctor here?	Gibt es hier einen homöopathischen Arzt?

acupuncture	Akupunktur (f)
aromatherapy	Aromatherapie (f)
Chinese medicine	chinesische Medizin (f)
herbalist	Naturheilkundiger/ Naturheilkundige
herbal medicine	Kräuterheilkunde (f)
homoeopathy	Homöopathie (f)
homoeopathic medicine	homöopathisches Mittel (neut)
natural remedy	Naturheilverfahren (neut)
naturopath	Heilpraktiker/in
non-medical practitioner	Heilpraktiker/in
physiotherapist	Physiotherapeut/in

HEALTH

TONGUE TWISTERS

Fischer Fritz fischt frische Fische, frische Fische fischt Fischer Fritz.
  Fisher Fritz is fishing fresh fish, fresh fish is being fished by fisher Fritz.

In Ulm und um Ulm und um Ulm herum.
  In Ulm and at Ulm and around Ulm.
  (Ulm is a small town in Swabia.)

Blaukraut bleibt Blaukraut und Brautkleid bleibt Brautkleid.
  Red cabbage stays red cabbage and a wedding dress stays a wedding dress.

Es reiten drei Reiter um den Ararat herum.
  There are three horse riders riding around the Ararat.

PARTS OF THE BODY

My ... hurt/s.	Mir tut ... weh.
ankle	mein Knöchel
appendix	mein Blinddarm
arm	mein Arm
back	mein Rücken
chest	mein Brustkorb
ear	mein Ohr
eye	mein Auge
finger	mein Finger
foot	mein Fuß
hand	meine Hand
head	mein Kopf
heart	mein Herz
kidney	meine Niere
knee	mein Knie
leg	mein Bein
liver	meine Leber
lung	meine Lunge
nose	meine Nase
skin	meine Haut
stomach	mein Magen
throat	mein Hals
tooth	mein Zahn

HEALTH

AT THE CHEMIST

Which chemist is open at night/at the weekend?	Welche Apotheke hat Nachtdienst/am Wochenende geöffnet?
Could you give me something for ..., please?	Können Sie mir bitte etwas gegen ... geben?
I need medication for ...	Ich brauche etwas gegen ...
I have a prescription.	Ich habe ein Rezept.
Do I need a prescription for ...?	Brauche ich ein Rezept für ...?

antiseptic
  Antiseptikum (neut)
bandage
  Verbandsmaterial (neut)
cough mixture
  Hustensaft (m)
laxative
  Abführmittel (neut)
painkillers
  Schmerzmittel (neut)

plaster	**Pflaster** (neut)
something for diarrhoea	**Durchfallmittel** (neut)
vitamins	**Vitamine** (pl)

> ### PLURALS
>
> There are a number of ways to make nouns plural in German. To learn these see page 22.

HEALTH

Instructions & Labels

äußerlich	for external use
bei Bedarf	as needed
innerlich	to be taken internally
nach Anweisung des Arztes	according to doctor's instructions
nüchtern	on an empty stomach
unzerkaut schlucken	swallow whole

AT THE DENTIST

I have a toothache.	Ich habe Zahnschmerzen.
I've lost a filling.	Ich habe eine Füllung verloren.
I've broken a tooth.	Mir ist ein Zahn abgebrochen.
My gums hurt.	Das Zahnfleisch tut mir weh.
I don't want it extracted.	Ich will ihn mir nicht ziehen lassen.
Please give me an anaesthetic.	Geben Sie mir bitte eine Betäubungsspritze.

My dentures are broken.	Mein Gebiss ist zerbrochen.
Can you fix it temporarily?	Können Sie es provisorisch behandeln?

abscess	Abszess (m)
anaesthetic	Betäubung (f)
bridge	Brücke (f)
crown	Krone (f)
to extract	ziehen
to fill	plombieren
infection	Entzündung (f)
jaw	Kiefer (m)
nerve	Nerv (m)
root treatment	Wurzelbehandlung (f)
tooth	Zahn (m)
toothache	Zahnschmerzen (pl)
wisdom tooth	Weisheitszahn (m)

HEALTH

SWEARING

The most common swearword is **Scheiße**, 'shit'. If you want to tone it down, use **Mist**, 'blast'; to emphasise it, say **verdammte Scheiße**. **Verdammt**, which means 'damn', is a very versatile word.

In addition, there are many English swearwords in use, eg 'fuck' and 'shit'. The German verb for 'fuck' is **ficken**. It's most vulgar usage is in the expression **Fick dich doch ins Knie**, 'fuck off'.

Another popular swearword is **Arschloch**, 'asshole', or the abbreviation **Arsch**, 'ass'. Like **scheiß-** you can also use **arsch-** as an adjective and put it in front of every noun or adjective you want to comment on, eg **es ist arschkalt**, 'it's bloody cold'.

Arschkriecher (m)	creep	**Penner** (m)	bum
Kacke (f)	shit	**Scheiße** (f)	shit

CROSSWORD – HEALTH

HEALTH

Across
3. Institution where surgeons work
4. Physical discomfort
7. Wound
9. Invasion of the body by microbes

Down
1. Tooth doctor
2. Vital fluid
3. Part of body furthest from ground
5. Four-chambered organ
6. Joint with silent K
8. Could be a molar or incisor

Answers on page 290.

DISABLED TRAVELLERS

What services are available for disabled travellers?	Was für Leistungen gibt es für behinderte Reisende?
I need assistance.	Ich brauche Hilfe.
Could you help me please?	Könnten Sie mir bitte helfen?

I'm ...
Ich bin ...

handicapped	behindert
blind	blind
deaf	taub
hard of hearing	schwerhörig
mute	stumm

Is there wheelchair access?	Gibt es die Möglichkeit, mit dem Rollstuhl zu kommen?
Is there an elevator?	Gibt es einen Aufzug?
Are guide dogs allowed?	Ist es erlaubt, Blindenhunde mitzubringen?
Could you please talk more slowly/clearly?	Könnten Sie bitte langsamer/deutlicher reden?
Speak into my other ear please.	Sprechen Sie bitte in mein anderes Ohr.
I wear a hearing aid.	Ich trage ein Hörgerät.

SPECIFIC NEEDS

DID YOU KNOW ... In Germany, all InterCity Express (ICE), InterCity/EuroCity (IC/EC) and InterRegio (IR) trains, suburban (S-Bahn) and underground (U-Bahn) trains, and ferry services have easy wheelchair access.

GAY TRAVELLERS

Is there a gay bar/club here?	Gibt es hier eine Schwulendisco?
Am I likely to be harassed?	Werde ich belästigt?
What gay magazines are there?	Was für Zeitschriften für Homosexuelle gibt es?
drag queen	Transvestit
gay	schwul
lesbian	lesbisch

TRAVELLING WITH THE FAMILY

Is there a concession for children?	Gibt es Ermäßigungen für Kinder?
Is there a playground?	Gibt es einen Spielplatz?
Is there a caretaker/babysitter available?	Gibt es eine Kinderbetreuung /einen Babysitter?
Do you have highchairs?	Haben Sie Kinderstühle?
Is there a room where I can change nappies?	Gibt es einen Wickelraum?
We need an extra bed in our room.	Wir brauchen ein zusätzliches Bett in unserem Zimmer.

LOOKING FOR A JOB

Looking for a job is not much fun right now, with more than eight million people unemployed in Germany. However, there is quite a range of short-term jobs you can do even if your grasp of German is not excellent. You'll find classifieds in the Saturday edition of the local papers under the heading **Stellenangebote**. Beware of 'super offers', where you are likely to be exploited. Your employer must register you, so before looking for a job you need to get a work permit - which you can only get if you have a residence permit. Working without them is illegal! However, European nationals from the EU don't need a work or residence permit.

I'm looking for a job.
   Ich suche eine Arbeit.

Do I need a work permit?
   Brauche ich eine Arbeitserlaubnis?

What kind of work is it?
   Was für eine Arbeit ist es?

Is the work dangerous?
   Ist die Arbeit gefährlich?

Do I have insurance?
   Bin ich versichert?

How much will I earn?
   Wie viel verdiene ich?

How much do you pay per hour?
   Wie viel bezahlen Sie pro Stunde?

THEY MAY SAY ...

Haben Sie eine Arbeitserlaubnis?
   Do you have a work permit?

Haben Sie eine Behinderung?
   Do you have any handicaps?

Wie viel verlangen Sie pro Stunde?
   How much do you charge per hour?

---

application	**Bewerbung** (f)
application form	**Bewerbungsunterlagen** (pl)
assembly line	**Fließband** (neut)
employee	**Angestellter/Angestellte**
employer	**Arbeitgeber** (m)
factory	**Fabrik** (f)
factory worker	**Fabrikarbeiter** (m)
illicit work	**Schwarzarbeit** (f)
insurance	**Versicherung** (f)
job offer	**Stellenangebot** (neut)
part time job	**Teilzeitstelle** (f)
references	**Zeugnisse** (pl)
résumé (CV)	**Lebenslauf** (m)
work experience	**Arbeitserfahrung** (f)
working hours	**Arbeitszeit** (f)
work permit	**Arbeitserlaubnis** (f)

SPECIFIC NEEDS

ON BUSINESS

I need to send a fax/email.	Ich muss ein Fax/eine E-Mail abschicken.
I am on a course.	Ich nehme an einem Kurs teil.
We're attending a conference/ trade fair.	Wir besuchen eine Konferenz/Handelsmesse.
Here's my business card.	Hier ist meine Karte.
I have an appointment with ...	Ich habe einen Termin bei ...
I need an interpreter.	Ich brauche einen Dolmetscher.
I need to use a computer.	Ich muss einen Computer benutzen.
May I introduce you to ...	Darf ich Ihnen ... vorstellen?
Mr ...	Herr ...
Mrs ...	Frau ...
my colleague	meinen Kollegen/meine Kollegin
my collaborator	meinen Mitarbeiter/ meine Mitarbeiterin

Useful Words

branch office	Zweigstelle (f)
client	Kunde/Kundin
distributor	Großhändler (m)
loss	Verlust (m)
manager	Manager/in
mobile phone	Mobiltelefon (neut); Handy (neut)
modem	Modem (neut)
overhead projector	Tageslichtprojektor (m)
presentation	Präsentation (f)
profit	Gewinn (m)
profitability	Rentabilität (f)
proposal	Vorschlag (m)
sales department	Verkaufsabteilung (f)

SPECIFIC NEEDS

ON TOUR

We're part of a group.	Wir gehören zu einer Gruppe.
We're on tour.	Wir sind auf Tournee.
I'm with the band/team.	Ich gehöre zur Band/zum Team.
Please speak to our manager.	Bitte sprechen Sie mit unserem Manager.
We've lost our equipment.	Wir haben unsere Ausrüstung verloren.
We sent equipment on this train/flight/bus.	Wir haben die Ausrüstung mit diesem Zug/Flug/Bus geschickt.
I'm staying with a (host) family.	Ich wohne bei einer (Gast-) Familie.
I'm still a groupie after all these years.	Nach all den Jahren bin ich immer noch ein Groupie.

ON LOCATION

actor	Schauspieler/in
camera	Kamera (f)
catering	Verpflegung (f)
continuity	Anschluss (m)
director	Regisseur/in
editor	Cutter/in
location	Drehort (m)
makeup	Make-up (neut)
producer	Produzent (m)
rushes	erste Kopie (f)
script	Drehbuch (neut)
scriptwriter	Drehbuchaut-or/in
sound	Ton (m)
wardrobe	Kostüme (pl)

THEY MAY SAY ...

Wir drehen!
We're filming!

Action!
Action!

Schnitt!
Cut!

PILGRIMAGE & RELIGION

SIGNS	
GOTTESDIENST	SERVICE IN PROGRESS

Where can I pray/worship?	Wo kann ich beten/den Gottesdienst besuchen?
Is there somebody to hear my confession?	Gibt es jemanden, der mir die Beichte abnimmt?
Can I receive communion here?	Kann ich hier das Abendmahl bekommen?
Can I attend this service?	Kann ich bei dem Gottesdienst dabeisein?
Where can I find a ...?	Wo kann ich ... finden?
church	eine Kirche
mosque	eine Moschee
synagogue	eine Synagoge
temple	einen Tempel
Bible	die Bibel
chapel	Kapelle (f)
christening	Taufe (f)
church	Kirche (f)
funeral	Begräbnis (neut)
grave	Grab (neut)
pilgrimage	Pilgerfahrt (f)
prayer	Gebet (neut)
prayers	Andacht (f)
priest	Priester (m)
religion	Religion (f)
shrine	Schrein (m)
wedding	Hochzeit (f)

SPECIFIC NEEDS

SPECIFIC NEEDS

TRACING ROOTS & HISTORY

I think my father/my mother came from here.	Ich glaube, dass mein Vater/ meine Mutter von hier stammt.
Their family name was ...	Ihr Familienname war ...
I'd like to visit the cemetery.	Ich würde gerne den Friedhof besuchen.

In which cemetery would I find (Bertold Brecht's) grave?	Auf welchem Friedhof liegt (Bertold Brecht)?
I have a relative who fought/died in the war.	Ich habe einen Verwandten, der im Krieg gekämpft hat/gefallen ist.
We think he/she was imprisoned here.	Wir glauben, dass er/sie hier gefangengehalten wurde.
Is there a war memorial around here?	Gibt es hier in der Gegend eine Gedenkstätte?
Is there a concentration camp that you can visit?	Gibt es ein Konzentrationslager, das man besuchen kann?
Is there a war museum here?	Gibt es hier ein Kriegsmuseum?

TELLING THE TIME

What time is it?	Wie spät ist es?
Do you know the exact time?	Haben Sie die genaue Zeit?
It is ... o'clock.	Es ist ... Uhr.
It's 6.15.	Es ist Viertel nach 6.
It's 6.30.	Es ist halb 7.
It's 5.45.	Es ist drei viertel 6.

(half an hour) ago	vor (einer halben Stunde)
(five) days ago	vor (fünf Tagen)
in (seven) minutes/days	in (sieben) Minuten/Tagen in
the morning	morgens
in the afternoon	nachmittags
in the evening	abends

DATES

If you want to tell the date you use the article **der** in front of the ordinal number (see page 217), followed by the month:

the first of May	der erste Mai

Sometimes Germans replace the name of the month with a number. January becomes the first month and May the fifth month:

the first of May	der erste fünfte

In written form it looks like this: 1.5.1997

What date is it today?	Der Wievielte ist heute?
It's the 8th of May.	Heute ist der achte fünfte/Mai.
It's the 26th of March.	Heute ist der sechsundzwanzigste dritte/März

TIME & DATES

DID YOU KNOW ...	You will sometimes hear **zwei** ('two') pronounced as 'zwo', especially in phone conversations. This is to distinguish it from the similar sound of **eins** ('one').

MONTHS

January	Januar
February	Februar
March	März
April	April
May	Mai
June	Juni
July	Juli
August	August
September	September
October	Oktober
November	November
December	Dezember

PREPOSITIONS

When prepositions and articles are used together they often combine to become one word. See page 52 for these contracted prepositions.

DAYS

Monday	Montag
Tuesday	Dienstag
Wednesday	Mittwoch
Thursday	Donnerstag
Friday	Freitag
Saturday	Samstag
Sunday	Sonntag

PRESENT

today	heute
this morning	heute Morgen
this afternoon	heute Nachmittag
tonight	heute Abend
this week	diese Woche
this month	dieser Monat
this year	dieses Jahr
now	jetzt
immediately	sofort; gleich

TIME & DATES

PAST

yesterday	gestern
the day before yesterday	vorgestern
yesterday morning	gestern Morgen
last night	letzte Nacht
last week	letzte Woche
last year	letztes Jahr

FUTURE

tomorrow	morgen
day after tomorrow	übermorgen
tomorrow morning	morgen früh
tomorrow afternoon/evening	morgen Nachmittag/Abend
next week	nächste Woche
next year	nächstes Jahr

DURING THE DAY

afternoon	Nachmittag (m)
day	Tag (m)
early	früh
midnight	Mitternacht (f)
morning	Morgen (m)
night	Nacht (f)
noon	Mittag (m)
sundown	Sonnenuntergang (m)
sunrise	Sonnenaufgang (m)

NUMBERS & AMOUNTS

CARDINAL NUMBERS

0	null	15	fünfzehn
1	eins	16	sechzehn
2	zwei (zwo on	17	siebzehn
	the phone)	18	achtzehn
3	drei	19	neunzehn
4	vier	20	zwanzig
5	fünf	30	dreißig
6	sechs	40	vierzig
7	sieben	50	fünfzig
8	acht	60	sechzig
9	neun	70	siebzig
10	zehn	80	achtzig
11	elf	90	neunzig
12	zwölf	100	hundert
13	dreizehn	1000	tausend
14	vierzehn	one million	eine Million

ORDINAL NUMBERS

To form ordinal numbers add -(s)te to the cardinal numbers.
First, erste, 3rd, dritte, and 7th, siebte, are the only irregular
forms.

2nd	zweite
15th	fünfzehnte
30th	dreißigste

DID YOU KNOW ...	German numbers above a thousand are written with a full stop: 1.000; decimal points are written with a comma: 1,54.

NUMBERS & AMOUNTS

FRACTIONS

a quarter	ein Viertel
a third	ein Drittel
half	eine Hälfte
three-quarters	drei Viertel

USEFUL WORDS

a little (amount)	ein bisschen
double	doppelt
a dozen	ein Dutzend
Enough!	Genug!
a few	ein paar
less	weniger
a lot; much	viel
many	viele
more	mehr
once	einmal
a pair	ein Paar
percent	Prozent
some	einige
too much	zu viel
twice	zweimal

VARIETIES OF GERMAN

German is spoken in Germany, Austria and Switzerland, but also in the northern part of Italy (South Tyrol), in parts of Belgium, Luxembourg and Liechtenstein. There are German-speaking minorities in Romania, Hungary, Russia, France, Namibia, the USA, Canada, Australia and Brazil. Thus it is not surprising that due to different political, historical, geographical and cultural influences a lot of dialects and accents have emerged. Normally you should be understood using **Hochdeutsch**, the accepted standard or High German. However, if you come across dialect speakers, it might be helpful to recognise some of the main differences.

Despite a preponderance of German dialects and accents, there are basically three major groups. In general, dialects are spoken more widely in the south of Germany, Switzerland and Austria. In the centre of Germany a neutral variety is spoken, and the north (on the coast, around Hamburg) is bilingual, because the dialect spoken there (**Platt**) is almost a different language. It's a mixture of Old English and German with completely different words. For example, **lütt** means 'small', **schnacken** means 'talk', **Schmok** means 'smoke', and **Moin** is the common greeting.

Travelling through Germany you may also hear words from the former GDR, the **Neuen Bundesländer** (Sachsen, Sachsen-Anhalt, Thüringen, Mecklenburg-Vorpommern and Branden-burg). For example, High German **Plastik** (neut), 'plastic', is **Plaste** (f) and the word **Objekt** (neut) is used to describe any kind of building. A roast chicken is called **Broiler** (m), 'Aerobic' is trans-lated into **Popgymnastik** (f) and 'to surf' is **windsegeln**

IN GERMANY
Some Basic Differences

	Standard (north)	Dialect (south & centre)
Saturday	Sonnabend	Samstag
Hello	Guten Tag (or Tach)	Grüß Gott
9.15	Viertel nach neun	viertel zehn
9.45	Viertel vor zehn	drei viertel zehn

The North

Apart from Platt, Hochdeutsch is spoken but with the following colloquial constructions and variations.

• Combination of verb and pronoun:

	German	Dialect
do you have	hast du	ha-ste
are you	bist du	bi-ste
do you want	willst du	will-ste

• Use of the t instead of the s, as in Dutch and English:

	German	Dialect
what	was	wat
this/that	das	dat

• Especially in Berlin, the g at the beginning of a word is pronounced like a j:

	German	Dialect
Are we going?	Gehen wir?	Yehn wa?
good	gut	juht
Impossible!	Das gibt es	Dat jihbts
	doch nicht!	doch nich!

• In Hamburg, the s before p and t at the beginning of a word
are pronounced s not sh. Spi-tze stei-ne instead of shpi-tze
shtei-ne (phonetic spelling) 'sharp stones'.

The Centre

The dialects spoken around Frankfurt, Nürnberg, Leipzig and
Dresden are basically Fränkisch, Sächsisch and Thüringisch. In
all three the p is pronounced like b, t like d and k like g

	German	Dialect
Please	Bitte	bidde
cake	Kuchen	guhchn
tea	Tee	deh

When it's in the middle of a word, and sometimes when it's at
the end of a word, the letter g is pronounced ch, eg Frage, 'question', is frah-che, and Nürnberg is nürn bech.

The South-west

Schwäbisch-Alemannisch (Swabian) covers a few dialects and
accents spoken around Stuttgart, from the Bodensee to Augsburg.
   Swabian, together with Saxon, are dialects with strong accents,
making Swabians and Saxons immediately recognisable in Germany.
Like the Austrians and Swiss, the Swabians love the diminutive
form, made by adding -le to the end of a word, eg Spätzle
(famous Swabian noodles). For this reason, the unfortunate
Swabians have been called miserly, which is not true! In contrast
to Bavarian, Austrian and Swiss, -le is not only used with nouns,
but often at the end of adjectives or verbs. Sometimes it is added
to the greeting Ade (bye-bye), making it Ade-le.
   In pronunciation, the ei is changed to oi (as in English boil),
for example, nein, 'no', is spelled noi and klein, 'small', is spelled
gloi. See also German in Switzerland on page 230.

The South-east

In Bavarian (**Bayerisch**) dialect, which is spoken around Munich (**München**), the main difference is in the pronunciation of consonants. As with Austrian dialects, no difference is made between **p** and **b**, **k** and **g**, and **t** and **d** when they fall at the beginning of a word. For example, **ich backe**, 'I bake', and **ich packe**, 'I pack' are pronounced in the same way as a mixture between **p** and **b**. The **st** and **sp** are pronounced as 'sht' and 'shp' even in the middle of a word and between syllables. High German **Wurst** (sausage) is pronounced 'vursht' and **Astrid** (a girl's name) becomes 'Ash-trid'.

The pronoun **wir**, 'we', is often pronounced **mir**. Verbs are shortened and contracted, for example, **wir haben**, 'we have', becomes **mir ham** and **wir sind**, 'we are', is **mir san** (phonetic spelling).

See also Austrian German on page 226.

VARIETIES OF GERMAN

GERMAN SPECIALITIES

Rest assured, there's more than Sauerkraut in Germany. Here's a small, selective list of specialities.

Bread

There are some 400 different sorts of bread and 1200 types of rolls in Germany. Typical breads include:

Roggenbrot
> made from rye, a bit of wheat and sour dough (**Sauerteig**), it has a strong and sour taste.

Weizenbrot or Weißbrot
> made from wheat, a bit of milk, fat or sugar. It's golden brown and crispy on the outside and white inside.

Mischbrot
> This one is Germany's best selling bread; it's a mixture of rye and wheat with sour dough or yeast. It is named after the predominant type of grain, **Roggenmischbrot** or Weizenmischbrot.

Vollkornbrot
> bread with specially ground ingredients, using either grain, coarse wholemeal or flour in various mixtures. Even oats, sesame, nuts, onions or herbs and spices are mixed in.

Rolls

Brötchen is the generic term for rolls, which are made of wheat and are golden and crispy. They're known by different names in the various regions:

Baden-Württemberg	Weckle
Bavaria	Semmel
Berlin	Schrippe & Schusterjunge (rye-based)
Hamburg	Rundstück

VARIETIES OF GERMAN

Other types of rolls are:

Käsebrötchen	(with cheese)
Zwiebel- or Speckbrötchen	(with roasted onions or bacon)
Sesam- or Mohnbrötchen	(with sesame or poppy-seed topping)
Roggenbrötchen	(with rye)

Good with marmalade or jam are süße Hörnchen (croissants) and Rosinenbrötchen (rolls with raisins).

In addition, there are pretzels (Brezel or Brezen), originally Bavarian but sold all over Germany.

Sausages

In Bavaria try the Weißwurst (veal sausage). The special Bavarian Weißwurstfrühstück (breakfast with white sausages) consists of sausages and a Brezen 'pretzel', usually accompanied by a glass of beer (Weißbier or Weizen). Experts enjoy them before noon.

In Berlin there's the Currywurst (sausage with curry and ketchup); in Nürnberg, Nürnberger Rostbratwürstchen (pork sausages); in Sachsen, Salami; and in Thüringen, Bratwürste (roasted sausages).

Regional Meat & Fish Specialities

Rheinischer Sauerbraten mit Kartoffelklößen
    marinated meat, slightly sour, and roasted, often served
    with potato dumplings
Schweinshaxen
    the very Bavarian dish! Leg of pork, very crispy and served
    with dumplings (Knödel).
Pfälzer Saumagen
    stuffed stomach of pork (this dish is former Bundeskanzler
    Kohl's favourite)
Kieler Sprotten
    small herring, smoked

Regional Vegetable Specialities

These are mostly vegetable-based but also include some meat. (If you are a vegetarian, see the Food chapter page 151 for some helpful phrases.)

Grünkohl mit Pinkel
  kale with sausages (around Bremen)
Leipziger Allerlei
  mixed vegetable stew (around Leipzig)
Linsen mit Spätzle
  lentil stew with noodles and sausages (around Stuttgart)

In the south-west, where Spargel (asparagus) is cultivated, restaurants offer dishes with fresh asparagus often accompanied by ham. This is usually during spring (April to June) when asparagus is at its best.

Sweets

There are cakes, such as Schwarzwälder Kirschtorte (Black Forest cake) and Frankfurter Kranz (sponge cake with rum, butter cream and cherries) but also – especially at Christmas time – the Nürnberger Lebkuchen and the Aachener Printen (cakes with chocolate, nuts, candied orange or lemon peel, honey, syrup and spices like caraway, cinnamon and vanilla). Not forgetting Lübeck's famous delicacy, Lübecker Marzipan.

Wine

Wein is cultivated in the south-west part of Germany along the Rhine, Moselle, Main and Neckar rivers. The smallest German wine-cultivating area is in Sachsen. Some interesting German wines are the Frankenwein or Bocksbeutel (a white wine with a dry and individual taste cultivated around Bamberg, Nürnberg, Aschaffenburg and Schweinfurt, named after the region Franken) and the Trollinger which is cultivated around Stuttgart.

VARIETIES OF GERMAN

Each year from the end of September to the beginning of October, the very young wine, **Federweißer** (named after its cloudy milky colour), is enjoyed. In some regions it's called **Suser**. Try it with a **Zwiebelkuchen**, or onion tart.

In Hessen, around Frankfurt, especially in the district of Sachsenhausen, you find the **Ebbelwoi**. It's made of apples, fresh and sour, with some 5% alcohol. It's said that the first glass tastes awful, but you get hooked after the second or at least the third glass!

Beer

Germany has about 5000 different kinds of **Bier**. All of them adhere to the **Deutsche Reinheitsgebot** of 1516, a law which decrees that only hop, malt, yeast and water should be used for brewing beer. In the north **Pils** is common, in Cologne you find the **Kölsch** and in Bavaria, where the normal amount for a beer is one litre (**Maß**), **Weißbier** or **Weizen** (cloudy with a lot of yeast) is popular. You can try some light ones with low calories and reduced alcohol, such as the **leichtes Weizen**, or go for **alkohol-freies Bier**, a 'non-alcoholic beer'.

AUSTRIAN GERMAN

High German is Austria's *lingua franca*. It is taught in schools but is used mainly for writing, whereas the spoken language contains a lot of local words which are often only understood in Austria. It's not surprising that German, which is used in several states, institutions, TV programs and the media, developed several varieties. Nine dialects exist, corresponding to Austria's nine **Bundesländer** (states). Eight are similar to Germany's Bavarian dialect, while the **Vorarlberg** has some Swiss influences. But they all share a common Austrian idiom.

Although phonetically similar to the Bavarian dialect, the **österreichische Umgangssprache** (Austrian colloquial language) has some peculiarities that differentiate it. For example, in weights Austrians use the **Dekagramm**, abbreviated to **Deka** or **dag**, which is equivalent to 10 grams. This term is not used in Germany and it's not even understood in Bavaria. **Jause** (second breakfast or snack), too, is uniquely Austrian, and **heuer** ('this year') is almost never used in Germany.

Thanks to tourism and the media, some High German words such as **Tomate**, 'tomato', **Kartoffel**, 'potato' or **Sahne** 'cream' are almost as common as their Austrian equivalents **Paradeiser**, **Erdäpfel** and **Obers**.

One typical and often imitated characteristic is the Austrians' love of diminutives. **Mädchen** (young girl) becomes **Mäderl**, **Bub** (boy) is **Buberl** and **Hase** (hare) is **Haserl**. But a **Schwammerl** (**Pilz**) is not necessarily a small mushroom and a **Momenterl** (**Moment**) can take a very long time. Sweets are called **Zuckerln** (**Bonbons**) and a croissant is a **Kipferl**

Pronunciation

Some vowels are pronounced differently. In words of French origin, Austrians do not pronounce the e at the end of a word: eg **Blamage** (embarrassment), pronounced '*bla-ma-she*' in High German, becomes '*blam-ahsh*' in Austrian.

The diphthong ei is pronounced ah, eg **Heim** (home) is '*hahm*', and **klein** (small) becomes '*klahn*'.

Greetings

There are several ways to greet people. **Servus** or **Grüß dich** 'hello', **Grüß Gott** (pol), **Küss die Hand**, **gnädige Frau** (literally, 'a kiss on the hand'; only said by a man to a woman; it's polite and a bit old-fashioned).

Herzig means 'nice' and **schiech**, pronounced '*shiach*', means 'awful' or 'ugly'. **Januar** (January) becomes **Jänner**, **Februar** (February) is **Feber**

T NOT TH
In German th is always pronounced as 't' and not 'th'. So a word like **Thema** ('subject'), is pronounced as 'tema' and not 'thema'.

Food

Beuschel	heart and lungs of pork, veal or beef
Blunzn	black pudding, blood sausage
Faschiertes	minced meat
Germ	yeast
G'spritzter	wine mixed with water
Hendl	roast chicken
Krügerl	0.5 litre beer
Obers	cream
Schlagobers	whipped cream

AUSTRIAN SPECIALITIES
Coffee Shops

In the 1920s the Wiener Kaffeehaus ('Vienna Coffee Bars')
were highly renowned institutions where intellectuals met and
famous books were written. Thanks to high rents in the inner
city, nowadays they're simply high-priced tourist attractions.
But if you are lucky, you can still find some of the old-
fashioned cafés. Kaffee (m), 'the drink' and Café (f), 'the place'
are both pronounced ka-feh. You may be a bit confused by the
different varieties of coffee specialities. Here's what you may
find on the menu:

Einspänner	sweet, strong mocha with whipped cream: lit 'carriage'
Fiaker	sweet mocha
Großer Brauner	big (cup of) coffee with a little milk
Kapuziner	coffee with lots of milk; lit. 'monk'
Kleiner Schwarzer	mocha without milk
Kleiner Goldener	mocha with milk
Kleiner Brauner	small (cup of) coffee with a bit of milk
Melange	one part coffee, one part milk, with a bit of frothed milk

Food

Austrian food specialities are:

Wiener Schnitzel	veal coated with breadcrumbs and egg
Wiener Tafelspitz	cooked beef served with Kren (German Meerrettich), a horseradish sauce
Knödel	dumplings
Serviettenknödel	dumplings made of meat, rolls and eggs
Topfenknödel	sweet dumpling with cheese curd
Germknödel	flour, yeast and poppy seed dumpling
Marillenknödel	potato dumplings stuffed with apricot

Mehlspeisen ('desserts made with flour') include Apfelstrudel, Kaiserschmarren, Palatschinke, Salzburger Nockerln and Sachertorte.

Wine

Austria's wine-growing areas are the Burgenland, Niederöster-reich, Steiermark and Wien (Vienna) in the east of the country. The Vienna speciality is Heuriger. Legend has it that wine-growers didn't want to take the trouble to store the wine, and therefore needed to get rid of it quickly. Heuriger means a young and fresh wine and is also the name of the restaurants where it's drunk. Both exist for only four months a year. Some special Jausen (snacks) are served with the wine, for example, the Brettljause or Heurigenplatte, which consist of bread, cheese, sausages, pickled gherkins and onions.

VARIETIES OF GERMAN

DID YOU KNOW ...	Austria is also famous for its lager beer. Well-known brands are Gösser, Schwechater, Stiegl, Zipfer and Weizenbier (which is wheat beer).

VARIETIES OF GERMAN

GERMAN IN SWITZERLAND

Switzerland has four official languages: German, French, Italian and Romansch. The most widely spoken of these, both in population and regional coverage (spoken by about 75% of the population), is German. Though German-speaking Swiss have no trouble with standard High German, they use Swiss German, or **Schwyzerdütsch**, even in quite formal situations: the strong accent can be heard in news broadcasts as well as in conversation.

Swiss German covers a wide variety of melodic dialects that can differ quite markedly from High German. It's an oral language for which there is no standard written form. Newspapers and books almost invariably use High German. The only significant difference in spelling is the use of **ss** instead of **ß**.

The Germans themselves often have trouble understanding **Schwyzerdütsch**. To English speakers' ears High German sounds as if it were full of rasping 'ch' sounds, but even Germans think that Swiss German sounds like a lot of throat-clearing. A reason for this is that the letter k, pronounced 'ch' in High German only when it's in the middle or at the end of a word, is always pronounced as 'ch' in Swiss German. Hence the word **Küchenkästli** (kitchen cupboard), relatively manageable when pronounced in High German, is almost unpronounceable in Swiss German as 'chu-chi-chäsht-li'.

Here are some characteristics of Swiss German that may be helpful. Since French is one of the national languages of Switzerland, a lot of foreign words in everyday use are French.

	Swiss German	German
bicycle	das Velo	das Fahrrad
ice-cream	das Glace	das Eis
platform	der Perron	der Bahnsteig

The Swiss seem to love the -i/-li ending. They use it as a diminutive form, but also in first names, for example, **Marieli**, or in second names like **Sprüngli** (a famous chocolate maker). A lot of other words end with i: **Rüebli** 'carrots', **Weggli** 'roll', **Maidli** 'girl', and **Leckerli** 'sweets'.

You can impress your walking companions, however, by using the following Swiss German terms (literal spelling):

Grüe-zi.	Hello.
Uff Wie-der-lue-ge.	Goodbye.
Vi guhts?	How are you?
Gu-et.	I'm fine.

Swiss Specialities

Apart from cheese and chocolate, it's hard to find common Swiss foods because of the four different cultures. French, Italian and of course German influences are obvious, but also obvious is the rejection of foreign traditions. Italian-speaking Switzerland does not have a pasta culture, nor does German-speaking Switzerland mainly eat Swabian noodles (instead they eat potatoes in every possible form).

Don't miss the **Rösti** ('*röhsh-di*), crunchy pieces of potato cakes, sometimes with cheese, onions or bacon. They are great as a side dish to **Zürcher Geschnetzeltes**, strips of veal with mushroom cream sauce.

A popular Romansch (a Latin-based language spoken around Graubünden) dish is **Bündner Fleisch**, or **Bresaola**: specially dried beef served with bread, butter and pepper.

Cheese

The most popular varieties are **Schweizer Käse** 'Swiss cheese', **Appenzeller** and **Greyezer**, and in the French region, *Gruyère*. Probably the best known cheese dish is **Käsefondue** – different sorts of cheese and white wine cooked together and served in a big pot with white bread to dip. Another traditional speciality is the Raclette, where large slices are scraped from a melted piece of cheese and are served with potatoes and mixed pickles, usually onions and cucumbers. It goes very well with Fendant, a young fresh white wine from the Wallis, a Swiss wine-growing district in the south.

Sweets

Famous Swiss sweets are Basler Leckerli, 'honey biscuits' and Rüeblitorte, 'carrot cake'.

If you like Schokolade (or Shoh-chi), 'chocolate', you'll never leave Switzerland again. Milk-chocolate was invented here, and some of the world's best chocolate bars still come from Switzerland. Lindt and Cailler are popular labels. Swiss confectionery also tastes great. Forget the calories - they'll be worth it!

EMERGENCIES

Help!	Hilfe!
Thief!	Dieb!
Fire!	Feuer!

Could you help me, please?	Könnten Sie mir bitte helfen?
Could I please use the telephone?	Könnte ich bitte das Telefon benutzen?
It's an emergency!	Es ist ein Notfall!
There's been an accident!	Es hat einen Unfall gegeben!
I am ill.	Ich bin krank.
My friend is ill.	Mein/e Freund/in ist krank.
Call a doctor!	Holen Sie einen Arzt!
Call an ambulance!	Rufen Sie einen Krankenwagen!

I have medical insurance.	Ich bin bei einer Krankenkasse.

I've been raped!	Ich bin vergewaltigt worden!
I've been robbed!	Ich bin bestohlen worden!
My possessions are insured.	Meine Sachen sind versichert.

I've lost ...	Ich habe ... verloren.
my backpack	meinen Rucksack
my bags	meine Reisetaschen
my camera	meinen Fotoapparat
my credit card	meine Kreditkarte
my handbag	meine Handtasche
my money	mein Geld
my travellers cheques	meine Reiseschecks
my passport	meinen Pass

Go away!	Gehen Sie weg!
Leave me alone!	Lassen Sie mich in Ruhe!
I'll call the police!	Ich rufe die Polizei!
Please call the police!	Rufen Sie bitte die Polizei!

If you need stronger words to get rid of unwanted people, see Swear Words & Slang page 116.

I am lost.	Ich habe mich verirrt.
Where are the toilets?	Wo ist die Toilette?
I'm sorry. I apologise.	Es tut mir Leid. Entschuldigen Sie bitte.
I didn't do it.	Ich habe es nicht getan.
I speak English.	Ich spreche Englisch.
I didn't realise I was doing anything wrong.	Ich war mir nicht bewusst, etwas Unrechtes getan zu haben.
I wish to contact my embassy/ consulate.	Ich möchte mich mit meiner Botschaft/meinem Konsulat in Verbindung setzen.

DEALING WITH THE POLICE

Where is the nearest police station?	Wo ist das nächste Polizeirevier?
I want to report ...	Ich möchte ... melden.
an accident	einen Unfall
an attack	einen Überfall
a loss	einen Verlust
a theft	einen Diebstahl
My car has been broken into.	Mein Auto ist aufgebrochen worden.
I've been attacked/raped.	Ich wurde angegriffen/ vergewaltigt.
I want to see a lawyer.	Ich möchte einen Anwalt sprechen.
What is the charge?	Wegen was werde ich angeklagt?

EMERGENCIES

| Can I make a phone call? | Kann ich mal telefonieren? |
| I want to have an interpreter. | Ich möchte einen Dolmetscher. |

cell	Zelle (f)
charge	Anklage (f)
complaint	Klage (f)
drugs	Rauschgift (neut)
gun	Pistole (f)
illegal possession of weapons/ drugs	unerlaubter Waffenbesitz (m)/ Drogenbesitz (m)
knife	Messer (neut)
police station	Polizeirevier (neut)
thief	Dieb (m)
theft	Diebstahl (m)
weapon	Waffe (f)

THEY MAY SAY ...

Ihren Ausweis, bitte!	Show me your identification!
Sie sind verhaftet.	You have been arrested.
Sie bekommen einen Strafzettel.	You're getting a traffic fine.
Ihre Personalien, bitte.	What is your name and address?
Zeigen Sie bitte ...	Show me your ...
Ihren Pass	passport
Ihre Ausweispapiere	identity papers
Ihren Führerschein	driver's licence
Ihre Arbeitserlaubnis	work permit
Sie müssen mit aufs Revier kommen.	You must come with us to the police station.
Sie haben das Recht zu schweigen, bis Ihr Anwalt anwesend ist.	You don't have to say anything until you are in the presence of a lawyer.

EMERGENCIES

In this dictionary the gender is either indicated by (m), (f) or (neut) after the word or the masculine (-er, -r), feminine (-in, -e) and neuter (-s) endings are separated by a slash. Synonyms and alternative meanings are separated by a semicolon. To work out the appropriate article – whether definite ('the') or indefinite ('a/an') – see page 20.

A

able (to be)	können
Can I walk there?	
Kann ich zu Fuß gehen?	
Can you show me (on the map)?	
Können Sie es mir (auf der Karte)	
zeigen?	
Can I see the room?	
Kann ich das Zimmer sehen?	
abortion	Abtreibung (f)
above	oben; über
abroad	im Ausland
accident	Unfall (m)
accommodation	Unterkunft (f);
	Zimmer (neut)
according to	zufolge; entsprechend
accountant	Buchhalter/in
across (from)	herüber
across (to)	hinüber
actor	Schauspieler/in
adaptor	Adapter (m)
addict	Süchtige/r
addiction	Abhängigkeit (f)
address	Adresse (f)
to adjust	anpassen
to admire	bewundern
adventure	Abenteuer (neut)

advice	Rat (m)
to advise	raten
aerogram	Luftpostbrief (m)
aeroplane	Flugzeug (neut)
(to be) afraid	Angst (haben)
after	nach
again	wieder
against	gegen; wider
age	Alter (neut)
to agree	übereinstimmen;
	zustimmen
I agree.	
Der Meinung bin ich auch.	
Do you agree?	
Meinen Sie nicht auch?	
agriculture	Landwirtschaft (f)
ahead	vor uns
aid (help)	Hilfe (f)
afternoon	Nachmittag (m)
air	Luft (f)
air-conditioned	Klimaanlage (f)
airline	Fluglinie (f)
air mail	Luftpost (f)
air pollution	Luftverschmutzung (f)
airport tax	Flughafengebühr (f)
airsickness	Luftkrankheit (f)
aisle seat	Platz am Gang
alarm clock	Wecker (m)

alcoholic	Alkoholiker/in
all	alle
allergy	Allergie (f)
to allow	erlauben; gestatten
It's not allowed.	
Es ist verboten.	
almost	fast
alone	allein/e
also	auch
alternative	Alternative (f)
always	immer
amazing	erstaunlich
ambassador	Botschafter/in
ambulance	Krankenwagen (m)
among	unter
amount	Betrag (m)
anaesthetic	Betäubung (f)
ancient	alt
and	und
I am angry.	Ich bin böse.
ankle	Knöchel (m)
answer (n)	Antwort (f)
to answer	antworten
ant	Ameise (f)
antique (adj)	antik
antique (n)	Antiquität (f)
antiseptic	Antiseptikum (neut)
anything	irgendetwas
anywhere	irgendwo
apart from	außer
(besides)	
apartment	Wohnung (f)
appendix	Blinddarm (m)
appointment	Verabredung (f);
	Termin (m)
apprentice	Lehrling (m)
approximately	ungefähr
April	April (m)
archeology	Archäologie (f)
architect	Architekt/in
architecture	Architektur (f)
area code	Vorwahl (f)

to argue	streiten
argument	Auseinandersetzung (f)
arm	Arm (m)
to arrive	ankommen
What time does ... arrive?	
Wann kommt ... an?	
art	Kunst (f)
art collection	Kunstsammlung (f)
art dealer	Kunsthändler (m)
art gallery	Kunstgalerie (f)
artist	Künstler/in
arts & crafts	Kunstgewerbe (neut)
as far as ...	bis zu ...
ashtray	Aschenbecher (m)
to ask	fragen
aspirin	Kopfschmerztablette (f)
asylum	Obdachlosenunter-
	kunft (f);
	Asylheim (neut)
asylum seeker	Asylbewerber/in
at	an; auf; bei
ATM card	Scheckkarte (f)
attic	Dachboden (m)
August	August (m)
aunt	Tante (f)
Australia	Australien (neut)
Austria	Österreich (neut)
author	Autor/in
automatic	automatisch
avalanche	Lawine (f)
axe	Axt (f)

B

B&W (film)	Schwarzweißfilm (m)
baby	Kind (neut);
	Baby (neut)
babysitter	Babysitter (m)
back (as in 'go back')	zurück
backpack	Rucksack (m)
bad	schlecht; übel
badger	Dachs (m)

bags	Reisetaschen (pl)
bait	Köder (m)
baker	Bäcker/in
bakery	Bäckerei (f)
balcony	Balkon (m)
ball	Ball (m)
ballet	Ballett (neut)
bandage	Verbandsmaterial (neut)
bank	Bank (f)
bank account	Bankkonto (neut)
banknote	Geldschein (m)
bank statement	Kontoauszug (m)
bar	Lokal (neut); Bar (f)
a bargain	Schnäppchen (neut)
to bargain	feilschen
bath	Bad (neut)
bathroom	Badezimmer (neut)
bath towel	Badetuch (neut)
batteries	Batterien (pl)
battery	Batterie (f)
bay	Bucht (f)
to be	sein
beach	Strand (m)
bear	Bär (m)
beautiful	schön
because	weil
because of	wegen
to become	werden
bed	Bett (neut)
bedroom	Schlafzimmer (neut)
bee	Biene (f)
before	vor
beggar	Bettler (m)
begin	beginnen; anfangen
beginner	Anfänger/in
at the beginning	am Anfang
behind	hinter
below	unter
belt	Gürtel (m)
beside	neben; an
best	beste/r/s

better	besser
between	zwischen
bible	Bibel (f)
bicycle	Fahrrad (neut)
big	groß
bike chain	Schloss (neut)
bill (account)	Rechnung (f)
bird	Vogel (m)
birthday	Geburtstag (m)
birthplace of...	das Geburtshaus von ...
bite (n; dog)	Biss (m)
bite (n; insect)	Stich (m)
bitter	bitter
black	schwarz
blackbird	Amsel (f)
black comedy	schwarze Komödie (f)
blanket	Wolldecke (f)
blind	blind
blister	Blase (f)
blue	blau
boar	Wildschwein (neut)
board	Spielbrett (neut)
boarding pass	Bordkarte (f)
boot	Boot (neut)
to boil	kochen
bomb	Bombe (f)
bookshop	Buchhandlung (f); Buchladen (m)
boot	Kofferraum (m)
bore (n)	Langweiler (m)
I'm bored.	
Ich langweile mich.	
boring	langweilig
borrow	ausleihen
boss	Chef (m); Boss (m)
botanic garden	botanischer Garten (m)
both	beide
bottle	Flasche (f)
bottle opener	Flaschenöffner (m)

at the bottom	ganz unten
bouncer (club heavy)	Türsteher (m)
box	Karton (m); Kiste (f)
boy	Junge (m)
boyfriend	Freund (m)
bra	Büstenhalter (m); BH (m)
brake fluid	Bremsflüssigkeit (f)
brakes	Bremsen (pl)
branch office	Zweigstelle (f)
brass	Messing (neut)
bread	Brot (neut)
breakdown service	Abschleppdienst (m)
breakfast	Frühstück (neut)
breast	Brust (f)
bricklayer	Maurer (m)
bridge	Brücke (f)
bridle-path	Reitweg (m)
bright (day)	heiter
bright (sun, eyes)	strahlend
bring	bringen
broken	zerbrochen; kaputt
brother	Bruder (m)
brown	braun
brush	Pinsel (m)
budgie	Wellensittich (m)
building	Gebäude (neut)
bum	Penner (m; derogative)
bus	Bus (m)
business	Geschäft (neut)
businessperson	Geschäftsmann/ Geschäftsfrau
busy	beschäftigt
but	aber
butcher	Metzger/in
butter	Butter (f)
butterfly	Schmetterling (m)
button	Knopf (m)
to buy	kaufen
Bye	Tschüss (S)

cable car	Seilbahn (f)
calmness	Ruhe (f)
camera	Kamera (f); Fotoapparat (m)
camera shop	Fotogeschäft (neut)
to camp	zelten
camping ground	Campingplatz (m)
camping stove	Kocher (m)
can (tin)	Kanister (m)
canary	Kanarienvogel (m)
candle	Kerze (f)
can opener	Dosenöffner (m)
canteen	Mensa (f)
cape (offshore)	Kap (neut)
capitalism	Kapitalismus (m)
carburettor	Vergaser (m)
cards	Kartenspiel (neut)
to care (about)	sich kümmern
I don't care. Es ist mir egal.	
careful	sorgsam; vorsichtig
carpenter	Schreiner/in
carriage (train)	Waggon (m)
to carry	tragen
cash	bar/Bargeld (neut)
cashier	Kassierer/in
castle	Schloss (neut); Burg (f)
cat	Katze (f)
cathedral	Dom (m)
cave	Höhle (f)
cellar	Keller (m)
cemetery	Friedhof (m)
central heating	Zentralheizung (f)
certificate	Schein (m)
chain	Kette (f)
chair	Stuhl (m)
chance	Zufall (m)
change (coins)	Wechselgeld (neut)
to change (money)	wechseln; umtauschen
to change (trains, etc)	umsteigen

chapel	Kapelle (f)	coins	Münzen (pl)
cheap	billig	a cold (illness)	Erkältung (f)
cheese	Käse (m)	cold	kalt
chemist	Apotheke (f)	I am cold.	
cheque card	Scheckkarte (f)	Mir ist kalt.	
chess	Schach (neut)	cold water	kaltes Wasser
chest	Brustkorb (m)	collar	Kragen (m)
chicken	Huhn (neut)	colour film	Farbfilm (m)
children	Kinder (pl)	colour slide film	Farbfilm für Dias (m)
chocolate	Schokolade (f)	comb	Kamm (m)
to choose	auswählen	to come	kommen
christening	Taufe (f)	comedy	Komödie (f)
Christmas	Weihnachten (neut)	comfortable	bequem;
Christmas tree	Weihnachtsbaum (m);		komfortabel
	Christbaum (m)	communism	Kommunismus (m)
church	Kirche (f)	companion;	Freund/in
cigarette papers	Zigarettenpapiere (pl)	friend	
cigarettes	Zigaretten (pl)	concert	Konzert (neut)
cinema	Kino (neut)	concert hall	Konzerthalle (f)
citizenship	Staatsbürgerschaft (f)	conditioner	Spülung (f)
city	Stadt (f)	condoms	Kondome (pl)
city centre	Innenstadt (f);	conductor	Schaffner/in
	Stadtmitte (f)	Congratulations!	Glückwünsche!
civil servant	Beamte/Beamtin	connection	Anschluss (m)
class system	Klassensystem (neut)	(transport)	
classical music	klassische Musik (f)	constellation	Sternbild (neut)
clean	sauber	constipation	Verstopfung (f)
client	Kunde/Kundin	constitution	Verfassung (f)
climate	Klima (neut)	contact lens	Kontaktlinse (f)
close (nearby)	nahe	contemporary	Gegenwartsliteratur
to close	schließen	literature	(f)
clothing	Kleidung (f)	contemporary	zeitgenössische
clothing store	Bekleidungsgeschäft	music	Musik (f)
	(neut)	contraceptive	Verhütungsmittel (m)
cloudy	wolkig	conversation	Konversation (f);
clutch (car)	Kupplung (f)		Gespräch (neut)
coal heating	Kohleheizung (f)	cook	Koch/Köchin
coat	Mantel (m)	to cook	kochen
cocaine	Kokain (neut);	corner	Ecke (f)
	Koks (neut)	cotton	Baumwolle (f)
coffee	Kaffee (m)	couchette	Liegeplatz (m)

cough	Husten (m)	dealer	Drogenhändler (m); Dealer (m)
cough mixture	Hustensaft (m)	death	Tod (m)
to count	zählen	December	Dezember (m)
cousin	Cousin/e	to decide	sich entscheiden
cow	Kuh (f)	decision	Entscheidung (f)
cramp	Krampf (m)	deer	Reh (neut); Hirsch (m)
crampons	Steigeisen (pl)	deforestation	Abholzung (f)
crazy	verrückt	delicatessen	Feinkostladen (m)
credit card	Kreditkarte (f)	delicious	köstlich
crop (agriculture)	Ernte (f)	demand	Forderung (f)
crowded	überfüllt	democracy	Demokratie (f)
cuckoo	Kuckuck (m)	demonstration (protest)	Demonstration (f)
cuckoo clock	Kuckucksuhr (f)	dentist	Zahnarzt/Zahnärztin
cupboard	Schrank (m)	to deny	bestreiten
currency	Währung (f)	to depart	abfahren; abreisen
customs (officials)	Zoll (m)	department store	Kaufhaus (neut)
customs declaration	Zollerklärung (f)	departure	Abfahrt (f)
to cut	schneiden	deposit	Kaution (f)
cycling	Radsport (m)	desert	Wüste (f)
		destination	Bestimmungsort (m); Zielflughafen (m)

D

daily	täglich	to destroy	zerstören
dairy products	Milchprodukte (pl)	detail (n)	Detail (neut)
damp	feucht	development	Entwicklung (f)
dance music	Tanzmusik (f)	diabetes	Zuckerkrankheit (f)
dancing	tanzen	diarrhoea	Durchfall (m)
dangerous	gefährlich	dictatorship	Diktatur (f)
dark	dunkel	dictionary	Wörterbuch (neut)
date (time)	Datum (neut)	different	anders; verschieden
daughter	Tochter (f)	difficult	schwierig; schwer
daughter-in-law	Schwiegertochter (f)	dining car	Speisewagen (m)
dawn	Morgen-dämmerung (f)	dining room	Esszimmer (neut)
day	Tag (m)	dinner	Abendessen (neut)
day after tomorrow	übermorgen	direct	direkt
day before yesterday	vorgestern	direction	Richtung (f)
dead	tot	director (film)	Regisseur/in
deaf	taub		

directory enquiries	Telefonauskunft (f)
dirt	Schmutz (m)
dirty	schmutzig
disadvantage	Nachteil (m)
discount	Rabatt (m); Skonto (neut; m)
discover	entdecken; finden
discrimination	Diskriminierung (f)
distant	fern
distributor (car)	Verteiler (m)
diving	Tauchen (neut)
doctor	Arzt/Ärztin
document	Urkunde (f)
documentary	Dokumentarfilm (m)
dog	Hund (m)
dole	Stempelgeld (neut)
I'm on the dole.	
Ich gehe stempeln.	
donkey	Esel (m)
dope	Dope (neut); Stoff (m)
double	doppelt
double bass	Kontrabass (m)
double bed	Doppelbett (neut)
down (there)	unten
downtown	Innenstadt (f); Zentrum (neut)
a dozen	ein Dutzend
drama	Schauspiel (neut)
dream (n)	Traum (m)
dress	Kleid (neut)
drink (n)	Getränk (neut)
to drink	trinken
driver	Fahrer/in
drug addict	Drogenabhängige/r
drug counselling service	Drogenberatungsstelle (f)

drug pusher	Dealer (m)
drugs	Rauschgift (neut)
drugstore	Drogeriemarkt (m)
drunk (inebriated)	betrunken
dry	trocken
drycleaner	chemische Reinigung (f)
duck	Ente (f)
during	während
dusk	Abenddämmerung (f)
dust	Staub (m)
dustbin	Mülltonne (f)
duty-free goods	zollfreie Waren (pl)

E

each	jede/r/s
eagle	Adler (m)
ear	Ohr (neut)
early	früh
to earn	verdienen
earnings	Verdienst (m)
earrings	Ohrringe (pl)
earth (soil)	Erde (f); Boden (m)
Earth (world)	Erde (f)
earthquake	Erdbeben (neut)
east	Osten (m); östlich
Easter	Ostern (neut)
easy	leicht
to eat	essen
I don't eat meat.	
Ich esse kein Fleisch.	
economical	wirtschaftlich
economics	Betriebswirtschaft (f)
economy	Wirtschaft (f)
education	Ausbildung (f)
eel	Aal (m)
eight	acht
eighteen	achtzehn
eighty	achtzig
election	Wahl (f)

electorate	Wähler (pl); Wählerschaft (f)
electrician	Elektriker/in
electricity	Elektrizität (f)
elevator	Lift (m); Aufzug (m)
eleven	elf
to embark	einsteigen
embassy	Botschaft (f)
embroidery	Stickerei (f)
employee	Angestellte/r
employer	Arbeitgeber (m)
empty	leer
end (n)	Ende (neut)
at the end	am Ende
energy	Energie (f)
engine	Motor (m)
engineer	Ingenieur/in
English	Englisch (neut)
to enjoy (oneself)	sich amüsieren
enough	genug
to enter	eintreten
entertaining	unterhaltsam
envelope	Briefumschlag (m)
environment	Umwelt (f)
equality	Gleichberechtigung (f)
evening	Abend (m)
every	jede/r/s
every day	alltäglich
everyone	alle
everything	alles
excellent	ausgezeichnet
excess baggage	Übergepäck (neut)
to exchange	umtauschen; wechseln
exchange office	Wechselstube (f)
exchange of money	Geldwechsel (m)
exchange rate	Kurs (m)
excluding	außer; ausgenommen
Excuse me	Entschuldigung
exhaust	Auspuff (m)

exhaust fumes	(Auto)Abgase (pl)
exile	Exil (neut)
expensive	teuer
experience	Erfahrung (f)
to export	exportieren
express train	Schnellzug (m)
eye	Auge (neut)

F

factory	Fabrik (f)
factory sale	Fabrikverkauf (m)
factory worker	Fabrikarbeiter/in
fair	Messe (f)
false	falsch
family	Familie (f)
fan	Ventilator (m)
fan belt	Keilriemen (m)
far	weit
farm	Bauernhof (m)
farmer	Bauer/Bäuerin
fast (quick)	schnell
fast train	Eilzug (m)
fat	dick
father	Vater (m)
fax	Fax (neut)
fear (n)	Angst (f)
feature film	Spielfilm (m)
February	Februar (m)
fee	Benutzungsgebühr (f)
feelings	Gefühle (pl)
I feel like ...	Ich habe Lust ...
female (animal)	Weibchen (neut)
festival	Fest (neut)
fever	Fieber (neut)
a few	ein paar
fiancé/e	Verlobte/r
fiction	Prosaroman (m)
field	Feld (neut)
fifteen	fünfzehn
fifty	fünfzig

film (movie)	Film (m)
film (roll of)	eine Rolle Film
film noir	Film-noire (m)
filtered (cigarette)	mit Filter
fine (good)	schön
fine (penalty)	Geldbuße (f); Verwarnung (f)
finger	Finger (m)
fire	Feuer (neut)
firewood	Brennholz (neut)
first	erste/r/s
fish	Fisch (m)
fishing	Fischen (neut)
fishing rod	Angel (f)
five	fünf
flash	Blitz (m)
flashlight (torch)	Taschenlampe (f)
flat (new)	Neubauwohnung (f)
flat (old)	Altbauwohnung (f)
flea-market	Flohmarkt (m)
flood	Flut (f)
floor	Boden (m)
flower shop	Blumenladen (m)
flute	Flöte (f)
fly	Fliege (f)
foam mattress	Isomatte (f)
fog	Nebel (m)
foggy	neblig
follow	folgen
food	Essen (neut)
food poisoning	Lebensmittelvergiftung (f)
foot	Fuß (m)
for	für
foreign	ausländisch
forever	immer
to forget	vergessen

I'll never forget this.
Ich vergesse das nie.
Don't forget to write!
Vergiss nicht zu schreiben!

to forgive	verzeihen
formal	formell
forty	vierzig
fountain	Brunnen (m)
four	vier
fourteen	vierzehn
fox	Fuchs (m)
frame	Rahmen (m)
France	Frankreich (neut)
free (of charge)	gratis; frei
free (not bound)	frei
to freeze	frieren
French	Französisch (neut)
fresh (not stale)	frisch
Friday	Freitag (m)
friend	Freund/in
friendly	freundlich
frog	Frosch (m)
from	aus; von
in front of	vor
frosty	frostig
fruit	Frucht (f)
frying pan	Bratpfanne (f)
fuel	Brennstoff (m)
full	voll
fun	Spaß (m)
funeral	Begräbnis (neut)
funny	komisch
furnished	möbliert
fuse	Sicherung (f)

G

game	Spiel (neut)
game show	Unterhaltungsshow (f)
gaol (jail)	Gefängnis (neut)
garbage	Abfall (m)
garbage dump	Müllkippe (f)
garden	Garten (m)
gardener	Gärtner/in
gas; petrol	Benzin (neut)

gas cartridge	Gaskartusche (f)
gas heating	Gasheizung (f)
gay	schwul
gear	Gang (m)
gears	Gangschaltung (f)
generator	Lichtmaschine (f)
German	Deutsch (neut)

  I don't speak German.
  Ich spreche kein Deutsch.
  I speak a little German.
  Ich spreche ein bisschen Deutsch.

Germany	Deutschland (neut)
Germany's federal parliament	der Bundestag
girlfriend	Freundin (f)
to give	geben; schenken

  Please give me ...
  Geben Sie mir bitte ...

glacier	Gletscher (m)
glass (of water)	Glas (neut)
glasses (for eyes)	Brille (f)
global warming	globale Erwärmung (f)
gloves	Handschuhe (pl)
to go	gehen; fahren

  Go straight ahead.
  Gehen Sie geradeaus.
  Does this bus go to ...?
  Fährt dieser Bus nach ...?
  I want to go to ...
  Ich möchte nach ... fahren.

goat	Ziege (f)
god	Gott (m)
gold	Gold (neut)
good	gut

  Good luck!
  Viel Glück!

goose	Gans (f)
gorge	Schlucht (f)
government	Regierung (f)
grandchildren	Enkel(kinder) (pl)
granddaughter	Enkelin (f)
grandfather	Großvater (m); Opa (m)
grandmother	Großmutter (f); Oma (f)
grandparents	Großeltern (pl)
grandson	Enkel (m)
grant	Studienförderung (f)
graphic arts	Grafik (f)
grateful	dankbar

  I am grateful.
  Ich bin dankbar.

grave (tomb)	Grab (neut)
green	grün
grey	grau
grocery	Lebensmittelladen (m)
to grow	wachsen
to guess	raten
guidebook	Handbuch (neut)
guilty	schuldig
guitar	Gitarre (f)
gulf	Golf (m)

H

hairbrush	Haarbürste (f)
hairdresser	Friseur/Friseuse
half	Hälfte (f)
ham	Schinken (m)
hammock	Hängematte (f)
hamster	Hamster (m)
hand	Hand (f)
handbag	Handtasche (f)
handicraft	Kunsthandwerk (neut)
handlebars	Lenker (m)
handmade	handgearbeitet
handsome	gut aussehend
hang-gliding	Drachenfliegen (neut)
happy	glücklich

  I am happy.
  Ich bin glücklich.

harbour	Hafen (m)
hard (difficult)	schwer
hard (not soft)	hart
to hate	hassen
to have	haben
I have .../you have ...	
ich habe .../du hast ...	
Have you (got) ...?	
Haben Sie ...?	
head	Kopf (m)
headache	Kopfschmerzen (pl)
health	Gesundheit (f)
to hear	hören
heart	Herz (neut)
heat	Hitze (f)
heating	Heizung (f)
heavy	schwer
Hello	Guten Tag; Hallo
to help	helfen
here	hier
herring	Hering (m)
Hi	Hallo
high	hoch
high blood pressure	hoher Blutdruck (m)
to hike	wandern
hill	Hügel (m)
to hire	mieten
I'd like to hire a car.	
Ich möchte ein Auto mieten.	
history	Geschichte (f)
to hitchhike	per Anhalter fahren; trampen
holiday (vacation)	Urlaub (m); Ferien (pl)
holy	heilig
home	Heim (neut)
homeless people	Obdachlose (pl)
to be homesick	Heimweh haben
homoeopathic medicine	homöopathisches Mittel (neut)
homosexual	homosexuell

honest	ehrlich
hope	Hoffnung (f)
horoscope	Horoskop (neut)
horse	Pferd (neut)
horse riding	Reiten (neut)
hospital	Krankenhaus (neut)
hot	heiß
I am hot.	
Mir ist heiß.	
hotel	Hotel (neut)
hot water	warmes Wasser
house	Haus (neut)
housewife	Hausfrau (f)
housework	Hausarbeit (f)
how	wie
How much is it?	
Wie viel kostet es?	
How do I get to ...?	
Wie komme ich nach ...?	
How are you?	
Wie geht es Ihnen?/dir? (pol/inf)	
human	menschlich
human rights	Menschenrechte (pl)
hundred	hundert
hurry (to be in a)	(in) Eile (sein)
I am in a hurry.	
Ich habe es eilig.	
to hurt (yourself)	sich weh tun
husband	Ehemann (m)
hut	Hütte (f)

I

ice; ice-cream	Eis (neut)
ice axe	Eispickel (m)
ice skating	Eis laufen (neut)
idea	Idee (f)
I.D. (identification card)	Personalausweis (m)
if	wenn; falls
ignition	Zündung (f)
ignition key	Zündschlüssel (m)
ill	krank

illegal	unerlaubt; illegal
imagination	Fantasie (f)
imitation	Imitation (f)
immediately	sofort
immigration	Immigration (f);
	Einwanderung (f)
to import	einführen
important	wichtig

It's (not) important.
Es ist (nicht) wichtig.

impossibility	Unmöglichkeit (f)
impossible	unmöglich
in	in
included	inbegriffen
indicator	Blinker (m)
indigestion	Magenverstimmung (f)
indoors	drinnen; im Haus
industry	Industrie (f)
inequality	Ungleichheit (f)
infection	Infektion (f)
inflammation	Entzündung (f)
influenza	Grippe (f)
informal	leger; informell
information	Auskunft (f)
in front of	vor
injection	Injektion (f); Spritze (f)
injury	Verletzung (f)
insect repellant	Insektenbekämpfungsmittel (neut)
inside	innen
instead of	(an)statt
insurance	Versicherung (f)
to insure	versichern

I have medical insurance.
Ich bin bei einer Krankenkasse.
My possessions are insured.
Meine Sachen sind versichert.

intelligent	intelligent
interesting	interessant
intermission	Pause (f)
interpreter	Dolmetscher/in
island	Insel (f)
IUD	Spirale (f)

J

jacket	Jacke (f)
jail (gaol)	Gefängnis (neut)
January	Januar (m)
jewellery	Schmuck (m)
job	Stelle (f); Job (m)
job market	Arbeitsmarkt (m)
job offer	Stellenangebot (neut)
joke	Witz (m)
journalist	Journalist/in
July	Juli (m)
jumper	Pullover (m); Pulli (m)
June	Juni (m)
Just a minute!	Ein Moment!
justice	Gerechtigkeit (f)

K

kettle	Kessel (m)
key	Schlüssel (m)
to kill	töten
kind (sentiment)	freundlich
kind (type)	Art (f); Sorte (f)
king	König (m)
to kiss	küssen
kitchen	Küche (f)
knee	Knie (neut)
knife	Messer (neut)
know (a person)	kennen
know (how to)	wissen; kennen

L

lake	See (m)
land	Land (neut)
landing	Landung (f)
landlady	Vermieterin (f)
landlord	Vermieter (m)
landslide	Erdrutsch (m)

languages	Sprachen (pl)
lark	Lerche (f)
last	letzte/r/s
last night	letzte Nacht
last week	letzte Woche
last year	letztes Jahr
When is the last bus to ...?	
Wann fährt der letzte Bus nach ...?	
late	spät
late show	Spätvorstellung (f)
latest collection	aktuelle Kollektion (f)
laugh	Lachen (neut)
to laugh	lachen
laundry	Wäscherei (f)
law	Jura; Gesetz (neut)
lawyer	Rechtsanwalt/ Rechtsanwältin
laxative	Abführmittel (neut)
lazy	faul
leaded fuel	verbleites Benzin (neut)
to learn	lernen
lease	Mietvertrag (m)
leather	Leder (neut)
to leave (depart)	verlassen
What time does ... leave?	
Wann fährt ... ab?	
lecture	Vorlesung (f)
lecturer	Dozent/in
left (not right)	links
Turn left ...	
Biegen Sie ... links ab.	
left-luggage office	Gepäckaufbewahrung (f)
left-luggage withdrawals	Gepäckausgabe (f)
left-wing	links stehend
leg	Bein (neut)
legal	legal; gesetzlich
legislation	Wahlperiode (f)
lens	Objektiv (neut)

lesbian	lesbisch
less	weniger
less (not as much/ many)	nicht so viel/viele
letter	Brief (m)
library	Bücherei (f); Bibliothek (f)
lice	Läuse (pl)
life	Leben (neut)
life jacket	Schwimmweste (f)
lift	Lift (m); Aufzug (m)
light (not dark)	hell
light (not heavy)	leicht
light bulb	Glühbirne (f)
lighter	Feuerzeug (neut)
light meter	Belichtungsmesser (m)
lightning	Blitz (m)
lights	Scheinwerfer (m)
like (similar)	ähnlich
to like	mögen
I (don't) like ...	
Ich mag ... (nicht).	
line	Linie (f)
linen	Leinen (neut)
to listen	hören
little (adj)	klein
to live	leben
liver	Leber (f)
living room	Wohnzimmer (neut)
local train	Nahverkehrszug (m)
location	Drehort (m)
lock	Schloss (neut)
locksmith	Schlosser (m)
lodger	Untermieter (m)
lonely	einsam
I am lonely.	
Ich bin einsam.	
long (thing)	lang
long (way)	weit
long ago	vor langer Zeit
long-sleeved	langärmelig

to look (at)	ansehen
to look for	suchen
I'm looking for ...	
Ich suche ...	
loose change	Kleingeld (neut)
to lose	verlieren
loss	Verlust (m)
loud	laut
to love	lieben
I love you.	
Ich liebe dich.	
love film	Liebesfilm (m)
love story	Liebesgeschichte (f)
low blood	niedriger
pressure	Blutdruck (m)
luggage locker	Schließfach (neut)
lunch	Mittagessen (neut)

M

machine	Maschine (f)
mad (crazy)	wahnsinnig
It is made of ...	Es ist aus ...
mailbox	Briefkasten (m)
main square	Hauptplatz (m)
majority	Mehrheit (f)
to make	machen
manager	Manager/in
many	viele
Many thanks	
Vielen Dank	
map	Karte (f)
March	März (m)
marches (demon-	Demonstrationen (pl);
strations)	Demos (abbr)
market	Markt (m)
marriage	Ehe (f)
to marry	heiraten
mass	Messe (f)
matches	Streichhölzer (pl)

material	Material (neut)
mathematics	Mathematik (f)
mattress	Matratze (f)
May	Mai
May I?	Darf ich?
maybe	vielleicht
mechanic	Mechaniker/in
medicine	Medizin (f)
to meet	treffen; begegnen
When should we meet?	
Wann wollen wir uns treffen?	
Where should we meet?	
Wo wollen wir uns treffen?	
member of	Abgeordnete/r
parliament	
menstruation	Menstruation (f);
	Periode (f); Tage (pl)
menthol	Menthol (neut)
menu	Menü (neut)
message	Mitteilung (f)
Middle East	Naher Osten (m)
midnight	Mitternacht (f)
milk	Milch (f)
mind (n)	Geist (m)
Do you mind?	Macht es Ihnen
	etwas aus?
mineral water	Mineralwasser (neut)
(without bubbles)	(ohne Kohlensäure)
minute	Minute (f)
mirror	Spiegel (m)
miss (to feel the	vermissen
absence of)	
miss (the bus, etc)	verpassen
mistake	Fehler (m)
to mix	(ver)mischen
mobile phone	Mobiltelefon (neut);
	Handy (neut)
modem	Modem (m)
modern art	moderne Kunst (f)
moisturising cream	Feuchtigkeitscreme (f)
monastery	Kloster (neut)

Monday	Montag (m)
money	Geld (neut)
monument	Denkmal (neut)
moon	Mond (m)
more	mehr
morning	Morgen (m)
mosque	Moschee (f)
mother	Mutter (f)
mountain	Berg (m)
mountain hut	Berghütte (f)
mountain range	Gebirgszug (m); Gebirgskette (f)
mouse	Maus (f)
movement	Bewegung (f)
movie	Film (m)
muggy	schwül
museum	Museum (neut)
music	Musik (f)
musician	Musiker/in

N

name	Name (m)
What is your name?	
Wie heißen Sie?;	
Wie ist Ihr Name?	
My name is ...	
Ich heiße ...;	
Ich bin ...;	
Mein Name ist ...	
natural gas	Erdgas (neut)
nature	Natur (f)
nature reserve	Naturschutzgebiet (neut)
nausea	Übelkeit (f)
near	nahe
necessary	notwendig
necklace	Halskette (f)
neither	keine/r/s
nephew	Neffe (m)
nerve	Nerv (m)
never	nie
new	neu

New Year's Eve	Silvester (m/neut)
New Zealand	Neuseeland (neut)
news	Nachrichten (pl)
newsagency	Zeitungshändler (m)
newspaper	Zeitung (f)
next	nächste/r/s
next to	neben
next week	nächste Woche
next year	nächstes Jahr
What is the next station?	
Wie heißt der nächste Bahnhof?	
nice	nett
niece	Nichte (f)
night	Nacht (f)
nine	neun
nineteen	neunzehn
ninety	neunzig
no	nein
noise	Geräusch (neut)
noisy	laut
none	keine/r/s
noon	Mittag (m)
north	Norden (m); nördlich
nose	Nase (f)
not any more	nicht mehr
nothing	nichts
Not so good.	Nicht so gut.
Not too bad.	Es geht.
novel	Roman (m)
November	November (m)
now	jetzt
nuclear energy	Atomenergie (f)
nuclear power station	Atomkraftwerk (neut)
nuclear waste	Atommüll (m)
nurse	Krankenpfleger/ Krankenschwester

O

oarsman	Ruderer (m)
obvious	offensichtlich; klar
occupation	Beruf (m)

ocean Ozean (m)
October Oktober (m)
to offend kränken
to offer anbieten
office Büro (neut)
office worker Büroangestellte/r
often häufig
oil Öl (neut)
oil-based paint Ölfarbe (f)
oil heating Ölheizung (f)
old alt
old buildings alte Gebäude
old part of the city Altstadt (f)
on an; auf
  On Sale
  Im Sonderangebot
  On Strike!
  Wir streiken!
once einmal
one eins
only einzige/r/s
to open öffnen
open (adj) offen; auf
  What time does it open?
  Wann macht es auf?
  I can't open the window.
  Ich kann das Fenster nicht aufmachen.
  Is the hotel open all night?
  Ist das Hotel die ganze Nacht geöffnet?
opera Oper (f)
opera house Opernhaus (neut)
opera singer Opernsänger/in
opinion Meinung (f)
opposite gegenüber; entgegengesetzt
optometrist Optiker (m)
or oder
order (system) Ordnung (f)
ordinary normal; gewöhnlich
organ Orgel (f)
to organise organisieren
other andere/r/s

out aus
over über
overdose Überdosis (f)
overnight über Nacht
to owe schulden
owner Besitzer/in

package Paket (neut)
a pack of cigarettes eine Schachtel Zigaretten
padlock Vorhängeschloss (neut)
pain Schmerz (m)
painful schmerzhaft
painkillers Schmerzmittel (neut)
painter Maler/in
painting Gemälde (neut)
paints Farben (pl)
pair Paar (neut)
palace Palast (m)
paper Papier (neut)
paperback Taschenbuch (neut)
parachuting Fallschirmspringen (neut)
paragliding Gleitschirmfliegen (neut)
paralysed gelähmt
parcel Paket (neut)
parents Eltern (pl)
park Park (m)
parliament Parlament (neut)
parrot Papagei (m)
part Teil (m)
to participate sich beteiligen
part-time job Teilzeitstelle (f)
party Fest (neut)
passenger (bus; taxi) Fahrgast (m)
passenger (plane) Fluggast (m)

passenger (train)	Reisende/r
passport	Pass (m)
past (time)	früher
path; track	Pfad (m)
patio	Terrasse (f)
to pay	bezahlen
to pay (into an account)	einzahlen
pay phone	Münztelefon (neut)
peace	Frieden (m)
peak	Gipfel (m)
pen (ballpoint)	Kugelschreiber (m)
pencil	Bleistift (m)
peninsula	Halbinsel (f)
penknife	Taschenmesser (neut)
pensioner	Rentner/in
people	Menschen (pl)
percent	Prozent (neut)
performance	Aufführung (f)
permanent	fest; ständig
permission	Erlaubnis (f)
to permit	erlauben
persecution	Verfolgung (f)
person	Mensch (m); Person (f)
personal	persönlich
personality	Persönlichkeit (f)
petrol	Benzin (neut)
petrol can	Benzinkanister (m)
pharmacy	Apotheke (f)
phone book	Telefonbuch (neut)
phone box	Telefonzelle (f)
phonecard	Telefonkarte (f)
photograph (n)	Fotografie (f)
to photograph	fotografieren
Can I take photographs?	
Darf ich fotografieren?	
photo shop	Fotogeschäft (neut)
physics	Physik (f)
piano	Klavier (neut)
piece	Stück (neut)
pilgrimage	Pilgerfahrt (f)

pillow	Kissen (neut)
pink	rosa
pipe	Pfeife (f)
place	Stelle (f); Platz (m)
plain	Ebene (f)
plane	Flugzeug (neut)
planet	Planet (m)
plant	Pflanze (f)
plateau	Hochebene (f)
platform	Gleis (neut)
to play (games; music)	spielen
Please	Bitte
plenty	viel
plumber	Installateur/in
poetry	Poesie (f); Gedichte (pl)
to point	richten; zeigen
police	Polizei (f)
police station	Polizeirevier (neut)
policy	Politik (f)
politician	Politiker/in
politics	Politik (f)
pollution	Umweltverschmutzung (f)
pony	Pony (neut)
pool (the game)	Billard (neut)
pool (indoors)	Hallenbad (neut)
pool (outdoors)	Freibad (neut)
pool attendant	Bademeister (m)
pool for nonswimmers	Nichtschwimmerbecken (neut)
pool for swimmers	Schwimmbecken (neut)
poor	arm
porter	Gepäckträger (m)
possible	möglich
It's (not) possible.	
Es ist (nicht) möglich.	
postcard	Postkarte (f)
poste restante	postlagernd

postman	Briefträger/in
post office	Postamt (neut)
post office box	Postfach (neut)
pot	Topf (m)
pottery	Töpferware (f)
poverty	Armut (f)
power	Kraft (f)
practical	praktisch
prayer	Gebet (neut)
to prefer	vorziehen
pregnant	schwanger
prepare	vorbereiten
present (gift)	Geschenk (neut)
present (time)	gegenwärtig
president	Präsident (m)
pretty	hübsch
to prevent	verhindern
price	Preis (m)

Can you write down the price?
Könnten Sie den Preis aufschreiben?
Could you lower the price?
Könnten Sie den Preis reduzieren?

priest	Priester (m); Pfarrer (m)
prime minister	Bundeskanzler (m)
print (artwork)	Abzug (m); Stich (m)
prison	Gefängnis (neut)
prisoner	Gefangene/r
private	privat
problem	Problem (neut)
to produce	produzieren
producer	Produzent (m)
profession	Beruf (m)
profit	Gewinn (m)
profitability	Rentabilität (f)
program	Programm (neut)
to promise	versprechen
proposal	Vorschlag (m)
prostitute	Prostituierte (f)

protected area	Landschaftsschutz-gebiet (neut)
protected species	geschützte Tierarten (pl)
protest	Protest (m)
psychology	Psychologie (f)
pub	Kneipe (f)
public beach	öffentlicher Strand (m)
public toilet	öffentliche Toilette (f)
to pull	ziehen
pump	Luftpumpe (f)
puncture	Reifenpanne (f)
pure	rein
purple	lila
to push	schieben

Q

quality	Qualität (f)
quarter	Viertel (neut)
question (n)	Frage (f)
quick	schnell
quiet	ruhig

R

rabbit	Kaninchen (neut)
race (contest)	Rennen (neut)
racist	Rassist/in
radiator	Kühler (m)
radio	Radio (neut)
rain	Regen (m)

It's raining.
Es regnet.

raincoat	Regenmantel (m)
rape (n)	Vergewaltigung (f)
to rape	vergewaltigen
rapids	Stromschnellen (pl)
rare	rar; selten
raw	roh

razor	Rasierapparat (m)
reading	Lesung (f)
ready	bereit; fertig
reason	Grund (m)
receipt	Quittung (f)
recently	vor kurzem
to recharge	aufladen
to recommend	empfehlen
recycling	Wiederverwertung (f)
	Recycling (neut)
red	rot
reduced price	herabgesetzter
	Preis (m)
reduction	Ermäßigung (f)
references	Zeugnisse (pl)
referendum	Volksentscheid (m)
refugee	Flüchtling (m)
to refund	zurückerstatten
to refuse	verweigern
region	Gebiet (neut)
registered mail	per Einschreiben
regulation	Vorschrift (f)
relative (family)	Verwandte/r
relatives;	Verwandtschaft (f)
relationship	
to relax	entspannen
religion	Religion (f)
to remember	sich erinnern
remote	entfernt
remote control	Fernbedienung (f)
rent (n)	Miete (f)

How much is the rent?

Wie hoch ist die Miete?

to rent	mieten
rent increase	Mieterhöhung (f)
renting out	Vermietung (f)
republic	Republik (f)
reservation (for	Reservierung (f)
a meal, a seat)	
to reserve	reservieren

I'd like to book a seat to ...

**Ich möchte einen Platz nach ...
reservieren lassen.**

residential area	Wohnviertel (neut)
respect (neut)	Respekt (m)
responsibility	Verantwortung (f)
restaurant	Restaurant (neut)
résumé (CV)	Lebenslauf (m)
retired	pensioniert
to return	zurückkommen
return flight	Rückflug (m)
revolution	Revolution (f)
rich	reich
riding school	Reitschule (f)
riding stable	Reitstall (m)
ridge	Grat (m)
right (not left)	rechts

Turn right ...

Biegen Sie ... rechts ab.

right (not wrong)	richtig

I am right.

Ich habe recht.

right there	gleich dort
right-wing	rechts stehend
ring	Ring (m)
risk	Risiko (neut)
river	Fluss (m)
road	Straße (f)
road map	Straßenkarte (f)
rob	bestehlen; berauben

I've been robbed!

Ich bin bestohlen worden!

robbery	Raub (m)
robin	Rotkehlchen (neut)
rock	Fels (m)
rock-climbing/	Bergsteigen (neut)
mountaineering	
roof	Dach (neut)
room	Zimmer (neut)
double room	Doppelzimmer
	(neut)
single room	Einzelzimmer
	(neut)
room number	Zimmernummer (f)
rope	Seil (neut)
round	rund

route	Strecke (f)
row	Reihe (f)
rowing	Rudern (neut)
rubber	Radiergummi (m)
ruins	Ruinen (pl)

S

sad	traurig
I am sad.	
Ich bin traurig.	
saddle	Joch (neut); Sattel (m)
safe (for valuables)	Safe (m/neut)
safe (adj)	sicher
safety	Sicherheit (f)
sailing	Segeln (neut)
salary	Gehalt (neut); Lohn (m)
On Sale	Im Sonderangebot
sales department	Verkaufsabteilung (f)
same	der/die/das gleiche
sanitary facilities	sanitäre Einrichtungen (pl)
sanitary napkins	Damenbinden (pl)
satin	Satin (m)
Saturday	Samstag (m)
to save (money)	sparen
to save (someone)	retten
scarf	Halstuch (neut)
scenery	Landschaft (f)
scientist	Wissenschaftler/in
scissors	Schere (f)
screwdriver	Schraubenzieher (m)
script	Drehbuch (neut)
scriptwriter	Drehbuchautor/in
sculptor	Bildhauer/in
sculpture	Skulptur (f)
sea	See (f); Meer (neut)
seagull	Möwe (f)
seal	Dichtung (f)
seasick	seekrank

seat	(Sitz)Platz (m)
seat belt	Sicherheitsgurt (m)
second	zweite/r/s
second-hand bookshop	Antiquariat (neut)
second-hand shop	Secondhandladen (m)
secret	Geheimnis (neut)
secretary	Sekretär/in
selfish	egoistisch
to sell	verkaufen
semi-detached house	Doppelhaus (neut)
seminar	Seminar (neut)
to send	senden
sender	Absender (m)
September	September (m)
serial	Serie (f)
serious	ernst
seven	sieben
seventeen	siebzehn
seventy	siebzig
several	einige
sexist	Sexist/in
shade (n)	Schatten (m)
shampoo	Shampoo (neut)
shape	Form (f)
to share	teilen
shaving cream	Rasiercreme (f)
sheep	Schaf (neut)
sheet	Bettlaken (neut)
shirt	Hemd (neut)
shoes	Schuhe (pl)
shoeshop	Schuhgeschäft (neut)
shooting	Schießsport (m)
shopkeeper	Kaufmann/Kauffrau
short	kurz
shortage	Knappheit (f)
shortcut	Abkürzung (f)
short-sleeved	kurzärmelig

short story	Kurzgeschichte (f)
to shout	schreien
to show	zeigen
Can you show me (on the map)?	
Könnten Sie es mir (auf der Karte) zeigen?	
shower (in bathroom)	Dusche (f)
shower (of rain)	Regenschauer (m)
shrine	Schrein (m)
shut	schließen
shy	schüchtern
sick	krank
side	Seite (f)
sign	Schild (neut)
signature	Unterschrift (f)
signpost	Wegweiser (m)
silk	Seide (f)
silver	Silber (neut)
similar	ähnlich
since	seit
single (unmarried)	unverheiratet
sister	Schwester (f)
sisters and brothers	Geschwister (pl)
to sit	sitzen
situation	Lage (f)
six	sechs
sixteen	sechzehn
sixty	sechzig
size	Größe (f)
to skate	Eis laufen
to ski	Ski fahren, Ski laufen
skin	Haut (f)
skirt	Rock (m)
sleep (n)	Schlaf (m)
to sleep	schlafen
sleeping bag	Schlafsack (m)
sleeping car	Schlafwagen (m)
sleepy (to be)	müde sein
I am sleepy.	
Ich bin müde.	
slide (photo)	Dia (neut)

slippery	glatt
slope	Hang (m)
slow	langsam
slowly	langsam
slow train	Personenzug (m)
small	klein
smear	Abstrich (m)
to smell	riechen
smog	Smog (m)
snail	Schnecke (f)
snake	Schlange (f)
snow	Schnee (m)
snowfield	Schneefeld (neut)
soap	Seife (f)
socialism	Sozialismus (m)
social security	Sozialunterstützung (f)
social worker	Sozialarbeiter/in
sociology	Soziologie (f)
solar energy	Solarenergie (f)
sold out	ausverkauft
solid	fest
some	einige
somebody	jemand
something	etwas
sometimes	manchmal
son	Sohn (m)
song	Lied (neut)
son-in-law	Schwiegersohn (m)
soon	bald
sore throat	Halsschmerzen (pl)
Sorry!	Entschuldigung!
I'm sorry.	
Es tut mir Leid.	
south	Süden (m); südlich
souvenir	Souvenir (neut); Andenken (neut)
souvenir shop	Souvenirladen (m)
spade	Spaten (m)
spare parts	Ersatzteile (pl)
spare tyre	Reservereifen (m)
spark plug	Zündkerze (f)

S

| sparrow | Spatz (m) |
| to speak | sprechen |

Do you speak English?

Sprechen Sie Englisch?

I don't speak German.

Ich spreche kein Deutsch.

I speak a little German.

Ich spreche ein bisschen Deutsch.

special	speziell
special offer	Sonderangebot (neut)
spicy	würzig
spider	Spinne (f)
spirit	Spiritus (m)
spokes	Speichen (pl)
sport	Sport (m)
sprain	Muskelzerrung (f)
spring	Quelle (f)
squash	Squash (neut)
squash racket	Squashschläger (m)
stadium	Stadion (neut)
stamp	Briefmarke (f)
standing room	Stehplatz (m)
star	Stern (m)
star sign	Sternzeichen (neut)
to start	anfangen mit; beginnen
state	Staat (m)
stationery	Schreibwaren (pl)
statues	Statuen (pl)
to stay (hotel)	übernachten
to stay (in a place)	bleiben
to steal	stehlen
stomach	Magen (m)
stone	Stein (m)
to stop	anhalten

Does this train stop at ...?

Hält dieser Zug in ...?

Please stop at the next corner.

Halten Sie bitte an der nächsten Ecke.

Stop here!

Halten Sie hier!

| stopover | Zwischenlandung (f) |

stork	Storch (m)
storm	Sturm (m)
stormy	stürmisch
story (tale)	Geschichte (f)
straight	gerade

Go straight ahead.

Gehen Sie geradeaus.

strange	fremd
stranger	Fremde/r
street	Straße (f)
street kids	Straßenkinder (pl)
On Strike!	Wir streiken!
strong	stark
student	Student/in
student card	Studentenausweis (m)
studio	Atelier (neut)
to study	studieren
stupid	dumm; blöd
style	Stil (m)
suburban train	Vorortzug (m); S-Bahn (f)
suddenly	plötzlich
sugar	Zucker (m)
suitcase	Koffer (m)
summer sale	Sommerschlussverkauf (m)
sun	Sonne (f)
sunblock cream	Sonnenschutzmittel (neut)
sunburn	Sonnenbrand (m)
sun cream	Sonnencreme (f)
Sunday	Sonntag (m)
sunglasses	Sonnenbrille (f)
sunrise	Sonnenaufgang (m)
sunset	Sonnenuntergang (m)
supermarket	Supermarkt (m)
supplement	Zuschlag (m)
Sure.	Klar!
surface mail	gewöhnliche Post
surname	Nachname (m)
surprise	Überraschung (f)

I'm surprised.

Ich bin überrascht.

to survive	überleben
sweater; jumper	Pullover (m); Pulli (m)
sweet	süß
to swim	schwimmen
swimming cap	Badekappe (f)
swimming costume	Badeanzug (m)
swimming pool	Schwimmbad (neut)
swimming trunks	Badehose (f)
switchboard	Telefonzentrale (f)
Switzerland	Schweiz (f)
synagogue	Synagoge (f)

T

table	Tisch (m)
table tennis	Tischtennis (neut)
tailor	Schneider/in
to take	bringen

Can you take me to ...?
Könnten Sie mich zu ... bringen?

takeoff	Abflug (m)
to talk	sprechen
tall	groß
target	Zielscheibe (f)
tasty	schmackhaft
tax	Steuer (f)
tea	Tee (m)
teacher	Lehrer/in
technique	Technik (f)
teeth	Zähne (pl)
telegram	Telegramm (neut)
telephone (n)	Telefon (neut)
to telephone	telefonieren; anrufen

Where can I make a phone call?
Wo kann ich telefonieren?

telephone book	Telefonbuch (neut)
telephone centre	Telefonzentrale (f)
telescope	Teleskop (neut)
television	Fernsehen (neut)
temperature	Temperatur (f)

temple	Tempel (m)
ten	zehn
tenant	Mieter/in
tennis	Tennis (neut)
tennis court	Tennisplatz (m)
tennis racket	Tennisschläger (m)
tent	Zelt (neut)
tent pegs	Heringe (pl); Zeltpflöcke (pl)
term	Semester (neut)
terminus	Endstation (f)
term of office	Wahlperiode (f)
test (n)	Test (m)
Thank you	Danke
theatre	Theater (neut)
theft	Diebstahl (m)
there	dort
thermos	Thermosflasche (f)
thick	dick
thief	Dieb (m)
thin	dünn
to think	denken
third	dritte/r/s
a third	ein Drittel
thirsty (to be)	Durst haben
thirteen	dreizehn
thirty	dreißig
this morning	heute Morgen
this street	diese Straße
this suburb	dieser Vorort
this week	diese Woche
this year	dieses Jahr
thousand	tausend
three	drei
three-quarters	drei Viertel
thriller	Krimi (m)
throat	Hals (m)
through	durch
thunder	Donner (m)
Thursday	Donnerstag (m)
ticket – one-way	Einfachfahrkarte (f)
ticket – return	Rückfahrkarte (f)

T

D
I
C
T
I
O
N
A
R
Y

tide	Gezeiten (pl)
time	Zeit (f)

What time is it?
Wie spät ist es?
Do you know the exact time?
Haben Sie die genaue Zeit?
What time is the ... bus?
Wann fährt der ... Bus?

tip (gratuity)	Trinkgeld (neut)
to tire	ermüden

I'm tired.
Ich bin müde.

tissues	Papiertücher (pl)
tobacco (pipe)	(Pfeifen)Tabak (m)
toboggan	Schlitten (m)
today	heute
together	zusammen
toilet	Toilette (f)

Where are the toilets?
Wo ist die Toilette?

toilet paper	Toilettenpapier (neut)
tomb	Grab (neut)
tomorrow	morgen

tomorrow afternoon
morgen Nachmittag
tomorrow evening
morgen Abend
tomorrow morning
morgen früh

tonight	heute Abend
too (also)	auch
tools	Werkzeug (neut)
too much/many	zu viel/viele
tooth	Zahn (m)
toothache	Zahnschmerzen (pl)
toothbrush	Zahnbürste (f)
toothpaste	Zahnpasta (f)
at the top	ganz oben
torch (flashlight)	Taschenlampe (f)
to touch	berühren

Don't touch.
Bitte nicht berühren.

tour	Tour (f); Fahrt (f); Führung (f)
tourist	Tourist/in
tourist information office	Fremdenverkehrsbüro (neut)
to tow	abschleppen
towards	auf ... zu
towel	Handtuch (neut)
tower	Turm (m)
town	Stadt (f)
toxic waste	Giftmüll (m)
toy	Spielzeug (neut)
track (path)	Pfad (m)
at the traffic lights	bei der Ampel
tragedy	Tragödie (f)
train	Zug (m)
tram	Straßenbahn (f)
transfer	Überweisung (f)
transit	Transit (m)
to translate	übersetzen
travel agency	Reisebüro (neut)
travellers cheque	Reisescheck (m)
travelling	Reisen (neut)
travel writing	Reisebericht (m)
trip	Reise (f)
true	wahr
to trust	trauen
to try	versuchen
Tuesday	Dienstag (m)
TV	Fernseher (m)
TV guide	Fernsehzeitung (f)
tweezers	Pinzette (f)
twelve	zwölf
twenty	zwanzig
twice	zweimal
two	zwei (zwo on phones)
typical	typisch
tyre (outer)	Mantel (m)
tyres	Reifen (pl)

260

U

umbrella	Regenschirm (m)
uncle	Onkel (m)
uncomfortable	unbequem
under	unter
underground	U-Bahn (f)
understand	verstehen

Do you understand me?
Verstehen Sie mich?
I understand.
Ich verstehe.

unemployed	arbeitslos
unemployment	Arbeitslosigkeit (f)
unemployment benefits	Arbeitslosengeld (neut)
unfurnished	unmöbliert
universe	Universum (neut)
university	Universität (f)
unleaded fuel	unverbleites Benzin (neut)
unsafe	nicht sicher; gefährlich
until	bis
up	oben
upbringing	Erziehung (f)
upstairs	oben
USA	Vereinigte Staaten (pl)
useful	nützlich

V

vacant	frei; offen
vacation	Urlaub (m); Ferien (pl)
vaccination	Schutzimpfung (f)
valley	Tal (neut)
valuable	wertvoll
value (price)	Wert (m)
vegetable shop	Gemüseladen (m)
venereal disease	Geschlechtskrankheit (f)
very	sehr
view	Aussicht (f)

village	Dorf (neut)
violin	Geige (f)
to visit	besuchen
to vomit	sich erbrechen
to vote	wählen

W

to wait	warten

Wait!
Warten Sie mal!

waiter	Kellner/in
waiting room	Wartesaal (m)
to walk	spazieren gehen

Can I walk there?
Kann ich dorthin zu Fuß gehen?

to want	mögen; wollen

I want a room with a ...
Ich möchte ein Zimmer mit ...
I want to go to ...
Ich möchte nach ... fahren.
I want to hire a car.
Ich möchte ein Auto mieten.

war	Krieg (m)
warm	warm
wash (clothes, etc)	waschen
wash (yourself)	sich waschen
washing powder	Waschpulver (neut)
wasp	Wespe (f)
waste	Abfall (m)
to watch	beobachten; zusehen
to watch TV	fernsehen
water	Wasser (neut)
water bottle	Feldflasche (f)
waterfall	Wasserfall (m)
wave	Welle (f)
way	Weg (m)

Can you show me the way to ...?
Könnten Sie mir den Weg nach ... zeigen?

W

weak	schwach
wealthy	reich
weapon	Waffe (f)
weather	Wetter (neut)
wedding	Hochzeit (f)
Wednesday	Mittwoch (m)
week	Woche (f)
welcome	Willkommen (neut)
welfare	Sozialhilfe (f)
welfare state	Sozialstaat (m)

I am (un)well.
Ich fühle mich (nicht) wohl.

well translated	gut übersetzt
west	Westen (m); westlich
wet	nass
what	was

What is that?
Was ist das?
What's this called?
Wie heißt das?
What's up?
Was ist los?
What work do you do?
Als was arbeitest du? (inf)
What is your name?
Wie ist Ihr Name? (pol)

wheel	Rad (neut)
when	wann

When does ... leave?
Wann fährt ... ab?
What time does it open/close?
Wann macht es auf/zu?
What time is the ... bus?
Wann fährt der ... Bus?

whenever	wann immer
where	wo

Where is ...?
Wo ist ...?

white	weiß
who?	wer/wen/wem?
whole	ganz

why	warum
wide	breit
wife	Frau (f); Ehefrau (f)
wild	wild
to win	gewinnen
wind	Wind (m)
window	Fenster (neut)
window seat	Fensterplatz (m)
windscreen	Windschutzscheibe (f)
windscreen wiper	Scheibenwischer (m)
windy	windig
winter sale	Winterschlussverkauf (m)
wire	Draht (m)
wise	weise
with	mit
without	ohne
wolf	Wolf (m)
wood	Holz (neut)
wool	Wolle (f)
work	Arbeit (f)
worker	Arbeiter/in
work of art	Kunstwerk (neut)
work permit	Arbeitserlaubnis (f)
world	Welt (f)
worry	Sorge (f)

I am worried.
Ich mache mir Sorgen.

worse	schlechter
wrestling	Ringkampf (m); Ringen (neut)
to write	schreiben
writer	Schriftsteller/in
writing paper	Briefpapier (neut)
wrong	falsch

Y

year	Jahr (neut)
years ago	vor Jahren
yellow	gelb
yes	ja

yesterday	**gestern**
yesterday morning	
gestern Morgen	
yet	noch; bis jetzt
yoghurt	Jogurt (m)
young	jung

Z

zero	null
zipper	Reißverschluss (m)
zoo	Zoo (m);
	Tiergarten (m)

In this dictionary the gender is either indicated by (m), (f) or (neut) after the word or the masculine (-er, -r), feminine (-in, -e) and neuter (-s) endings are separated by a slash. Synonyms and alternative meanings are separated by a semicolon. To work out the appropriate article – whether definite ('the') or indefinite ('a/an') – see page 20.

A

Aal (m)	eel
Abend (m)	evening
Abenddämmerung (f)	dusk
Abendessen (neut)	dinner
Abenteuer (neut)	adventure
aber	but
abfahren; abreisen	to depart
Abfahrt (f)	departure
Abfall (m)	garbage; waste
Abflug (m)	takeoff
Abführmittel (neut)	laxative
(Auto)Abgase (pl)	exhaust fumes
Abgeordnete/r	member of parliament
Abhängigkeit (f)	addiction
Abholzung (f)	deforestation
Abkürzung (f)	shortcut
Abmeldung (f)	notice of departure
Abschleppdienst (m)	breakdown service
abschleppen	to tow
Absender (m)	sender
Abstrich (m)	smear
Abtreibung (f)	abortion
Abzug (m)	print (artwork)

acht	eight
achtzehn	eighteen
achtzig	eighty
Adler (m)	eagle
ähnlich	like (similar)
aktuelle Kollektion (f)	latest collection
Alkoholiker/in	alcoholic
alle	all; everyone
allein	alone
Allergie (f)	allergy
alles	everything
alltäglich	every day
alt	ancient; old
Altbauwohnung (f)	old flat
alte Gebäude (pl)	old buildings
Alter (neut)	age
Alternative (f)	alternative
Altstadt (f)	old part of the city
am Anfang	at the beginning
am Ende	at the end
Ameise (f)	ant
Amsel (f)	blackbird
(sich) amüsieren	to enjoy (oneself)
an	on; at
anbieten	to offer
Andenken (neut)	souvenir
andere/r/s	other

anders; verschieden	different
anfangen mit; beginnen	to start; begin
Anfänger/in	beginner
Angel (f)	fishing rod
Angestellte/r	employee
Angst (f)	fear (n)
Angst (haben)	(to be) afraid
anhalten	to stop
ankommen	to arrive
anpassen	to adjust
anrufen; telefonieren	to telephone
Anschluss (m)	connection (transport)
ansehen	to look (at)
(an)statt	instead of
antik	antique (adj)
Antiquariat (neut)	second-hand bookstore
Antiquität (f)	antique (n)
Antiseptikum (neut)	antiseptic
Antwort (f)	answer (n)
antworten	to answer
Apotheke (f)	pharmacy
Arbeit (f)	work
Als was arbeitest du? (inf) What work do you do?	
Arbeiter/in	worker
Arbeitgeber (m)	employer
Arbeitserlaubnis (f)	work permit
arbeitslos	unemployed
Arbeitslosengeld (neut)	unemployment benefits
Arbeitslosigkeit (f)	unemployment
arbeitslos sein	to be unemployed
Ich bin arbeitslos. I'm unemployed.	
Arbeitsmarkt (m)	job market

Archäologie (f)	archeology
arm	poor
Armut (f)	poverty
Art (f); Sorte (f)	kind (type)
Arzt/Ärztin	doctor
Aschenbecher (m)	ashtray
Asylbewerber/in	asylum seeker
Atelier (neut)	studio
Atomenergie (f)	nuclear energy
Atomkraftwerk (neut)	nuclear power station
Atommüll (m)	nuclear waste
auch	too (also)
auf	on; at
Aufführung (f)	performance
aufladen	to recharge
auf ... zu	towards
Aufzug (m)	lift
Auge (neut)	eye
aus	out
aus; von	from
Es ist aus ...	It is made of ...
Ausbildung (f)	education
Auseinandersetzung (f)	argument
ausgezeichnet	excellent
Auskunft (f); Information (f)	information
im Ausland	abroad
ausländisch	foreign
Auspuff (m)	exhaust
außer	apart from (besides)
außer; ausgenommen	excluding
Aussicht (f)	view
Australien (neut)	Australia
ausverkauft	sold out
auswählen	to choose
automatisch	automatic
Autor/in	author
Axt (f)	axe

266

B

Bäcker/in	baker
Bäckerei (f)	bakery
Bad (neut)	bath; bathroom
Badeanzug (m)	swimming costume
Badehose (f)	swimming trunks
Badekappe (f)	swimming cap
Bademeister (m)	pool attendant
Badetuch (neut)	bath towel
bald	soon
Balkon (m)	balcony
Ball (m)	ball
Ballett (neut)	ballet
Bank (f)	bank
Bankkonto (neut)	bank account
Banknote (f)	banknote
Bär (m)	bear
bar/Bargeld (neut)	cash
Batterien (pl)	batteries
Bauer/Bäuerin	farmer
Bauernhof (m)	farm
Baumwolle (f)	cotton
Beamter/Beamtin	civil servant
begegnen; treffen	to meet
beginnen; anfangen mit	begin; to start
Begräbnis (neut)	funeral
bei der Ampel	at the traffic lights
beide	both
Bein (neut)	leg
Bekleidungsgeschäft (neut)	clothing store
Belichtungsmesser (m)	light meter
Benutzungsgebühr (f)	fee
Benzin (neut)	petrol; gas
Benzinkanister (m)	petrol can
beobachten; zusehen	to watch

bequem; komfortabel	comfortable
bereit; fertig	ready
Berg (m)	mountain
Berghütte (f)	mountain hut
Bergsteigen (neut)	mountaineering; rockclimbing
Beruf (m)	occupation; profession
berühren	to touch
beschäftigt	busy
Besitzer/in	owner
besser	better
beste/r/s	best
bestehlen; berauben	rob
Ich bin bestohlen worden!	I've been robbed!
etwas bestellen	to order (a meal)
Bestimmungsort (m); Zielflughafen (m)	destination
bestreiten	to deny
besuchen	to visit
Betäubung (f)	anaesthetic
(sich) beteiligen	to participate
Betrag (m)	amount
Betriebswirtschaft (f)	economics
betrunken	drunk (inebriated)
Bett (neut)	bed
Bettlaken (neut)	sheet
Bettler (m)	beggar
bewundern	to admire
bezahlen	to pay
Bibel (f)	bible
Bibliothek (f)	library
Biegen Sie ... links ab.	Turn left ...
Biegen Sie ... rechts ab.	Turn right ...
Biene (f)	bee
Bildhauer/in	sculptor
Billard (neut)	pool (the game)
billig	cheap

bis	until
bisherig	previous
Biss (m)	bite (n; dog)
ein bisschen	a bit; a little
bis zu ...	as far as ...
Bitte	Please
blank	shiny; shining
Blase (f)	blister
blau	blue
bleiben	to stay; remain
Bleistift (m)	pencil
Blinddarm (m)	appendix
Blinker (m)	indicator
Blitz (m)	flash; lightning
blöd	stupid
Blumenladen (m)	flower shop
Boden (m)	earth (soil); floor
Bombe (f)	bomb
Boot (neut)	boat
Bordkarte (f)	boarding pass
borgen	to borrow
Boss (m)	boss
botanischer Garten (m)	botanic garden
Botschaft (f)	embassy
Botschafter/in	ambassador
Bratpfanne (f)	frying pan
braun	brown
breit	wide
Bremsen (pl)	brakes
Bremsflüssigkeit (f)	brake fluid
Brennholz (neut)	firewood
Brennstoff (m)	fuel
Brief (m)	letter
Briefkasten (m)	mailbox
Briefmarke (f)	stamp
Briefpapier (neut)	writing paper
Briefträger/in	postman

Briefumschlag (m)	envelope
Brille (f)	glasses (eyes)
bringen	to bring; to take
Brot (neut)	bread
Brücke (f)	bridge
Bruder (m)	brother
Brunnen (m)	fountain
Brust (f)	breast
Brustkorb (m)	chest
Bücherei (f)	library
Buchhalter/in	accountant
Buchhandlung (f); Buchladen (m)	bookshop
Bucht (f)	bay
Bundeskanzler (m)	prime minister
Bundestag (m)	federal parliament
Burg (f); Schloss (neut)	castle
Büro (neut)	office
Büroangestellte/r	office worker
Bus (m)	bus
Büstenhalter (m); BH (m)	bra
Butter (f)	butter
bützen	to kiss

C

Campingplatz (m)	camping ground
chaotisch	chaotic
Chef (m)	boss
chemische Reinigung (f)	drycleaner
Computerkunst (f)	computer/ technological art
Computerspiel (neut)	computer game
Cousin/e	cousin

D

Dach (neut)	roof
Dachboden (m)	attic
Dachs (m)	badger
Damenbinden (pl)	sanitary napkins
Dämmerung (f)	dawn; dusk
Danke	Thank you
Ich bin dankbar.	
I am grateful.	
Datum (neut)	date (time)
Demonstrationen (pl)	marches
denken	to think
Denkmal (neut)	monument
Deutsch	German
Ich spreche kein Deutsch.	
I don't speak German.	
Ich spreche ein bisschen Deutsch.	
I speak a little German.	
Deutschland (neut)	Germany
Dezember (m)	December
Dia (neut)	slide (film)
dick	fat; thick
Dieb (m)	thief
Diebstahl (m)	theft
Dienstag (m)	Tuesday
diese/r/s	this
diese Straße	this street
diese Woche	this week
dieser Vorort	this suburb
dieses Jahr	this year
Diktatur (f)	dictatorship
direkt	direct
Diskriminierung (f)	discrimination
Dokumentarfilm (m)	documentary
Dolmetscher/in	interpreter
Dom (m)	cathedral
Donner (m)	thunder
Donnerstag (m)	Thursday
Dope (neut)	dope

Doppelbett (neut)	double bed
Doppelhaus (neut)	semi-detached house
doppelt	double
Doppelzimmer (neut)	double room
Dorf (neut)	village
dort	there
Dosenöffner (m)	can opener
Dozent/in	lecturer
Drachenfliegen (neut)	hang-gliding
Draht (m)	wire
Drehbuch (neut)	script
Drehbuchautor/in	scriptwriter
Drehort (m)	location
drei	three
dreißig	thirty
drei Viertel	three-quarters
dreizehn	thirteen
dritte/r/s	third
Drittel (neut)	a third
Drogenabhängige/r	drug addict
Drogenberatungs-stelle (f)	drug counselling service
Drogeriemarkt (m)	drugstore
dumm	stupid
dunkel	dark
dünn	thin
durch	through
Durchfall (m)	diarrhoea
Durst haben	thirsty (to be)
Dusche (f)	shower (in bathroom)
Dutzend (neut)	a dozen

E

Ebene (f)	plain
Ecke (f)	corner
Es ist mir egal.	
I don't care.	

egoistisch	selfish
Ehe (f)	marriage
Ehemann (m)	husband
ehrlich	honest
Eifer (m)	enthusiasm
eigentlich	really; actually
Eile (f)	hurry (to be in a)
Ich habe es eilig.	
I'm in a hurry.	
Eilzug (m)	fast train
Einfachfahrkarte (f)	ticket - one way
einführen	to import
einige	several; some
einmal	once
Ein Moment!	
Just a minute!	
eins	one
Ich bin einsam.	
I am lonely.	
einsteigen	to embark
eintreten	to enter
Einwanderung (f)	immigration
einzahlen	to pay
	(into account)
Einzelzimmer (neut)	single room
einzige/r/s	only
Eis (neut)	ice; ice-cream
Eis laufen (neut)	ice skating;
	to skate
Eispickel (m)	ice axe
Elektriker/in	electrician
Elektrizität (f)	electricity
elf	eleven
Eltern (pl)	parents
empfehlen	to recommend
Ende (neut)	end (n)
Endstation (f)	terminus
Enkel(kinder) (pl)	grandchildren

Enkel (m)	grandson
Enkelin (f)	granddaughter
entdecken; finden	discover
Ente (f)	duck
entfernt	remote
entscheiden	to decide
Entscheidung (f)	decision
Entschuldigung	Excuse me;
	Sorry
entspannen	to relax
Entwicklung (f)	development
Entzündung (f)	inflammation
sich erbrechen	to vomit
Erdbeben (neut)	earthquake
Erde (f)	Earth (world);
	earth (soil)
Erdgas (neut)	natural gas
Erdrutsch (m)	landslide
Erfahrung (f)	experience
sich erinnern	to remember
Erkältung (f)	a cold (illness)
erlauben	to permit;
	to allow
Erlaubnis (f)	permission
Ermäßigung (f)	reduction
ernst	serious
Ernte (f)	harvest
Ersatzteile (pl)	spare parts
erstaunlich	amazing
erste/r/s	first
Erziehung (f)	upbringing
Esel (m)	donkey
Essen (neut)	food
essen	to eat
Esszimmer (neut)	dining room
etwas	something
exportieren	to export

F

German	English
Fabrik (f)	factory
Fabrikarbeiter/in	factory worker
Fabrikverkauf (m)	factory sale
Fahrer/in	driver
Fahrgast (m)	passenger (bus; taxi)
Fahrrad (neut)	bicycle
Fahrt (f)	tour
Fallschirmspringen (neut)	parachuting
falsch	false; wrong
Fantasie (f)	imagination
Farben (pl)	paints
Farbfilm (m)	colour film
Farbfilm für Dias	colour slide film
fast	almost
faul	lazy
Fax (neut)	fax
Februar (m)	February
Fehler (m)	mistake
feilschen	to bargain
Feinkostladen (m)	delicatessen
Feld (neut)	field
Feldflasche (f)	water bottle
Fels (m)	rock
Fenster (neut)	window
Fensterplatz (m)	window seat
Ferien (pl)	holiday; vacation
fern	distant
Fernbedienung (f)	remote control
Fernsehen (neut)	television
fernsehen	to watch TV
Fernseher (m)	TV
Fernsehzeitung (f)	TV guide
fertig	ready
Fest (neut)	festival; party
fest	solid; permanent
feucht	damp

German	English
Feuchtigkeitscreme (f)	moisturising cream
Feuer (neut)	fire
Feuerzeug (neut)	lighter
Fieber (neut)	fever
mit Filter	filtered (cigarette)
finden	discover
Fischen (neut)	fishing
Fixer (m)	drug addict
Flasche (f)	bottle
Flaschenöffner (m)	bottle opener
Fleisch (neut)	meat
Ich esse kein Fleisch.	I don't eat meat.
Fliege (f)	fly
Flohmarkt (m)	flea-market
Flöte (f)	flute
Flüchtling (m)	refugee
Fluggast (m)	passenger (plane)
Flughafengebühr (f)	airport tax
Fluglinie (f)	airline
Flugzeug (neut)	(aero)plane
Fluss (m)	river
Flut (f)	flood
folgen	follow
Forderung (f)	demand (n)
Form (f)	shape
formell	formal
Fotogeschäft (neut)	camera shop
Fotografie (f)	photograph (n)
fotografieren	to photograph
Frage (f)	question (n)
fragen	to ask
Frankreich (neut)	France
Französisch (neut)	French
Frau (f)	woman; wife
frei	free (not bound)
Freibad (neut)	outdoor swimming pool
Freitag (m)	Friday
fremd	strange
Fremde/r	stranger

Fremdenverkehrsbüro (neut)	tourist information office
Freund/in	friend; boy/girlfriend
freundlich	friendly; kind (sentiment)
Frieden (m)	peace
Friedhof (m)	cemetery
frieren	to freeze
frisch	fresh (not stale)
Friseur/Friseuse	hairdresser
Frosch (m)	frog
frostig	frosty
Frucht (f)	fruit
früh	early
früher	past (time)
Frühstück (neut)	breakfast
Fuchs (m)	fox
fünf	five
fünfzehn	fifteen
fünfzig	fifty
für	for
Fuß (m)	foot

G

Gämse (f)	chamois
Gang (m)	gear
Gangschaltung (f)	gears
Gans (f)	goose
ganz	whole
Garten (m)	garden
Gärtner/in	gardener
Gasheizung (f)	gas heating
Gaskartusche (f)	gas cartridge
Gebäude (neut)	building
geben	to give
Geben Sie mir bitte ...	
Please give me ...	
Gebet (neut)	prayer
Gebiet (neut)	region

Gebirgszug (m); Gebirgskette (f)	mountain range
Geburtshaus von ...	birthplace of ...
Geburtstag (m)	birthday
Gedicht (neut)	poem
gefährlich	dangerous
Gefangene/r	prisoner
Gefängnis (neut)	jail; prison
Gefühle (pl)	feelings
gegen	against
gegenüber	opposite
gegenwärtig	present (time)
Gegenwartsliteratur (f)	contemporary literature
Gehalt (neut)	salary
Geheimnis (neut)	secret
gehen	to go
Gehen Sie geradeaus.	
Go straight ahead.	
Wie geht´s?	
How are you?	
Es geht.	
Not too bad.	
Geige (f)	violin
Geist (m)	mind (n)
gelähmt	paralysed
gelb	yellow
Geld (neut)	money
Geldbuße (f)	fine (penalty)
Geldschein (m)	banknote
Geldwechsel (m)	exchange of money
Gemälde (neut)	painting
Gemüseladen (m)	vegetable shop
genug	enough
Gepäckaufbewahrung (f)	left-luggage office
Gepäckausgabe (f)	left-luggage withdrawals
Gepäckträger (m)	porter
gerade	straight
Geräusch (neut)	noise
Gerechtigkeit (f)	justice

Geschäft (neut)	business
Geschäftsmann/ Geschäftsfrau	businessperson
Geschenk (neut)	present (gift)
Geschichte (f)	history; story (tale)
Geschlechtskrankheit (f)	venereal disease
geschützte Tierarten (pl)	protected species
Geschwister (pl)	brothers & sisters
Gespräch (neut)	conversation
gestatten	to allow
gestern	yesterday
gestern Morgen	yesterday morning
Gesundheit (f)	health
Getränk (neut)	drink (n)
Gewinn (m)	profit
gewinnen	to win
gewöhnliche Post	surface mail
Gezeiten (pl)	tide
Giftmüll (m)	toxic waste
Gipfel (m)	peak
Gitarre (f)	guitar
Glas (neut)	glass (of water)
glatt	slippery
Gleichberechtigung (f)	equality
gleich dort	right there
der/die/das gleiche	same
Gleis (neut)	platform; track
Gleitschirmfliegen (neut)	paragliding
Gletscher (m)	glacier
globale Erwärmung (f)	global warming
glücklich	happy
Ich bin glücklich.	I am happy.
Glückwünsche!	Congratulations!
Glühbirne (f)	light bulb

Gold (neut)	gold
Golf (m)	gulf
Gott (m)	god
Gottesdienst (m)	service
Grab (neut)	grave (tomb)
Grafik (f)	graphic arts
Grat (m)	ridge
gratis	free (of charge)
grau	grey
Grippe (f)	influenza
groß	big, tall
Großeltern (pl)	grandparents
Großmutter (f)	grandmother
Großvater (m)	grandfather
Grube (f)	hole; hollow
grün	green
Grund (m)	reason
Gurt (m)	seat belt
Gürtel (m)	belt
gut	good
gut aussehend	handsome
Guten Tag	Hello; Good day

H

Haarbürste (f)	hairbrush
haben	to have
Ich habe ...	I have ...
Haben Sie ...?	Have you (got) ...?
Haben Sie die genaue Zeit?	Do you know the exact time?
Hafen (m)	harbour
Halbinsel (f)	peninsula
Hälfte (f)	half
Hallenbad (neut)	indoor swimming pool
Hallo	Hello

Hals (m)	throat
Halskette (f)	necklace
Halstuch (neut)	scarf
Halt!	Stop!
Hält dieser Zug in ...?	
Does this train stop at ...?	
Halten Sie bitte an der nächsten Ecke.	
Please stop at the next corner.	
Halten Sie hier!	
Stop here!	
handgearbeitet	handmade
Handschuhe (pl)	gloves
Handtasche (f)	handbag
Handtuch (neut)	towel
Hang (m)	slope
Hängematte (f)	hammock
hart	hard (not soft)
hassen	to hate
häufig	often
Hauptplatz (m)	main square
Haus (neut)	house
Hausarbeit (f)	housework
Hausfrau (f)	housewife
Haut (f)	skin
heilig	holy
Heim (neut)	home
Heimweh haben	to be homesick
heiraten	to marry
heiß	hot
Mir ist heiß.	
I am hot.	
heiter	bright (day)
Heizung (f)	heating
helfen	to help
hell	light (not dark)
Hemd (neut)	shirt
herabgesetzter Preis	reduced price
Hering (m)	herring
Heringe (pl)	tent pegs
herüber	across (from)
Herz (neut)	heart
heute	today

heute Abend	tonight
heute Morgen	this morning
hier	here
Hilfe (f)	help; aid
hinter	behind
hinüber	across (to)
Hirsch (m)	deer (stag)
Hitze (f)	heat
hoch	high
Hochebene (f)	plateau
Hochzeit (f)	wedding
Hoffnung (f)	hope
hoher Blutdruck (m)	high blood pressure
Höhle (f)	cave
Holz (neut)	wood
homöopathisches Mittel (neut)	homoeopathic medicine
homosexuell	homosexual
hören	to hear; to listen
Horoskop (neut)	horoscope
Hotel (neut)	hotel
hübsch	pretty
Hügel (m)	hill
Huhn (neut)	chicken
Hund (m)	dog
hundert	hundred
hungrig	hungry
Hunger haben	to be hungry
Hast du Hunger?	
Are you hungry?	
Husten (m)	cough
Hustensaft (m)	cough mixture
Hütte (f)	hut

I

Idee (f)	idea
im Haus	indoors
immer	always; forever
Immigration (f)	immigration
in	in
inbegriffen	included
Industrie (f)	industry
Infektion (f)	infection

K

informell	informal
Ingenieur/in	engineer
Injektion (f)	injection
innen	inside
Innenstadt (f)	downtown
Insektenbekämp- fungsmittel (neut)	insect repellant
Insel (f)	island
Installateur/in	plumber
instant	instant
irgendetwas	anything
irgendwo	anywhere
Isomatte (f)	foam mattress

J

ja	yes
Jacke (f)	jacket
Jahr (neut)	year
jede/r/s	every; each
jemand	somebody
jetzt	now
Job (m)	job
Joch (neut)	saddle
Jogurt (m)	yoghurt
Journalist/in	journalist
Juli (m)	July
jung	young
Junge (m)	boy
Juni (m)	June
Jura	law

K

Kajak fahren (neut)	kayaking
kalt	cold (temperature)
Mir ist kalt.	
I am cold.	
kaltes Wasser	cold water
Kamm (m)	comb
Kanarienvogel (m)	canary
Kaninchen (neut)	rabbit

Kanister (m)	can (tin)
Kap (neut)	cape (offshore)
Kapelle (f)	chapel
Kapitalismus (m)	capitalism
kaputt	broken
Karte (f)	map
Kartenspiel (neut)	cards
Käse (m)	cheese
Kassierer/in	cashier
Katze (f)	cat
kaufen	to buy
Kaufhaus (neut)	department store
Kaufmann/Kauffrau	shopkeeper
Kaution (f)	deposit
Keilriemen (m)	fan belt
keine/r/s	none; neither
Keller (m)	cellar
Kellner/in	waiter
kennen	to know (a person)
Kerze (f)	candle
Kessel (m)	kettle
Kette (f)	chain
Kind (neut)	baby
Kinder (pl)	children
Kino (neut)	cinema
Kirche (f)	church
Kissen (neut)	pillow
klar	sure
Klassensystem (neut)	class system
klassische Musik (f)	classical music
Klavier (neut)	piano
Kleid (neut)	dress
Kleidung (f)	clothing
klein	little; small
Kleingeld (neut)	loose change
Klima (neut)	climate
Klimaanlage (f)	air-conditioned
Kloster (neut)	monastery
Knappheit (f)	shortage
Kneipe (f)	pub
Knie (neut)	knee
Knöchel (m)	ankle

K

D
I
C
T
I
O
N
A
R
Y

Knopf (m)	button
Koch/Köchin	cook
kochen	to boil; to cook
Kocher (m)	camping stove
Köder (m)	bait
Koffer (m)	suitcase
Kofferraum (m)	boot
Kohleheizung (f)	coal heating
Kokain (neut); Koks (neut)	cocaine
Kollege/Kollegin	colleague
komfortabel	comfortable
komisch	funny
kommen	to come
Kommunismus (m)	communism
Komödie (f)	comedy
Kondome (pl)	condoms
König (m)	king
können	can (able to)
Kann ich das Zimmer sehen?	
Can I see the room?	
Kann ich zu Fuß gehen?	
Can I walk there?	
Könnten Sie den Preis aufschreiben?	
Can you write down the price?	
Könnten Sie den Preis reduzieren?	
Could you lower the price?	
Könnten Sie es mir (auf der Karte) zeigen?	
Can you show me (on the map)?	
Könnten Sie mich zu ... bringen?	
Can you take me to ...?	
Könnten Sie mir den Weg nach ... zeigen?	
Can you show me the way to ...?	
Kontaktlinse (f)	contact lens
Kontoauszug (m)	bank statement
Kontrabass (m)	double bass
Konversation (f)	conversation
Konzert (neut)	concert
Konzerthalle (f)	concert hall
Kopf (m)	head

Kopfschmerzen (pl)	headache
Kopfschmerztablette (f)	aspirin
köstlich	delicious
Kraft (f)	power
Kragen (m)	collar
Krampf (m)	cramp
krank	ill; sick
kränken	to offend
Krankenhaus (neut)	hospital
Krankenkasse (f)	medical insurance
Krankenpfleger/ Krankenschwester	nurse
Krankenwagen (m)	ambulance
Kreditkarte (f)	credit card
Krieg (m)	war
Krimi (m)	thriller
Küche (f)	kitchen
Kuckuck (m)	cuckoo
Kuckucksuhr (f)	cuckoo clock
Kugelschreiber (m)	pen (ballpoint)
Kuh (f)	cow
Kühler (m)	radiator
sich kümmern	to care (about)
Kunde/Kundin	client
Kundendienst (m)	service
Kunst (f)	art
Kunstgalerie (f)	art gallery
Kunstgewerbe (neut)	arts & crafts
Kunsthändler (m)	art dealer
Kunsthandwerk (neut)	handicraft
Künstler/in	artist
Kunstsammlung (f)	art collection
Kunstwerk (neut)	work of art
Kupplung (f)	clutch (car)
Kurs (m)	exchange rate
kurz	short
kurzärmelig	short-sleeved
Kurzgeschichten (pl)	short stories
küssen	to kiss

M

L

Lachen (m)	laugh
lachen	to laugh
Lage (f)	situation
Landschaft (f)	scenery
Landschaftschutz-gebiet (neut)	protected area
Landung (f)	landing
Landwirtschaft (f)	agriculture
lang	long (thing)
langärmelig	long-sleeved
langsam	slow; slowly
langweilig	boring
Ich langweile mich.	
I'm bored.	
Läuse (pl)	lice
laut	loud; noisy
Lawine (f)	avalanche
Leben (neut)	life
leben	to live
Lebenslauf (m)	résumé (CV)
Lebensmittelladen (m)	grocery
Lebensmittelver-giftung (f)	food poisoning
Leber (f)	liver
Leder (neut)	leather
leer	empty
legal	legal
leger	informal
Lehrer/in	teacher
Lehrling (m)	apprentice
leicht	easy
Es tut mir Leid.	
I'm sorry.	
Leinen (neut)	linen
Lenker (m)	handlebars
Lerche (f)	lark
lernen	to learn

lesbisch	lesbian
Lesung (f)	reading
letzte/r/s	last
letztes Jahr	last year
letzte Nacht	last night
letzte Woche	last week
Lichtmaschine (f)	generator
lieben	to love
Ich liebe dich.	
I love you.	
Liebesfilm (m)	love film
Liebesgeschichte (f)	love story
Lied (neut)	song
Liegeplatz (m)	couchette
Lift (m)	elevator
lila	purple
Linie (f)	line
links	left (not right)
Lohn (m)	salary
Lokal (neut)	bar
Luft (f)	air
Luftkrankheit (f)	airsickness
Luftpost (f)	airmail
Luftpumpe (f)	pump
Luftpostbrief (m)	aerogram
Luftverschmutzung (f)	air pollution

M

machen	to make
Magen (m)	stomach
Magenverstimmung (f)	indigestion
Mai (m)	May
Maler/in	painter
manchmal	sometimes
mein Mann	my husband
Mantel (m)	coat
März (m)	March
Markt (m)	market
Matratze (f)	mattress

Maus (f)	mouse
mehr	more
Mehrheit (f)	majority
Meinung (f)	opinion
Mensa (f)	canteen
Mensch (m)	person
Menschen (pl)	people
Menschenrechte (pl)	human rights
menschlich	human
Menü (neut)	menu
Messe (f)	fair; mass
Messer (neut)	knife
Messing (neut)	brass
Metzger/in	butcher
Miete (f)	rent (n)
mieten	to hire; to rent
Mieter/in	tenant
Mieterhöhung (f)	rent increase
Mietvertrag (m)	lease
Milch (f)	milk
Mineralwasser (neut)	mineral water
Minute (f)	minute
mit	with
mit Filter	filtered (cigarette)
Mittag (m)	noon
Mittagessen (neut)	lunch
Mitteilung (f)	message
Mitternacht (f)	midnight
Mittwoch (m)	Wednesday
möbliert	furnished
moderne Kunst (f)	modern art
mögen	to want

Ich möchte ein Auto mieten.
I want to hire a car.
Ich möchte ein Zimmer mit ...
I want a room with a ...
Ich möchte einen Platz nach ...
reservieren lassen.
I'd like to book a seat to ...
Ich möchte nach ... fahren.
I want to go to ...

möglich	possible

Es ist (nicht) möglich.
It's (not) possible.

Mond (m)	moon
Montag (m)	Monday
morgen	tomorrow
morgen Abend	tomorrow evening
Morgendämmerung (f)	dawn
morgen früh	tomorrow morning
morgen Nachmittag	tomorrow afternoon
morgens	in the morning
Moschee (f)	mosque
Motor (m)	engine
Möwe (f)	seagull
müde sein	sleepy (to be)

Ich bin müde.
I'm sleepy/tired.

Müllkippe (f)	garbage dump
Mülltonne (f)	dustbin
Münzen (pl)	coins
Münztelefon (neut)	pay phone
Museen (pl)	museums
Muskelzerrung (f)	sprain
Mutter (f)	mother

N

nach	after
Nachmittag (m)	afternoon
Nachname (m)	surname
Nachrichten (pl)	news
nächste/r/s	next
nächste Woche	next week
nächstes Jahr	next year
Nacht (f)	night
Nachteil (m)	disadvantage
nahe	close (nearby)

Naher Osten (m)	Middle East
Nahverkehrszug (m)	local train
Nase (f)	nose
nass	wet
Naturschutzgebiet (neut)	nature reserve
Nebel (m)	fog
neben	beside; next to
neblig	foggy
Neffe (m)	nephew
Nein	no
Nerv (m)	nerve
nett	nice
Netz (neut)	net
neu	new
Neubauwohnung (f)	new flat
neun	nine
neunzehn	nineteen
neunzig	ninety
Neuseeland (neut)	New Zealand
nicht	not
nicht mehr	not any more
nicht sicher	unsafe
nicht so gut	not so good
nicht so viel	less (not as much; many)
Nichte (f)	niece
nichts	nothing
Nichtschwimmerbecken (neut)	pool for non-swimmers
nie	never
niedriger Blutdruck (m)	low blood pressure
noch	yet; still
noch mal dasselbe	same again
Norden (m)	north
normal	ordinary
Notlandung (f)	emergency landing
notwendig	necessary
November (m)	November

Nuckel (m)	dummy; pacifier
nuklearfrei	nuclear-free
null	zero
nutzen	to use
nützlich	useful

O

Obdachlose (pl)	homeless people
Obdachlosenunterkunft (f)	asylum
oben	at the top; up; above
obgleich	although; though
Objektiv (neut)	lens
oder	or
offen	open (adj)
offensichtlich	obvious
öffentliche Toilette (f)	public toilet
öffentlicher Strand (m)	public beach
öffnen	to open
ohne	without
Ohr (neut)	ear
Ohrringe (pl)	earrings
Öl (neut)	oil
Ölfarbe (f)	oil-based paint
Ölheizung (f)	oil heating
Oma (f)	grandmother
Onkel (m)	uncle
Opa (m)	grandfather
Oper (f)	opera
Opernhaus (neut)	opera house
Opernsänger/in	opera singer
Optiker (m)	optometrist
ordnen	to organise
Ordnung (f)	order (system)
Orgel (f)	organ
Osten (m)	east
Ostern (neut)	Easter
Österreich (neut)	Austria
Ozean (m)	ocean

P

Paar (neut)	pair
paar	a few
Packriemen (m)	strap
Paket (neut)	packet
Palast (m)	palace
Papagei (m)	parrot
Papier (neut)	paper
Papiertücher (pl)	tissues
Pass (m)	passport
Pause (f)	intermission
Penner (m; derogative)	bum
pensioniert	retired
per Anhalter fahren	to hitchhike
per Einschreiben	registered mail
Performance (f)	performance art
Personalausweis (m)	I.D. (identification card)
Personenzug (m)	slow train
persönlich	personal
Persönlichkeit (f)	personality
Pfad (m)	path; track
Pfarrer (m)	priest
Pfeife (f)	pipe
Pferd (neut)	horse
Pflanze (f)	plant
Physik (f)	physics
Pilgerfahrt (f)	pilgrimage
Pinsel (m)	brush
Pinzette (f)	tweezers
Planet (m)	planet
Platz (m)	place; seat
Platz am Gang	aisle seat
plötzlich	suddenly
Poesie (f)	poetry
Politik (f)	policy; politics
Politiker/in	politician
Polizei (f)	police
Polizeirevier (neut)	police station
Postamt (neut)	post office

Postfach (neut)	post office box
Postkarte (f)	postcard
postlagernd	poste restante
praktisch	practical
Präsident (m)	president
Preis (m)	price
Priester (m)	priest
privat	private
Produzent (m)	producer
produzieren	to produce
Prostituierte (f)	prostitute
Prozent (neut)	percent
Psychologie (f)	psychology
Puder (m)	powder

Q

Quelle (f)	spring
Querele (f)	dispute; quarrel
quetschen	to squash; to crush
Quittung (f)	receipt

R

Rabatt (m)	discount
Radiergummi (m)	rubber
Radsport (m)	cycling
Rahmen (m)	frame
rar	rare
Rasierapparat (m)	razor
Rasiercreme (f)	shaving cream
Rassist/in	racist
Rat (m)	advice
raten	to advise; to guess
Raub (m)	robbery
Raumfahrt (f)	astronautics
Rauschgift (neut)	drugs
Rechnung (f)	bill (account)
rechtlich	legal

rechts	right (not left)
Rechtsanwalt/ Rechtsanwältin	lawyer
rechts stehend	right-wing
Recycling (neut)	recycling
Regen (m)	rain
Es regnet.	It's raining.
Regenmantel (m)	raincoat
Regenschauer (m)	shower (of rain)
Regenschirm (m)	umbrella
Regierung (f)	government
Regisseur/in	director (film)
Reh (neut)	deer
reich	rich
Reifen (pl)	tyres
Reifenpanne (f)	puncture
Reihe (f)	row
rein	pure
Reise (f)	trip
Reisebericht (m)	travel writing
Reisebüro (neut)	travel agency
Reisen (neut)	travelling
Reisende/r	passenger (train)
Reisescheck (m)	travellers cheque
Reisetaschen (pl)	bags
Reißverschluss (m)	zipper
Reiten (neut)	horse riding
Reitschule (f)	riding school
Reitstall (m)	riding stable
Reitweg (m)	bridle-path
Religion (f)	religion
Rennen (neut)	race (contest)
Rentabilität (f)	profitability
Rentner/in	pensioner
Reservereifen (m)	spare tyre
reservieren	to reserve
Reservierung (f)	reservation (for meal, seat)

Respekt (m)	respect (n)
retten	to save (someone)
Revolution (f)	revolution
richten	to point
richtig	right (not wrong)
Ich habe recht.	I am right.
Richtung (f)	direction
riechen	to smell
Ring (m)	ring
Ringen (neut); Ringkampf (m)	wrestling
Risiko (neut)	risk
Rock (m)	skirt
roh	raw
eine Rolle Film (f)	film (roll of)
Roman (m)	fiction; novel
rosa	pink
rot	red
Rotkehlchen (neut)	robin
Rückfahrkarte (f)	ticket - return
Rückflug (m)	return flight
Rucksack (m)	backpack
Ruderer (m)	oarsman
Rudern (neut)	rowing
Ruhe (f)	peace; calmness
ruhig	quiet
Ruinen (pl)	ruins
rund	round

S

Safe (m/neut)	safe (for valuables)
Samstag (m)	Saturday
Samt (neut)	velvet
sanitäre Einrichtungen (pl)	sanitary facilities
Satin (m)	satin
Sattel (m)	saddle

sauber	clean
S-Bahn (f)	suburban train
Schach (neut)	chess
eine Schachtel Zigaretten	a pack of cigarettes
Schaf (neut)	sheep
Schaffner/in	conductor
Schatten (m)	shade (n)
Schauspiel (neut)	drama
Schauspieler/in	actor
Scheckkarte (f)	ATM card; cheque card
Scheibenwischer (m)	windscreen wiper
Schein (m)	certificate
Scheinwerfer (m)	lights
schenken; geben	to give
Schere (f)	scissors
schieben	to push
Schießsport (m)	shooting
Schild (neut)	sign
Schinken (m)	ham
Schlaf (m)	sleep (n)
schlafen	to sleep
Schlafsack (m)	sleeping bag
Schlafwagen (m)	sleeping car
Schlafzimmer (neut)	bedroom
Schlange (f)	snake
Schlauch (m)	inner tube
schlecht	bad
schlechter	worse
schließen	shut; to close
Schließfach (neut)	luggage locker
Schlitten (m)	toboggan
Schloss (neut)	castle; bike chain; lock
Schlosser (m)	locksmith
Schlucht (f)	gorge
Schlüssel (m)	key
schmackhaft	tasty
Schmerz (m)	pain
schmerzhaft	painful

Schmerzmittel (neut)	painkillers
Schmetterling (m)	butterfly
Schmuck (m)	jewellery
Schmutz (m)	dirt
schmutzig	dirty
Schnake (f)	gnat
Schnäppchen (neut)	a bargain
Schnecke (f)	snail
Schnee (m)	snow
Schneefeld (neut)	snowfield
schneiden	to cut
Schneider/in	tailor
schnell	fast (quick)
Schnellzug (m)	express train
Schokolade (f)	chocolate
schön	beautiful; fine (good)
Schrank (m)	cupboard
Schraubenzieher (m)	screwdriver
schreiben	to write
Schreibwaren (pl)	stationery
schreien	to shout
Schrein (m)	shrine
Schreiner/in	carpenter
Schriftsteller/in	writer
schüchtern	shy
Schuhe (pl)	shoes
Schuhgeschäft (neut)	shoeshop
schulden	to owe
schuldig	guilty
Schutzimpfung (f)	vaccination
schwanger	pregnant
schwarz	black
schwarze Komödie (f)	black comedy
Schwarzweißfilm (m)	B&W (film)
Schweiz (f)	Switzerland
schwer	hard (difficult); heavy
Schwester (f)	sister
Schwiegersohn (m)	son-in-law
Schwiegertochter (f)	daughter-in-law
schwierig	difficult

German	English
Schwimmbad (neut)	swimming pool
Schwimmbecken (neut)	swimming pool
schwimmen	to swim
Schwimmer/in	swimmer
Schwimmweste (f)	life jacket
schwul	gay
schwül	muggy
sechs	six
sechzehn	sixteen
sechzig	sixty
See (m)	lake
See (f)	sea
seekrank	seasick
Seele (f)	soul
Segeln (neut)	sailing
sehen	to see
Seher (m)	seer
sehr	very
Seide (f)	silk
Seife (f)	soap
Seil (neut)	rope
Seilbahn (f)	cable car
sein	to be
seit	since
Seite (f)	side
seitwärts	sideways
Sekretär/in	secretary
Sekt (m)	sparkling wine
selten	rare
Semester (neut)	term
Seminar (neut)	seminar
senden	to send
September (m)	September
Serie (f)	serial
sicher	safe
Sicherheit (f)	safety
Sicherheitsgurt (m)	seat belt
Sicherung (f)	fuse
sieben	seven
siebzehn	seventeen
siebzig	seventy
Sicherheitsgurt (m)	seat belt
Silber (neut)	silver
Silvester (m/neut)	New Year's Eve
sitzen	to sit
Ski fahren	to ski
Skonto (neut/m)	discount
sofort	immediately
sofortig	instant
Solarenergie (f)	solar energy
Sommerschlussverkauf (m)	summer sale
Im Sonderangebot (neut)	On Sale
Sonne (f)	sun
Sonnenaufgang (m)	sunrise
Sonnenbrand (m)	sunburn
Sonnenbrille (f)	sunglasses
Sonnencreme (f)	sun cream
Sonnenschutzmittel (neut)	sunblock cream
Sonnenuntergang (m)	sundown; sunset
Sonntag (m)	Sunday
sorgsam	careful
Souvenirladen (m)	souvenir shop
Sozialarbeiter/in	social worker
Sozialhilfe (f)	welfare
Sozialismus (m)	socialism
Sozialstaat (m)	welfare state
Sozialunterstützung (f)	social security
Soziologie (f)	sociology
sparen	to save (money)
Spaß (m)	fun
spät	late
Spaten (m)	spade

Spätvorstellung (f)	late show
Spatz (m)	sparrow
spazieren gehen	to walk
Speichen (pl)	spokes
Speisewagen (m)	dining car
speziell	special
Spiegel (m)	mirror
Spiel (neut)	game
Spielbrett (neut)	board
spielen	to play (games; music)
Spielfilm (m)	feature film
Spinne (f)	spider
Spirale (f)	IUD
Spiritus (m)	spirit
Sport (m)	sport
Sprachen (pl)	languages
sprechen	to speak; to talk
Sprechen Sie Englisch?	
Do you speak English?	
Ich spreche kein Deutsch.	
I don't speak German.	
Ich spreche ein bisschen Deutsch.	
I speak a little German.	
Spritze (f)	injection
Spülung (f)	conditioner
Squashschläger (m)	squash racket
Staat (m)	state
Staatsbürgerschaft (f)	citizenship
Stadion (neut)	stadium
Stadt (f)	city; town
ständig	permanent
stark	strong
(an)statt	instead of
Statuen (pl)	statues
Staub (m)	dust
stehlen	to steal
Stehplatz (m)	standing room
Steigeisen (pl)	crampons
Stein (m)	stone
Stelle (f)	job; place; spot
stellen	to put; to place

Stellenangebot (neut)	job offer
Stempelgeld (neut)	dole
Ich gehe stempeln.	
I'm on the dole.	
sterblich	mortal
Stern (m)	star
Sternbild (neut)	constellation
Sternzeichen (neut)	star sign
Steuer (f)	tax
Stich (m)	bite (n; insect)
Stickerei (f)	embroidery
Stil (m)	style
Stoff (m)	dope
Storch (m)	stork
strahlend	bright (sun, eyes)
Strand (m)	beach
Straße (f)	road; street
Straßenbahn (f)	tram
Straßenkarte (f)	road map
Straßenkinder (pl)	street kids
Strecke (f)	route
Streichhölzer (pl)	matches
Wir streiken!	On Strike!
streiten	to argue
Stromschnellen (pl)	rapids
Stück (neut)	piece
Studentenausweis (m)	student card
Studentenwohnheim (neut)	hall of residence
Studienförderung (f)	grant
studieren	to study
Stuhl (m)	chair
Sturm (m)	storm
stürmisch	stormy
suchen	to look for
Ich suche ...	
I'm looking for ...	
Süchtige/r	addict
Süden (m)	south
Sumpf (m)	marsh
süß	sweet

T

Tabak (m)	tobacco (pipe)
Tag (m)	day
täglich	daily
Tal (neut)	valley
Tante (f)	aunt
tanzen	dancing
Tanzmusik (f)	dance music
Taschenbuch (neut)	paperback
Taschenlampe (f)	flashlight (torch)
Taschenmesser (neut)	penknife
taub	deaf
Tauchen (neut)	diving
Taufe (f)	christening
tauschen	to exchange
tausend	thousand
Teil (m)	part
teilen	to share
Teilzeitstelle (f)	part-time job
Telefon (neut)	telephone
Telefonauskunft (f)	directory enquiries
telefonieren	to telephone

Wo kann ich telefonieren?
Where can I make a phone call?

Telefonkarte (f)	phonecard
Telefonzelle (f)	phone box
Telefonzentrale (f)	switchboard
Telegramm (neut)	telegram
Teleskop (neut)	telescope
Tempel (m)	temple
Tennisplatz (m)	tennis court
Tennisschläger (m)	tennis racket
Termin (m)	appointment
teuer	expensive
Tinte (f)	ink
Tisch (m)	table
Tischtennis (neut)	table tennis
Tochter (f)	daughter
Tod (m)	death
Topf (m)	pot
Töpferwaren (pl)	pottery
tot	dead
töten	to kill
Tourist/in	tourist
tragen	to carry
Tragödie (f)	tragedy
trauen	to trust
Traum (m)	dream (n)
traurig	sad

Ich bin traurig.
I am sad.

treffen	to meet
trinken	to drink
Trinkgeld (neut)	tip (gratuity)
trocken	dry
Tschüss (S)	Bye
Turm (m)	tower
Türsteher (m)	bouncer (club heavy)
typische	typical

U

U Bahn (f)	underground
übel	bad
Übelkeit (f)	nausea
über	over; above
Überdosis (f)	overdose
übereinstimmen	to agree
überfüllt	crowded
Übergepäck (neut)	excess baggage
überleben	to survive
übermorgen	day after tomorrow
über Nacht	overnight
übernachten	to stay (accommodation)
Überraschung (f)	surprise

Ich bin überrascht.
I'm surprised.

übersetzen	to translate
Überweisung (f)	transfer
Umschlag (m)	envelope
umsteigen	to change (trains, etc)
Umwelt (f)	environment
Umweltverschmutzung (f)	pollution
unbequem	uncomfortable
und	and
unerlaubt	illegal
Unfall (m)	accident
ungefähr	approximately
ungelegen	inconvenient
Ungleichheit (f)	inequality
Universum (neut)	universe
unmöbliert	unfurnished
unmöglich	impossible
unten	at the bottom; down (there)
unter	among; below; under
unterhaltsam	entertaining
Unterkunft (f)	accommodation
Untermieter (m)	lodger
Unterschrift (f)	signature
unverbleites Benzin (neut)	unleaded fuel
unverheiratet	single (unmarried)
Urkunde (f)	document
Urlaub (m)	holiday

V

Vater (m)	father
Ventilator (m)	fan
Verabredung (f)	appointment
Verantwortung (f)	responsibility
Verbandsmaterial (neut)	bandage
verbleites Benzin (neut)	leaded fuel

verboten	forbidden; not allowed
verdienen	to earn
Verdienst (m)	earnings
vereinbaren	to agree
Vereinigte Staaten (pl)	USA
Verfassung (f)	constitution
Verfolgung (f)	persecution
vergessen	to forget

Ich vergesse das nie.
I'll never forget this.
Vergiss nicht zu schreiben!.
Don't forget to write!

vergewaltigen	to rape
Vergewaltigung (f)	rape (n)
verhindern	to prevent
verkaufen	to sell
Verkaufsabteilung (f)	sales department
verlassen	to leave (depart)

Wann fährt ... ab?
What time does ... leave?

verlieren	to lose
Verletzung (f)	injury
Verlobte/r	fiancé/e
Verlust (m)	loss
Vermieter (m)	landlord
Vermieterin (f)	landlady
Vermietung (f)	renting out
vermissen	miss (feel absence of)
verpassen	miss (the bus etc)
verrückt	crazy
versichern	to insure
Versicherung (f)	insurance
versprechen	to promise
verstehen	understand

Verstehen Sie mich?
Do you understand me?
Ich verstehe.
I understand.

Verstopfung (f)	constipation
versuchen	to try
Verteiler (m)	distributor
Verwandte/r	relative (family)
Verwandtschaft (f)	relationship; relatives
Verwarnung (f)	fine (penalty)
verzeihen	to forgive
viel	plenty
viele	many
Vielen Dank	Many thanks
vielleicht	maybe
vier	four
Viertel (neut)	quarter
vierzehn	fourteen
vierzig	forty
Vogel (m)	bird
Volksentscheid (m)	referendum
voll	full
vor	before; in front of
vorbereiten	prepare
vorgestern	day before yesterday
Vorhängeschloss (neut)	padlock
vor Jahren	years ago
vor kurzem	recently
vor langer Zeit	long ago
Vorlesung (f)	lecture
Vorortzug (m)	suburban train
Vorschlag (m)	proposal
Vorschrift (f)	regulation
vorsichtig	careful
vor uns	ahead
Vorwahl (f)	area code
vorziehen	to prefer

W

wachsen	to grow
Waffe (f)	weapon
Waggon (m)	carriage (train)

Wahl (f)	election
wählen	to vote
Wähler (pl)/ Wählerschaft (f)	electorate
Wahlperiode (f)	legislation; term of office
wahnsinning	mad (crazy)
wahr	true
während	during
Währung (f)	currency
wandern	to hike
wann	when

Wann fährt ... ab?
When does ... leave?
Wann fährt der ... Bus?
What time is the ... bus?
Wann kommt ... an?
When does ... arrive?
Wann macht es auf/zu?
What time does it open/close?

wann immer	whenever
Warenhaus (neut)	department store
warm	warm
warmes Wasser	hot water
warten	to wait

Warten Sie mal!
Wait!

Wartesaal (m)	waiting room
warum	why
was	what

Was ist das?
What is that?
Wie heißt das?
What's this called?
Was ist los?
What's up?

waschen	wash (clothes, etc)
sich waschen	wash (yourself)
Wäscherei (f)	laundry

Waschpulver (neut)	washing powder
Wasser (neut)	water
Wasserfall (m)	waterfall
Wechselgeld (neut)	change (coins)
wechseln	to change (money)
Wechselstube (f)	exchange office
Wecker (m)	alarm clock
Weg (m)	way
wegen	because of
Wegweiser (m)	signpost
sich weh tun	to hurt (yourself)
Weibchen (neut)	female (animal)
Weihnachten (neut)	Christmas
Weihnachtsbaum (m)	Christmas tree
weil	because
weise	wise
weiß	white
weit	far; long (way)
Welle (f)	wave
Wellensittich (m)	budgie
Welt (f)	world
weniger	less
wenn	if; when
wer	who
werden	to become
Werkzeug (neut)	tools
Wert (m)	value (price)
wertvoll	valuable
Wespe (f)	wasp
Westen (m)	west
Wetter (neut)	weather
wichtig	important

Es ist (nicht) wichtig.
It's (not) important.

wider; gegen	against
wie	how

Wie geht es Ihnen/dir? (pol/inf)
How are you?

Wie komme ich nach ...?
How do I get to ...?

Wie spät ist es?
What time is it?

Wie viel kostet es?
How much is it?

wieder	again
Wiederverwertung (f)	recycling
Wildschwein (neut)	boar
Willkommen (neut)	welcome
Wind (m)	wind
windig	windy
Windschutzscheibe (f)	windscreen
Wirtschaft (f)	economy
wirtschaftlich	economical
wissen	know (how to)
Wissenschaftler/in	scientist
Witz (m)	joke (neut)
wo	where

Wo ist ...?
Where is ...?

Wo ist die Toilette?
Where are the toilets?

Wo sollen wir uns treffen?
Where should we meet?

Wohnung (f)	apartment
Wohnviertel (neut)	residential area
Wohnzimmer (neut)	living room
wolkig	cloudy
Wolldecke (f)	blanket
Wolle (f)	wool
wollen	to want
Wörterbuch (neut)	dictionary
würzig	spicy
Wüste (f)	desert

Z

zählen	to count
Zahn (m)	tooth
Zahnarzt/Zahnärztin	dentist
Zahnbürste (f)	toothbrush
Zähne (pl)	teeth

GERMAN – ENGLISH

German	English
Zahnpasta (f)	toothpaste
Zahnschmerzen (pl)	toothache
zehn	ten
zeigen	to show
Zeit (f)	time
zeitgenössische Musik (f)	contemporary music
Zeitung (f)	newspaper
Zeitungshändler (m)	newsagency
Zelt (neut)	tent
zelten	to camp
Zoltheringe (pl); Zeltpflöcke (pl)	tent pegs
Zentralheizung (f)	central heating
Zentrum (neut)	downtown
zerbrochen	broken
zerstören	to destroy
Zeugnisse (pl)	references
Ziege (f)	goat
ziehen	to pull
Zielflughafen (m)	destination
Zielscheibe (f)	target
Zimmer (neut)	room
Zimmernummer (f)	room number
Zoll (m)	customs (officials)
Zollerklärung (f)	customs declaration

German	English
zollfreie Waren (pl)	duty-free goods
Zoo (m)	zoo
Zucker (m)	sugar
Zuckerkrankheit (f)	diabetes
Zufall (m)	chance
zufolge	according to
Zug (m)	train
Zündkerze (f)	spark plug
Zündschlüssel (m)	ignition key
Zündung (f)	ignition
zurück	back (as in 'go back')
zurückkommen	to return
zurückzahlen	to refund
zusammen	together
Zuschlag (m)	supplement
zusehen	to watch
zustimmen	to agree
zu viel/viele	too much/many
zwanzig	twenty
zwei (zwo on the telephone)	two
Zweigstelle (f)	branch office
zweimal	twice
zweite/r/s	second
zwischen	between
Zwischenlandung (f)	stopover
zwölf	twelve

CROSSWORD ANSWERS

GETTING AROUND (pg 80)

Across	Down
3. Bahnhof	1. fahren
4. Zündkerze	2. Luftkrankheit
6. nahe	3. Benzin
7. Flugzeug	5. dort
9. hinter	8. Gurt

SHOPPING (pg 148)

Across	Down
3. lila	1. Flohmarkt
4. Warenhaus	2. blau
7. Schokolade	5. Apotheke
8. Halskette	6. Schuhe
9. feilschen	

AROUND TOWN (pg 100)

Across	Down
3. Postamt	1. Denkmal
6. Palast	2. Statuen
7. Markt	4. Telefon
8. öffentliche	5. Messe
10. Münzen	9. um (the)

IN THE COUNTRY (pg 178)

Across	Down
1. Sonnenaufgang	2. Ochse
6. Hering	3. Norden
7. Ebene	4. Gletscher
9. Kocher	5. Nebel
10. Donner	8. Ahorn

INTERESTS (pg 128)

Across	Down
5. Reisen	1. Künstler
6. Sonne	2. Romane
7. Flöte	3. Kunst
8. Stier	4. Arbeiten
10. Tanzmusik	9. Stil

HEALTH (pg 204)

Across	Down
3. Krankenhaus	1. Zahnarzt
4. Schmerzen	2. Blut
7. Verletzung	3. Kopf
9. Infektion	5. Herz
	6. Knie
	8. Zahn

I
N
D
E
X

NOTES

LONELY PLANET

Phrasebooks

L onely Planet phrasebooks are packed with essential words and phrases to help travellers communicate with the locals. With colour tabs for quick reference, an extensive vocabulary and use of script, these handy pocket-sized language guides cover day-to-day travel situations.

- handy pocket-sized books
- easy to understand Pronunciation chapter
- clear & comprehensive Grammar chapter
- romanisation alongside script to allow ease of pronunciation
- script throughout so users can point to phrases for every situation
- full of cultural information and tips for the traveller

'...vital for a real DIY spirit and attitude in language learning'
– *Backpacker*

'the phrasebooks have good cultural backgrounders and offer solid advice for challenging situations in remote locations'
– *San Francisco Examiner*

Arabic (Egyptian) • Arabic (Moroccan) • Australian *(Australian English, Aboriginal and Torres Strait languages)* • Baltic States *(Estonian, Latvian, Lithuanian)* • Bengali • Brazilian • Burmese • British *(English, dialects, Scottish Gaelic, Welsh)* • Cantonese • Central Asia *(Kazakh, Kyrgyz, Pashto, Tajik, Tashkorghani, Turkmen, Uyghur, Uzbek & others)* • Central Europe *(Czech, German, Hungarian, Polish, Slovak, Slovene)* • Costa Rica Spanish • Eastern Europe *(Albanian, Bulgarian, Croatian, Czech, Hungarian, Macedonian, Polish, Romanian, Serbian, Slovak, Slovene)* • East Timor *(Tetun, Portuguese)* • Egyptian Arabic • Ethiopian *(Amharic)* • Europe *(Basque, Catalan, Dutch, French, German, Greek, Irish, Italian, Maltese, Portuguese, Scottish Gaelic, Spanish, Turkish, Welsh)* • Farsi (Persian) • Fijian • French • German • Greek • Hebrew • Hill Tribes *(Lahu, Akha, Lisu, Mong, Mien & others)* • Hindi/Urdu • Indonesian • Italian • Japanese • Korean • Lao • Latin American Spanish • Malay • Mandarin • Mongolian • Moroccan Arabic • Nepali • Papua New Guinea • Pidgin • Pilipino (Tagalog) • Polish • Portuguese • Quechua • Russian • Scandinavian *(Danish, Faroese, Finnish, Icelandic, Norwegian, Swedish)* • South-East Asia *(Burmese, Indonesian, Khmer, Lao, Malay, Tagalog Pilipino, Thai, Vietnamese)* • South Pacific *(Fijian, Hawaiian, Kanak languages, Maori, Niuean, Rapanui, Rarotongan Maori, Samoan, Tahitian, Tongan & others)* • Spanish *(Castilian, also includes Catalan, Galician & Basque)* • Sri Lanka • Swahili • Thai • Tibetan • Turkish • Ukrainian • USA *(US English, vernacular, Native American, Hawaiian)* • Vietnamese

COMPLETE LIST OF LONELY PLANET BOOKS

AFRICA Africa on a shoestring • Cairo • Cape Town • East Africa • Egypt • Ethiopia, Eritrea & Djibouti • The Gambia & Senegal • Healthy Travel Africa • Kenya • Malawi • Morocco • Mozambique • Read This First: Africa • South Africa, Lesotho & Swaziland • Southern Africa • Southern Africa Road Atlas • Tanzania, Zanzibar & Pemba • Trekking in East Africa • Tunisia • Watching Wildlife East Africa • Watching Wildlife Southern Africa • West Africa • World Food Morocco • Zimbabwe, Botswana & Namibia

AUSTRALIA & THE PACIFIC Aboriginal Australia & the Torres Strait Islands • Auckland • Australia • Australia Road Atlas • Bushwalking in Australia • Cycling Australia • Cycling New Zealand • Fiji • Healthy Travel Australia, NZ and the Pacific • Islands of Australia's Great Barrier Reef • Melbourne • Micronesia • New Caledonia • New South Wales & the ACT • New Zealand • Northern Territory • Outback Australia • Out to Eat – Melbourne • Out to Eat – Sydney • Papua New Guinea • Queensland • Rarotonga & the Cook Islands • Samoa • Solomon Islands • South Australia • South Pacific • Sydney • Sydney Condensed • Tahiti & French Polynesia • Tasmania • Tonga • Tramping in New Zealand • Vanuatu • Victoria • Walking in Australia • Watching Wildlife Australia • Western Australia

CENTRAL AMERICA & THE CARIBBEAN Bahamas, Turks & Caicos • Baja California • Bermuda • Central America on a shoestring • Costa Rica • Cuba • Dominican Republic & Haiti • Eastern Caribbean • Guatemala • Guatemala, Belize & Yucatán: La Ruta Maya • Havana • Healthy Travel Central & South America • Jamaica • Mexico • Mexico City • Panama • Puerto Rico • Read This First: Central & South America • World Food Mexico • Yucatán

EUROPE Amsterdam • Amsterdam Condensed • Andalucía • Austria • Barcelona • Belgium & Luxembourg • Berlin • Britain • Brussels, Bruges & Antwerp • Budapest • Canary Islands • Central Europe •Copenhagen • Corfu & the Ionians • Corsica • Crete • Crete Condensed • Croatia • Cycling Britain • Cycling France • Cyprus • Czech & Slovak Republics • Denmark • Dublin • Eastern Europe • Edinburgh • England • Estonia, Latvia & Lithuania • Europe on a shoestring • Finland • Florence • France • Frankfurt Condensed • Georgia, Armenia & Azerbaijan • Germany • Greece • Greek Islands • Hungary • Iceland, Greenland & the Faroe Islands • Ireland • Istanbul • Italy • Krakow • Lisbon • The Loire • London • London Condensed • Madrid • Malta • Mediterranean Europe • Milan, Turin & Genoa • Moscow • Mozambique • Munich • The Netherlands • Normandy • Norway • Out to Eat – London • Paris • Paris Condensed • Poland • Portugal • Prague • Provence & the Côte d'Azur • Read This First: Europe • Rhodes & the Dodecanese • Romania & Moldova • Rome • Rome Condensed • Russia, Ukraine & Belarus • Scandinavian & Baltic Europe • Scotland • Sicily • Slovenia • South-West France • Spain • St Petersburg • Sweden • Switzerland • Trekking in Spain • Tuscany • Venice • Vienna • Walking in Britain • Walking in France • Walking in Ireland • Walking in Italy • Walking in Spain • Walking in Switzerland • Western Europe • World Food France • World Food Ireland • World Food Italy • World Food Spain

COMPLETE LIST OF LONELY PLANET BOOKS

INDIAN SUBCONTINENT Bangladesh • Bhutan • Delhi • Goa • Healthy Travel Asia & India • India • Indian Himalaya • Karakoram Highway • Kerala • Mumbai (Bombay) • Nepal • Pakistan • Rajasthan • Read This First: Asia & India • South India • Sri Lanka • Tibet • Trekking in the Indian Himalaya • Trekking in the Karakoram & Hindukush • Trekking in the Nepal Himalaya

ISLANDS OF THE INDIAN OCEAN Madagascar &Comoros • Maldives • Mauritius, Réunion & Seychelles

MIDDLE EAST & CENTRAL ASIA Bahrain, Kuwait & Qatar • Central Asia • Dubai • Iran • Israel & the Palestinian Territories • Istanbul • Istanbul to Cairo on a Shoestring • Istanbul to Kathmandu • Jerusalem • Jordan • Lebanon • Middle East • Oman & the United Arab Emirates • Syria • Turkey • World Food Turkey • Yemen

NORTH AMERICA Alaska • Boston • Boston Condensed • British Colombia • California & Nevada • California Condensed • Canada • Chicago • Deep South • Florida • Great Lakes • Hawaii • Hiking in Alaska • Hiking in the USA • Honolulu • Las Vegas • Los Angeles • Louisiana & The Deep South • Miami • Montreal • New England • New Orleans • New York City • New York City Condensed • New York, New Jersey & Pennsylvania • Oahu • Out to Eat – San Francisco • Pacific Northwest • Puerto Rico • Rocky Mountains • San Francisco • San Francisco Map • Seattle • Southwest • Texas • Toronto • USA • Vancouver • Virginia & the Capital Region • Washington DC • World Food Deep South, USA • World Food New Orleans

NORTH-EAST ASIA Beijing • China • Hiking in Japan • Hong Kong • Hong Kong Condensed • Hong Kong, Macau & Guangzhou • Japan • Korea • Kyoto • Mongolia • Seoul • Shanghai • South-West China • Taiwan • Tokyo • World Food – Hong Kong

SOUTH AMERICA Argentina, Uruguay & Paraguay • Bolivia • Brazil • Buenos Aires • Chile & Easter Island • Colombia • Ecuador & the Galapagos Islands • Healthy Travel Central & South America • Peru • Read This First: Central & South America • Rio de Janeiro • Santiago • South America on a shoestring • Santiago • Trekking in the Patagonian Andes • Venezuela

SOUTH-EAST ASIA Bali & Lombok • Bangkok • Cambodia • Hanoi • Healthy Travel Asia & India • Ho Chi Minh City • Indonesia • Indonesia's Eastern Islands • Jakarta • Java • Laos • Malaysia, Singapore & Brunei • Myanmar (Burma) • Philippines • Read This First: Asia & India • Singapore • South-East Asia on a shoestring • Thailand • Thailand's Islands & Beaches • Thailand, Vietnam, Laos & Cambodia Road Atlas • Vietnam • World Food Thailand • World Food Vietnam

Also available; Journeys travel literature, illustrated pictorials, calendars, diaries, Lonely Planet maps and videos. For more information on these series and for the complete range of Lonely Planet products and services, visit our website at **www.lonelyplanet.com**.

LONELY PLANET

Series Description

travel guidebooks	in depth coverage with backgournd and recommendations
	download selected guidebook Upgrades at www.lonelyplanet.com
shoestring guides	for travellers with more time than money
condensed guides	highlights the best a destination has to offer
citySync	digital city guides for Palm TM OS
outdoor guides	walking, cycling, diving and watching wildlife
phrasebooks	don't just stand there, say something!
city maps and road atlases	essential navigation tools
world food	for people who live to eat, drink and travel
out to eat	a city's best places to eat and drink
read this first	invaluable pre-departure guides
healthy travel	practical advice for staying well on the road
journeys	travel stories for armchair explorers
pictorials	lavishly illustrated pictorial books
eKno	low cost international phonecard with e-services
TV series and videos	on the road docos
web site	for chat, Upgrades and destination facts
lonely planet images	on line photo library

LONELY PLANET OFFICES

Australia
Locked Bag 1, Footscray,
Victoria 3011
☎ 03 8379 8000
fax 03 8379 8111
email: talk2us@lonelyplanet.com.au

UK
10a Spring Place,
London NW5 3BH
☎ 020 7428 4800
fax 020 7428 4828
email: go@lonelyplanet.co.uk

USA
150 Linden St, Oakland,
CA 94607
☎ 510 893 8555
TOLL FREE: 800 275 8555
fax 510 893 8572
email: info@lonelyplanet.com

France
1 rue du Dahomey,
75011 Paris
☎ 01 55 25 33 00
fax 01 55 25 33 01
email: bip@lonelyplanet.fr
website: www.lonelyplanet.fr

World Wide Web: www.lonelyplanet.com *or* **AOL keyword: lp**
Lonely Planet Images: lpi@lonelyplanet.com.au